1968

Amid the crucible of war, revolt, and tragedy, sports helped soothe America's psyche

Sal Maiorana

Contents

Prologue - Welcome to Miami

As the sun began to take cover on the far side of the Galt Ocean Mile Hotel in Fort Lauderdale, casting a refreshing shade across the pool deck, Vince Lombardi shifted his weight in the chair he was occupying, took off his thick-rimmed eyeglasses and held them in his right hand, turned away from his view of the Atlantic Ocean toward the man sitting across from him and said, "Jack, wouldn't it be nice if it was this comfortable Sunday afternoon?"

Jack McDonald stirred the small cubes of ice in his vodka gimlet and smiled at the famous football coach of the Green Bay Packers who he'd known long before he'd become the famous football coach of the Green Bay Packers. "Jesus, coach," Jack said to the living legend who once mentored him on the gridiron at St. Cecilia High School in Englewood, New Jersey, "after what you went through a couple weeks ago, I'd think you wouldn't mind a little sun and heat."

Two weeks earlier, Lombardi had stood on the sidelines at Lambeau Field in Green Bay, leading his Packers to a 21-17 victory over the Dallas Cowboys in the NFL Championship Game, or, as Jack and the other members of the sporting press who were there that incredible day dubbed it, the Ice Bowl.

There had been countless bad-weather games in NFL history, but there had never been anything quite like this one. The temperature at kickoff in Green Bay was minus-thirteen degrees, and estimates regarding the wind-chill factor pegged it at around minus-forty-eight degrees. The $80,000 underground heating system the Packers had installed beneath the field prior to the start of the 1967 season - the one that Lombardi himself had said would never allow the surface to freeze regardless of how cold it got - was rendered useless due to a tactical error made by the grounds crew. With overnight flurries in the forecast, they had placed a tarp over the field to keep the snow off which worked just fine, except for one small detail. In the morning when it was pulled off, the condensation that had formed between the cover and the heated field instantly froze, turning the green and brown muck into a virtual skating rink. And once the damage had been done, it was so cold that the heating coils could not recover and they never put a dent in the glaciered surface.

The Wisconsin State University - La Crosse marching band was supposed to provide pre-game and halftime entertainment, but the woodwind instruments froze and could not produce sound, and the mouthpieces on the brass instruments were sticking to the kids' lips. Up in the stands, it was learned after the game that an elderly man had died from exposure. And in the press box, near where Jack had been sitting and shivering despite being protected from the elements, the former NFL star receiver turned television broadcaster, Frank Gifford, told his CBS audience, "I'm going to take a bite out of my coffee."

Even while they were thawing out for the past few days in South Florida as they prepared to play in the second AFL-

NFL Championship Game against the champions from the AFL, the Oakland Raiders, several Packers were still feeling the effects from the frostbite they had suffered, and figured they would for quite some time.

But Lombardi was a hard man, a man from the north who didn't like the heat and humidity that Florida was famous for. At least when it's cold, Lombardi reasoned, you can always put on some long underwear or slip on a sweater under your parka. When it's hot, what the hell are you supposed to do, walk around naked? So, once that sun dipped behind the team hotel, he was perfectly content to sit with Jack and discuss his intention to retire from coaching at the conclusion of this championship game that was now being referred to by some in the media as the Super Bowl.

"I told Pete a few weeks ago that I was stepping down at the end of the year," Lombardi told the nationally-known columnist of *SportsWorld*, the foremost weekly sports magazine in the United States, recounting his conversation with NFL commissioner Pete Rozelle. "My health hasn't been good, my goddamn hip hurts every day and the medicine is eating away at my stomach. Marie thinks enough is enough and she's on my ass to get out."

For several months, Jack had begun to ascertain that Lombardi was considering retirement. He could tell in his conversations throughout the 1967 season with the man who had guided the Packers to five NFL championships since his 1959 arrival in Green Bay - now known as Titletown, USA - that something was amiss. The bark in

Lombardi's distinctive voice wasn't as menacing; the intensity that once creased his weathered face as he stalked the sideline on Sunday afternoons had softened; and his practices were no longer reminiscent of boot camp days at Parris Island. He was only 54 years old, but the coaching life, or at least his coaching life, had clearly drained him because he poured so much into it. Hours and hours and hours spent watching film of Green Bay's opponents; the sleepless nights stressing over every aspect of the weekly game plans; demanding perfection from his finely-tuned team and erupting in anger when his players did not meet his Everest-like expectations; and then those exhausting three hours on game day when the cauldron burned so hot, even in the frigidity of Green Bay, no matter if the opponent was the impressive Cowboys or the lowly Cardinals.

"I'm tired, Jack," Lombardi said. "I think now's the time. We've won, we've done well, but the team is getting old and I'll admit we haven't done a good enough job of getting new blood into the organization. It might be time for a change, time for the club to hear a different voice."

As Jack listened intently, meeting Lombardi's gaze as he sipped his drink, the coach made one thing abundantly clear. "If I see any of this in that goddamn magazine of yours before next week, I'll rip out your eyeballs and feed 'em to the buzzards."

Lombardi had nothing to worry about, and he knew that. As well as being a good friend and trusted confidante, Jack was one of the most respected and principled sports columnists in the country, a man who, before landing the ultimate sports writing gig at *SportsWorld*, had cut his teeth in the jungle that was the newspaper industry of New York City at a time when there were nearly as many daily rags in Gotham as there were professional sports teams.

Jack's father, Arthur, never advanced past the eighth grade and spent the years that he should have been in high school working at his father's bakery in Hoboken, New Jersey. Willing to join the Army during World War I, he was rejected due to his flat feet and because he was the lone son born to his parents. Arthur was a common laborer who worked a variety of jobs including a harrowing four-year stint on the crew that built the Hudson River Bridge, later renamed for George Washington, one of the great civil engineering feats of the 20th century which held the title as the longest main span in the world until the Golden Gate Bridge opened in Northern California in 1937.

Jack's mother, Gloria, enlisted in the Army Nurse Corps when she was 22 years old and wound up serving her country primarily at a field hospital near London. During her time in England she spent her days listening to the terrifying sounds of war off in the distance, beyond the captive balloons that were visible from where she was stationed, while treating a never-ending parade of wounded soldiers, most younger than she, many who would never get to be as old as she.

Gloria and Arthur, both now deceased, were married in 1920, Jack was born in 1922, and his sister, Mary, came along in 1924. The family settled in a modest three-bedroom home in a quiet, middle-class neighborhood in Englewood, just across the Hudson from upper Manhattan and the lower Bronx, oblivious to the Great Depression because Arthur was a vital member of the bridge-building team, and there was always a need for nurses with Gloria's experience.

Jack was an avid sports fan, just like his father, and while baseball was his favorite game to follow in the daily newspapers, awed as he was by the exploits of Babe Ruth and Lou Gehrig and the dynastic New York Yankees, it was football that the sturdily-built Jack possessed the requisite skills for. When he graduated from public school and moved on to St. Cecilia, he made the freshmen football team, played a year of junior varsity, and then earned his spot on the varsity which was coached by former Fordham University quarterback Andy Palau, and Palau's old Rams teammate, Lombardi.

Who could have known then, during those days at St. Cecilia when Lombardi taught Jack chemistry in the morning and football in the afternoon, that 30 years later they would be sitting on a hotel pool deck in Fort Lauderdale, each among the most distinguished men in their respective fields, discussing the end of Lombardi's storied tenure as coach of the Packers.

"What are you going to do with yourself, coach?" Jack asked the man who he always had, and always would, call coach. "When training camp starts in the summer, what the hell are you going to do to scratch that itch?"

Lombardi looked across the table, and with a glint of sadness in those piercing brown Italian eyes admitted that he wasn't sure, but that he knew this was the right time to leave the Packers, as soon as they kicked the shit out of those minor-league Raiders from the AFL.

Two days later, Lombardi led the Packers onto the field at the Orange Bowl, and his men put on one last display of brilliance as they blew past the overmatched Raiders of up-and-coming coach John Madden, 33-14. Even though Green Bay was by far the superior team, it was evident to everyone who was there that this was the end of an era, the end of a dynasty. The Raiders kept it close in the first half as they forced the Packers to settle for three Don Chandler field goals, and when Green Bay quarterback and game MVP Bart Starr connected with Boyd Dowler on a 62-yard touchdown pass, the Raiders had an answer when their quarterback, the Mad Bomber, Daryle Lamonica, hit Bill Miller with a 23-yard touchdown. But after intermission the Packers flexed their NFL muscle and gradually and decisively expanded on their 16-7 lead.

Jerry Kramer, the great offensive guard whose textbook-perfect block on Dallas' Jethro Pugh had paved the way for Starr to sneak across the goal line for the winning touchdown in the waning seconds of the Ice Bowl, knew this was Lombardi's last game and he told Jack afterward that he had implored his teammates to "play the last 30 minutes for the old man." And the Packers played the second half like they had played so often during Lombardi's iconic tenure, dominating the line of scrimmage on both sides and rendering the explosive

Oakland offense utterly feeble. By the time Lamonica and Miller hooked up for a second touchdown late in the fourth quarter, the Packers were already mentally spending their winners' shares - or at least deducing how their wives were going to spend it.

When it was over Lombardi was carried off the field by two of his greatest players, Kramer and fellow offensive lineman Forrest Gregg, both of whom had played on every one of Lombardi's Green Bay teams. Long after the horde of reporters had returned to the press box to begin clickety-clacketing away on their Remington's, Jack was leaning against the wall outside the Green Bay locker room talking with Starr, Lombardi's quarterback.

"How's the thumb?" he asked the wily veteran who was now a two-time Super Bowl MVP.

"Can't feel a thing right now," Starr said with a smile of the injury he suffered that knocked him out of the game early in the fourth quarter. "I'm thinking I'll be fine by the time I need to throw a football again."

"Well, since you brought it up, I know you know Lombardi is announcing his retirement this week or next. Have you given any thought to what 1968 is gonna be like without him?"

"Jack, all I know is it's gonna be one hell of a year."

It sure was.

1 - Love and War

There had been no communication in nearly three weeks - Christmas Eve, to be exact. The last Jack and his wife, Olivia, knew, their son, Patrick, was just south of the DMZ on a mountain plateau near the key strategic city of Khe Sahn, his head perpetually on a swivel, an M-16 slung over his shoulder, fighting whatever fight his country was asking him to fight. More importantly, scared shitless like just about every American soldier over there, he was trying to stay alive, and thankfully, he was succeeding.

Three weeks is a long damn time in war. So, when Jack reached his hotel in downtown Houston and called home to Garden City to hear Olivia gleefully share the news that she'd received a letter from Patrick, postmarked six days earlier, saying that he was all right and things had been quiet in his Godforsaken jungle, Jack fell back onto the bed and let out a sigh of relief.

Monday morning Jack had finished his piece on the Super Bowl and Vince Lombardi's heretofore unreported impending retirement - a scoop which was sure to create shockwaves, not to mention sell a few extra newsstand copies of *SportsWorld*. Once it was filed to the office in midtown Manhattan so that the goddamned copy editors and fact checkers could take their swings at his finely crafted prose, he called Olivia to check in, but because the mail had not yet arrived on the west end of Long Island, she had no news to report regarding Patrick.

After a check with the office to make sure the pencil-necked geeks - who always seemed to think they knew more than he about the events he covered - did not change so much as the placement of a comma, he lounged around for a bit at the hotel pool, then packed his suitcase for the drive down to the Miami airport. There was a quick detour to Miami Beach to grab lunch at the popular Jewish-style deli, Wolfies, on the corner of 21st and Collins, a great old place Jack always tried to hit whenever he was down in the land of humidity. One pastrami on rye and two cups of coffee later, Jack was off to catch his early-evening flight bound for Houston where he would be covering the big college basketball showdown between unbeaten, top-ranked UCLA, and unbeaten, second-ranked Houston at the magnificent Astrodome.

Jack asked Olivia to recite the letter, which she did, and as he listened to the depressing tale his son was recounting, his heart ached because Jack could relate to what Patrick was going through. Jack knew war, he knew what it was like to live in a jungle, soaked by the rains, buffeted by the wind, to be caked in mud, and ravaged by mosquitos. He knew what it felt like to endure the pains of daily hunger because the C-rations didn't come close to satisfying a man's appetite. He understood completely why Patrick lived in fear that one of those Viet Cong sons-of-bitches would sneak up from behind and slit his throat or blow his brains out because Jack had the very same fears about Hitler's lunatic Nazi troops two-and-a-half decades earlier. And though he worried every day that he'd never again see Patrick alive, it was somewhat offset by the pride that surged through Jack's heart and soul. His only son went to Vietnam, already without question the most unpopular war in United States history, knowing that it was what he had to do, eager to do his part, even though he - like almost every American including the top American, President Lyndon B. Johnson - wasn't sure what the hell our boys were fighting for. Maybe it was true what they said about war, that it's God's way of teaching you geography, because what other explanation was there for war, especially this war?

Jack first learned the true horrors of war from his mother. When he and his sister Mary began learning in history class about what was then called The Great War, Gloria McDonald augmented their lessons with some of her remembrances from her days in England. Jack, in particular, was fascinated by those conversations, but hearing the anguish in his mother's voice and drawing mental pictures of the carnage she dealt with, he openly hoped and privately prayed that he would never have to go to a foreign country to kill people, or even worse, be killed.

However, in December 1941 when the Japanese bombed Pearl Harbor, 19-year-old Jack had a change of heart and like most boys his age felt the immediate need to join the military and contribute to the protection of the American way of life. He took a leave from Fordham University, where he'd just completed his fifth semester of study and his second season on the varsity football team, to enlist in the Army. By the fall of 1942 he was in the shit in the European theater.

Always a leader growing up, whether it was corralling his friends for the daily summer sandlot baseball games of his New Jersey youth, or co-captaining the St. Cecilia varsity football team when he was a senior, nothing changed in the Army. Jack rose in rank during his two years overseas and when it came time to execute the historic Normandy landings on D-Day, June 6, 1944, he was a First Lieutenant with the 4th Infantry Division. On that fateful morning, the men of the 4th were plotted to land at Utah Beach at the Tare Green and Uncle Red sectors, but instead, due to inclement weather that shifted the current in the English Channel, they came ashore a bit to the Southeast at the Victor sector and encountered very little resistance, especially compared to the horrific tumult that greeted those who landed at Omaha Beach. However, barely an hour after they disembarked and had pressed inland, Jack took a bullet to his left shoulder and only thanks to the expert work of the company medic who quickly stanched the gushing blood did he make it out of that hell hole alive. After two surgeries and a few weeks of recuperation in France, he was sent home to New Jersey, against his wishes, his service to his country fulfilled, though he felt like a failure, felt like he was abandoning his brothers when they needed him the most.

For the final year of the war, Jack had a tough time coming to terms with the fact that his comrades were still risking their lives while he was stateside, back at Fordham pursuing a degree in journalism. Only when President Truman dropped the atomic bombs on Hiroshima and Nagasaki in August 1945, bringing an abrupt end to the war, did Jack truly feel ready to move on with his life. Unable to resume his football career due to his injury, he concentrated on his studies and spent two summers working in the wire room at the *New York Herald-Tribune* learning about the business he was hoping to forge a career in. Impressed by his work, the newspaper brought him on full-time after he graduated with honors, kick-starting a journey that, 20 years later, had taken him to the top of his profession.

By 1948 he was working in the sports department at the *Herald-Tribune* where the great Red Smith was the lead sports columnist. He stayed until 1955 when the *New York Post* lured him away to cover the New York Football Giants where his old coach, Vince Lombardi, was working as the defensive coordinator. Jack was on the Giants' beat during a period when they were one of the NFL's preeminent teams with a roster filled with a cadre of stars including Charlie Conerly, Frank Gifford, Alex Webster, Kyle Rote, Sam Huff, Rosey Grier, and Andy Robustelli. They won the NFL championship in 1956 with a 47-7 trouncing of the Chicago Bears, then captured the East Division in 1958, '59 and '61, only to lose all three championship games, most notably the famous overtime battle in '58 at Yankee Stadium to the Baltimore Colts, the game that universally was credited with putting pro football on the map.

Following the title game loss in '61 to the Packers, by then coached by Lombardi who that day won the first of his five championships in Green Bay, Jack received a phone call - on New Years' Day 1962 - from Martin Abrams, the managing editor of *SportsWorld*, asking if he'd be interested in joining the world-renowned weekly magazine as its senior football writer. Within days of accepting the incredibly generous, life-changing offer, Jack was sent out on his first assignment - a 5,000-word cover story on none other than Lombardi.

Four distinguished years covering pro football led to his promotion to senior columnist, thus allowing Jack the freedom to travel around the country, and even the world, to write about the biggest sports events and the most famous athletes, next on his list being the most eagerly-awaited college basketball showdown in recent memory.

2 - *Big Lew Meets Big E*

A couple weeks before mighty UCLA arrived in Texas to
play the University of Houston in what was being billed as
college basketball's game of the century, Cougars coach
Guy Lewis - perhaps the only non-country clubber in
America who could pull off wearing bright red trousers
and red-and-white checkered sport coats - dispatched a
scout to the West Coast to watch John Wooden's
magnificent Bruins in person.

The assignment was to find a chink in the armor of this
magnificent machine, the defending NCAA champion,
winner of 47 games in a row, and led by the incomparable
giant, 7-foot-2 junior center Lew Alcindor, already
considered to be the greatest college basketball player in
history after not even a year-and-a-half as a varsity player.

"He saw 'em beat the livin' tar outta Washington and Washington State, and then he goes up to Cal and they beat 'em all by about 30, so he comes back and tells me, 'No college team can beat this team,'" Lewis recalled to Jack in his Texas drawl as they sat in Lewis' claustrophobic office inside Jeppesen Fieldhouse the day before the Cougars would try to prove that scout wrong. "What the hell do I do with that horseshit? I mean dadgummit, that's not gonna help us a lick when that big fella starts throwing up them hook shots of his. Well I told my players and ya know what they said? 'We'll beat 'em.'"

And beat 'em they did. In front of more than 52,000 fans at the Astrodome - the world's first indoor baseball/football stadium that was transformed into the world's largest basketball arena for this momentous occasion - Alcindor looked merely mortal and UCLA could not overcome his rare off night, not to mention the sublime play of Houston star Elvin Hayes, and lost, 71-69.

"This was the greatest victory our school has ever won," said Lewis, who certainly qualified as an expert on that topic as he'd been a Cougar ever since he came home from the war and played for the very first Houston basketball team in 1946, then became just the second coach in program history, a job he'd held since 1956.

In the days leading up to the first nationally-televised regular-season college basketball game, which would be viewed on approximately 150 stations in every state in the union except Hawaii, Jack spent plenty of time on the Houston campus trying to take the pulse of the place, and to learn more about this up-and-coming basketball power before the heretofore unbeatable Bruins sauntered into town.

Football was king in Texas, and Jack knew what they always said about basketball down there - it's just a way for football players to stay in shape until the start of spring practice. But for more than a decade Lewis had been trying to change the culture, and he was starting to succeed. Houston was not a member of the Southwest Conference, nor was it a member of any conference. Thus, as an independent, the Cougars' football squad was largely irrelevant in the Lone Star State. With a limit of 10 regular-season games, SWC teams had only three weeks where they could schedule non-conference foes, and most preferred to play schools from outside of SWC territory in order to help increase their recruiting footprint. Thus, the Texas-based SWC teams - Texas, Texas Tech, SMU, TCU, Baylor, Rice, and Texas A&M typically ignored Houston. Since the start of the 1960s, the only schools that scheduled Houston were Baylor and Texas A&M, and neither of them had done so since 1965.

So, Lewis saw an opportunity for basketball to make its mark at Houston. The SWC was a powerful football league, but it was not a strong basketball league, and Lewis' Cougars were consistently one of the best hardwood squads in Texas. None of his first four teams qualified for post-season play, but after exiting the rugged Missouri Valley Conference to go independent in 1960, things began to turn. In five of the next seven years the Cougars qualified for a tournament (once in the NIT, four times in the NCAA) and just last spring they'd advanced to the NCAA Final Four where they lost in the national semifinals, 73-58, to UCLA in a game played at Freedom Hall in Louisville.

One of the key reasons for the resurgence was the university administration's decision in 1964 to finally allow black athletes to play for Cougar teams. That seismic sociological breakthrough allowed Lewis to recruit star players like his senior co-captains, Don Chaney and Elvin Hayes, who arrived on campus from Louisiana in the fall of 1964 and, after sitting out their freshman year per NCAA rules, had led Houston to 66 victories in 76 games heading into the showdown with UCLA. After a decade-long absence from the national polls, the Cougars had not been outside the top 10 since November of 1966, and now, thanks to this monumental victory in front of the largest crowd to ever witness a college basketball game, they would be catapulting past the Bruins into the number one spot in the land.

Lewis hadn't exactly appreciated that piece of information his scout provided, but he admitted to Jack that he knew damn well it might have been the truth. The previous spring when UCLA blew past the Cougars in the NCAA on its way to its third national championship in four years, Hayes, just as he was in the Astrodome, was the best player on the court. He outscored Alcindor, 25-19, and out-rebounded him, 24-20, but the Bruins were just too good and they simply wore down Lewis' team.

"They hit you so many ways," Lewis said when he thought back to that game as he sat behind his metal desk drinking coffee while Jack listened intently and scribbled away in his notebook. "Last year at Louisville we placed too much emphasis on Alcindor. We were letting him pass to the open man. This time we have to make it tough for them to get the ball to him, and then cut off his passing lanes. There ain't no way we can stop him, but we gotta keep them other fellas from killing us."

And if that didn't work, Lewis had a couple other things up his sleeve. Before Jack visited with Lewis, he talked to various people in the Houston athletic department and he learned that Lewis wasn't leaving anything to chance. For instance, he sure wasn't going to haul out of his closet the same pink-and-white-checkered sport coat he wore in that tournament game because clearly, it had bad karma. Lewis also decided that because his team sat on the left side of the scorer's table against UCLA last year, also the same side they had been sitting on for their home games this year, that they would instead sit on the right side at the Astrodome. Further, Lewis arranged for the Bruins to be escorted into the cavernous stadium for their shoot-around a few hours later, which Jack would be attending, through unlucky gate number 13.

"Hey, if no college team can beat 'em then we're gonna have to get creative, and we're gonna have to change things up," Lewis said with a smile when he explained to Jack his seemingly lunatic superstitions.

None of that really mattered, though, when the game began because everything Hayes threw toward the hoop went in. Following the NCAA match when he'd outplayed Alcindor, Hayes was asked his opinion of the UCLA prodigy and Jack, who was standing just a few feet away, heard the man they called The Big E opine, "I can't really say Alcindor should be the No. 1 basketball player in the country." Pressed further, Hayes added, "He's not aggressive enough on the boards, particularly on offense. Defensively, he just stands around. He's not at all, you know, all they really put him up to be."

It was all chutzpah because actually, Alcindor was everything everyone said he was, a lithe athletic assassin who was the most dominant offensive player to come along since Kansas' own 7-foot-2 behemoth, Wilt Chamberlain, had laid waste to opponents a decade before. But while Wilt's game was all about power, Alcindor's was all about finesse. He could work inside to score amidst the flying elbows and the crafty hip checks that defenders tried to get away with, but he could also step out and knock down his incontestable hook shot with remarkable ease.

The only thing that could truly stop Alcindor was an injury, and wouldn't you know it, he had one when he took the court at the Astrodome. A week before, he'd suffered a scratched left eyeball and he sat out UCLA's last two games, routs of Stanford and Portland. For part of the week before the trip to Houston he stayed in bed and rested wearing an eyepatch, and the first time he practiced was during the Bruins' day-before-the-game workout. "I didn't feel as good physically as I should have," was the reticent Alcindor's lone comment after what was arguably the worst performance of his college career, and just the second defeat of his high school and college careers combined.

And it showed in his play. He made only 4 of 18 shots from the floor and finished with 15 points and 12 rebounds. Meanwhile, Hayes played like a man possessed. He pumped in 29 first-half points and finished with 39 points and 15 rebounds, prompting Lewis to say, "Isn't that Hayes great? Almost every game he plays is great."

Lewis called Hayes' first-half heroics, "The greatest I've ever seen in college basketball." That's because not only was he scoring in bunches to help give the Cougars a 46-43 halftime lead, he and teammate Ken Spain were taking turns in the low post of Houston's active 1-3-1 zone frustrating Alcindor. Hayes actually blocked three of Alcindor's shots and twice stole the ball from him.

"Our plan was to bottle up Alcindor and shut off his passing lanes to (Mike) Lynn and (Lynn) Shackelford," said Lewis. "Shackelford and Lynn killed us from the corners in last year's game. We knew we had to stop Alcindor, and we had to stop his feeds to the corner men."

Despite the one-sided nature of the marquee Hayes-Alcindor matchup, the Bruins remained close throughout. Houston had run off a 16-6 spurt in the first half with Hayes scoring 10 to open a 27-18 lead, but UCLA clawed back to within three at the half using its vaunted press to force turnovers that resulted in easy baskets.

With Hayes' scoring curtailed in the second half by constant double-teaming, the Bruins rallied on the wings of hot-shooting guard Lucious Allen (25 points), pulled even at 54-54, and the game was tense from then on. Alcindor made a free throw to forge a 65-65 tie with 3:02 remaining, and after Houston regained a four-point lead, Allen drove the lane for a basket, then made two free throws after Spain had missed a pair, and the score was 69-69 with 44 seconds to go.

The final half minute was simply frantic. With 28 seconds left, UCLA's Jim Nielsen fouled Hayes, and Hayes calmly sank both shots to produce what would be the last points of the night. UCLA threw a pass away for a turnover, got the ball back when the Cougars were charged with traveling, then turned it over again when the ball went out of bounds off a Bruin with 12 seconds to go. After a timeout, Houston inbounded the ball to Hayes, and he managed to dribble clear of trouble and avoided getting fouled as the clock struck zero and bedlam broke out on the Astrodome floor.

Oh, about that floor. Jack had learned that the playing court was trucked in from the Los Angeles Sports Arena, a 225-panel puzzle that weighed 18 tons and cost $10,000 to transport. After the game the floor was disassembled, loaded up and sent back to Los Angeles where in two months, the NCAA Final Four would be played on it. When Allen heard this, his first thought was that these two teams might be meeting on this very same hardwood with the national championship on the line, and that excited the senior. "I hope they come to L.A. undefeated," said Allen. "That would be very nice."

3 - Tet

The footage, even the edited version shown on NBC's *Huntley-Brinkley Report*, was so stunning, so horrifying, that Kathleen McDonald couldn't physically close her mouth after her jaw had drooped in disbelief.

Cupping her face as she sat in the first-floor dining room of her residence hall on the campus of Columbia University, her fertile mind could not process what she and at least 100 other students had just seen on the black and white television at the far end of the spacious room. Cold-blooded murder in the streets of Saigon, an image she was sure would never be eviscerated from her mind.

One day earlier the war in Vietnam had taken a stark turn when North Vietnamese Army and Viet Cong forces, estimated to be in excess of 80,000 strong, launched a massive wave of surprise attacks on South Vietnam, infiltrating more than 100 cities and towns including 36 of 44 provincial capitols. The most astonishing aspect of what became known as the Tet Offensive were the forays on the metropolis of Saigon where the Communist soldiers blanketed South Vietnam's capitol city and targeted the headquarters of the Army of the Republic of Vietnam, the Tan Son Nhut Air Base, the Independence Palace, the Long Binh Naval Headquarters, the National Radio Station, and the U.S. Embassy, as well as several police districts and individual homes of ARVN officers.

The allied troops, caught terribly off guard because the war was supposed to have been in a state of cease fire to observe the Tet Lunar New Year holiday, had regrouped after the initial insurgence and had begun to regain their footing. And on a street corner in the heart of Saigon, the South Vietnamese chief of national police, General Nguyen Ngoc Loan, made a statement to that effect. After his men had captured a Vietcong operative named Nguyen Van Lem, Loan walked over to the young handcuffed prisoner, raised his pistol, pointed it at his head, and pulled the trigger.

At the precise moment the bullet exploded into Lem's head, the shutter on the camera of an Associated Press photographer named Eddie Adams clicked, preserving a Pulitzer Prize-winning moment that was deemed unconscionable by the American public. Further, the execution was caught on video by an NBC cameraman, and as millions watched Chet Huntley and David Brinkley explain the horrific scene while warning of its graphic nature, the United States' tolerance of the war took a precipitous dip, and Kathleen was following right along.

Actually, it had been several months since Kathleen had been gripped with disquietude regarding Vietnam. Her grandma McDonald had served in World War I, her father, Jack, served in World War II, and now her older brother, Patrick, was there in Vietnam. The McDonalds had always done their part, and she was so proud to say that three generations had played a role in defending America's freedom. But this war, this war that was tearing the country apart, had conjured feelings she never thought she'd have to deal with.

On the one hand, she knew she had to back the effort - after all, that was the family ethos, all she'd ever known. And really, why wouldn't she, considering her big brother was over there. One year her elder, Patrick was in many ways her best friend as much as he was her sibling. He'd always watched over her in grammar school and later in high school; it was he who taught her how to throw a baseball, how to shoot a basketball, how to properly roll a joint (and made sure their parents never found out about their occasional dalliance with pot); and it was he who introduced her to Elvis Presley and Buddy Holly and The Beatles and The Rolling Stones. He was in the thick of this awful conflict and now he needed her love and support more than she had ever needed his which was saying something. Could anyone possibly expect her to march and chant against the war?

But on the other hand, she could not shake the omnipresent feeling that this war was wrong because no one seemed to know who we were actually fighting, or why, and our men and women were dying there every day, for what? The goals in World War I and World War II and in Korea had been clear and unmistakable; America knew its enemy, understood the cause our soldiers were undertaking, and stood shoulder to shoulder from Maine to California, from Florida to Washington, in countenance. Vietnam was different, the lines so blurry, the initiative so seemingly cryptic, and as more and more body bags were being filled with young Americans - who, if you listened to the vociferous anti-war faction, had no business fighting a battle the South Vietnamese should have been fighting themselves - Kathleen was wavering and questioning her own belief system. And the fact that she was a sophomore in the journalism school at Columbia certainly exacerbated her confusion and trepidation.

Like many universities and colleges across the country, Columbia was roiled by debate regarding Vietnam and almost daily there were protesters marching on the Morningside Heights campus. They carried their hand-made signs and their bullhorns and they chanted their disapproval of America's involvement. Most of the unrest was civil as campus security looked on, comforted to be backed by the New York City police department which was on constant alert, ready to intercede if needed. But on some days it escalated, especially when certain over-exuberant groups had the temerity to light the stars and stripes aflame, as if that vile act was going to bring Patrick and the other men and women home safely.

If the anti-war sentiment wasn't enough, the campus was also embroiled in a racially-fueled dispute over the school administration's plan to construct a gymnasium in the city-owned Morningside Park which was bordered by the campus on one side, and the largely African-American neighborhood of Harlem on the other. The facility was slated to be built on a steep slope in the park, with Harlem at the bottom of the hill and Morningside Heights at the top, and at issue was the proposed design of the building. It had been decided that Harlem residents would be allowed use of the facility, but they would have access only to a dedicated community area on the lower level through a "back door" entrance on their side of the gym, while Columbia students would enter from the main doors located on their side. This was unacceptable to many who felt the Harlem residents were being discriminated against, a form of blatant racism, and the protesters nicknamed the project "Gym Crow."

So, in the weeks leading up to Tet, the cauldron that was Columbia was bubbling more actively, the student uprisings had grown more intense, more divisive, more militant, and, to Kathleen's senses, more frightful. Ever since she had enrolled in the fall of 1966, the controversy surrounding Vietnam had always smoldered, and then in March 1967 it began to burn as hot as napalm when it came to light that Columbia was playing an important and heretofore secretive role in assisting the United States' involvement. An activist for Columbia's Students for a Democratic Society named Bob Feldman discovered documents in the International Law Library that mapped out the university's affiliation with the Institute for Defense Analyses (IDA), a weapons research think-tank that was part of the U.S. Department of Defense. When Feldman went public with his findings, the already overwhelmingly anti-war student body was whipped into a further froth and demanded the university resign its membership in the IDA.

The university did not bow to the pressure, much to the chagrin of the SDS, and plans were already in the works for a massive protest in the coming spring. There was no telling how far the SDS would go to make its point, but there was deep concern at Columbia that the university grounds could become a de facto battlefield. Now, on this night, students in the dining room of the John Jay residence hall, as well as Americans everywhere, were watching the atrocity of a human life, enemy or not, being taken. And with a camera capturing the repulsion for the world to see, the heat was turned up several more degrees.

When the broadcast was complete and Brinkley said, "Good night, Chet" and Huntley replied in kind as he always did, "Good night, David, and good night, for NBC News" there was nothing more than a murmuring amongst the dispersing students as they tried to digest what they'd just seen. Kathleen took the elevator up to her fourth-floor room, walked through the doors to the right and immediately went to the hall phone and called her parents in Garden City to ask if they'd watched the news, and to inquire about whether they'd heard anything from Patrick since his last letter had arrived a couple weeks earlier. Indeed, Jack and Olivia had seen the film clip, and Olivia could sense that her daughter was at once disturbed by the brutality and fearful for Patrick's safety. Olivia had read every word of coverage about the Tet Offensive in that day's edition of the *New York Times* and she, too, had waves of anxiety rush over her because with the attacks so broad in scope across South Vietnam, surely Patrick had to be in harm's way.

"Honey, we don't know where he is, but you know your brother - he's a survivor, he always finds a way," Olivia said, trying in vain to ease her daughter's worry, and perhaps even her own.

Like so many Americans, Olivia had concluded months ago that the United States should withdraw from Vietnam. She read about the speech made by General William Westmoreland to the National Press Club back in November of 1967 where he emphatically stated that the communists were, "...unable to mount a major offensive ... I am absolutely certain that whereas in 1965 the enemy was winning, today he is certainly losing. We have reached an important point when the end begins to come into view."

She didn't buy it, and she wanted to know to what end Westmoreland was referring. President Johnson had recently sent more troops to Vietnam and U.S. representation in the country was now more than 500,000, its highest total ever. Americans were watching this war and all of its hell on television, and the nightly dispatches from reporters on the scene, reciting the rhetoric that the U.S. military leaders were providing during the press briefings, had grown more and more difficult to believe. Westmoreland was saying that the enemy was being defeated, but Americans were watching their sons, daughters, nephews, nieces, or neighbors traipsing through forests and swamps, trying to find that ever-elusive bastard, Charlie. They saw them laid out on their bellies along the Ho Chi Minh Trail, M-16's at the ready, hoping the damn things wouldn't jam as they were known to do, eyes wide open and darting from side to side, unsure of where the next confrontation would be coming from. They saw soldiers carrying their wounded comrades, their faces filled with pain and anguish, to safety, but really, was anywhere truly safe over there? What end was Westmoreland talking about?

The general, sounding confident to the point of arrogant, had said just a couple weeks earlier, "I hope they try something, because we are looking for a fight." Well, he got his wish, and now, more than ever, as a Viet Cong man lie dead in a Saigon street, a hole blown through his head, and thousands of others on both sides of the conflict meeting a similar fate, the end of this Vietnam nightmare never seemed more distant.

4 – Greatness at Grenoble

It had been nearly a quarter of a century since Jack had stepped foot in France, and that was a step he would never forget for as long as he would live. It was D-Day, June 6, 1944, and he and the members of the 4th Infantry division were advancing inland from Utah Beach on their way to hooking up with the paratroopers of the 82nd Airborne unit near Sainte Mere-Eglise. Jack was just emerging from a tree-lined area along the main road when he was gunned down by a German sniper.

He left France on one of the specially-constructed war-time hospital trains that could transport hundreds of wounded soldiers from the front lines to the division hospitals. Weeks later he was shipped back across the Atlantic Ocean to Englewood from whence he'd come two years earlier, and he got on with the rest of his life, a life that now would have him returning to the country where he'd almost died.

Grenoble, the host city for the 10th Winter Olympiad, was a long way from Sainte Mere-Eglise, maybe 300 miles to the southeast tucked down near the borders of Northern Italy and Switzerland, and Jack really had no interest in taking a detour to reacquaint himself with the beaches of Normandy. He was interested, however, in this dashing French skier named Jean-Claude Killy, the two-time defending World Cup champion who was widely regarded as the greatest skier on the planet and would be the heavy favorite to win all three alpine skiing events, a feat accomplished only once in the nine previous Games. And while Jack was apathetic regarding figure skating, he knew the pretty American brunette, Peggy Fleming, was going to be a big story in these Olympics to the folks back home, and his editor, Mark Brantley, had already told him to brush up on his Salchows, axels, toe loops, and camel spins because he'd be writing about Miss Fleming, whether she won gold, silver, bronze, or catastrophe.

Brantley had tagged along on the flight from LaGuardia to Paris, and the subsequent train ride down to Grenoble, one of 19 *SportsWorld* staffers who would be on site though only three - Jack, Mitch McBride and Henry Lucchesi - would actually be providing copy for the magazine. There were five photographers on the team, three fact-checking researchers - one for each writer - and then there were guys like Brantley, managing editor Martin Abrams, and a few advertising and marketing stiffs who were only there to drink, eat and be merry while they hosted the parties that *SportsWorld* would be throwing in the never-ending pursuit of increased ad buys.

Jack was OK with that; business was business and he knew the wining and dining was all part of it. But what he really hated was when he was asked - as the senior columnist and, in many ways, the face of the magazine - to attend the parties and schmooze it up with the clients. "Tell 'em a few stories about life on the road, Jack Mac," is what Abrams would always say. Well, Jack enjoyed his vodka gimlets just like the next guy, but he much preferred to be drinking them with people he was fond of, or at least wanted to get to know. These blowhards he was forced to entertain didn't fit in either category, but he did it because he knew he had to.

Every once in a while, though, Jack enjoyed one of these soirees, such as the one that was held the night before the opening ceremonies. Jack was summoned to the magnificent Hôtel de l'Europe, Grenoble's oldest hotel situated right in the city's central square, for *SportsWorld*'s biggest shindig of the fortnight, and ol' Jack Mac went home pretty happy when it was done.

As he was working his way through his third vodka gimlet, and trying to plot his escape from a conversation with an oil baron from Texas who was representing Shell but was far more interested in talking about the golf club championship he'd won the previous summer, into the ballroom walked French actresses/models Catherine Deneuve and Brigitte Bardot. Olivia McDonald probably would have given Jack a serious stare down had she seen the drool meandering down from her husband's chin when those two beauties breezed past him. And oh, what she might have done if she could have read Jack's mind the moment he caught a glimpse of their glamourous gowns that revealed their naked backs for all to see. Even the wannabe Arnold Palmer shut his trap as the head-turning women sashayed their way over to give a hug and a kiss on each cheek to the host, Franklin Xavier Stevenson, the chief executive officer of *SportsWorld*, who was holding a bourbon on the rocks in one hand, an unfiltered Camel cigarette in the other, and looking very much like the unrefined, multi-millionaire that he was.

Damn, it's good to be the king, Jack thought to himself as he watched Stevenson greet his two most famous and certainly most beautiful guests. And it was good to be Jack, at least on this night, because about 15 minutes later, Abrams strolled over to Jack and told him that Stevenson wanted him to come by and not only meet the starlets, but tell them all he knew about the playboy quarterback of the New York Jets, Joe Namath.

Jack had just written a cover story on Namath at the conclusion of the 1967 pro football season, during which he'd become the first man in history to surpass 4,000 yards passing in a season. Jack had spent three days at the Jets' practice facility on Long Island getting to know the handsome gunslinger who was taking Broadway by storm, which explained why he was already nicknamed Broadway Joe. Miss Deneuve and Miss Bardot didn't know a thing about football, and barely even recognized the fact that Namath was a star quarterback, but they knew he was somebody. They had both appeared at a swanky fashion party at Sardi's on West 44th in midtown Manhattan a few months back and Namath was there as well. They were captivated by Joe's charisma and the way the models swooned when he fixed his gaze on them. Despite their own celebrity, they were admittedly intrigued. So, as Stevenson was pointing out various members of the *SportsWorld* team and he mentioned that "Jack over there" had just written a cover story about Namath, they asked to meet Jack.

Jack was not an awkward man, nor was he someone who was ever uncomfortable in a social setting, but this was a situation he hadn't encountered before. Typically at these things, he'd be talking up CEOs from Xerox or American Airlines or General Motors, regaling them with stories about Mickey Mantle or Jack Nicklaus or Jim Brown or Wilt Chamberlain. Dishing the inside scoop on Joe Namath to two of the most beautiful and well-known figures in fashion and entertainment was a new experience.

Jack walked back with Abrams, gave a firm handshake to Stevenson, politely turned down his offer of a Camel, and then was introduced to Miss Deneuve and Miss Bardot, taking each of their right hands and kissing them as he said hello. If any of his sports writer pals had seen that, he knew he would have paid holy hell, but it felt like the thing to do, the women certainly didn't pull back and, in fact, it seemed as if they were expecting it.

"Jack here's the man you ought to talk to," Stevenson said. "I didn't read the story myself - sorry Jack - but I'm sure he knows more about ol' Joe Willie than Joe Willie's mama. Jack's the best we got."

For the next 10 minutes, Jack spoke as authoritatively as he could on all things Namath. He spiced up the conversation with as much anecdotal information that he could remember from his time with Namath, answered a couple of their questions, and then, as if a timer went off in both of their heads, the moment came when he could clearly see they were placated and they'd had enough of his drivel. Sensing his dalliance with them was complete, Jack looked at his now empty glass and said, "Franklin, ladies, if you'll excuse me, I'm going to freshen this. It was a privilege to have met you."

"Thanks for stopping by, Jack, and good luck up there on that mountain," Stevenson said, a reference to Jack chronicling the exploits of the great Killy at Chamrousse. Jack nodded as both women smiled and said, "Au revoir."

"You kissed their hands?" Olivia said the next day when Jack called her from his hotel room. "You're such a cad."

He figured he'd get something like that, but it was worth it. After all, he kissed the hands of Catherine Deneuve and Brigitte Bardot. How many men would die for the chance to do that, let alone talk to them for 10 minutes? Millions, maybe? Hell yeah he kissed their hands.

The rest of his 12-day stay in France wasn't nearly as rewarding, but it offered up some terrific story lines that he was able to write the hell out of, the result of which was two more cover stories, one on Fleming, the other on Killy, both of whom, as expected, rose to the occasion and stole the show.

Prim and proper Peggy was up first, and Jack knew he'd be relying on *SportsWorld*'s crack researcher, Helen Habadasher, to get through Miss Fleming's pursuit of America's first Olympic figure skating gold medal since the 1960 Games in Squaw Valley. "Now, you know about 1961, right?" Helen had asked Jack on the train ride from Paris. Yes, Jack knew about 1961, but Helen really knew about 1961, and her notes provided tremendous perspective for Jack as he sought to capture the essence of Fleming's victory, and what it meant to the United States figure skating community.

On Valentine's Day 1961, less than a month after John F. Kennedy had been sworn in as President, the entire United States team, including 18 skaters and 16 coaches, officials, and family members, boarded Sabena Flight 548 at Idlewild Airport in New York City (which was now renamed in honor of JFK) bound for the World Championships in Prague. The plane never made it to Czechoslovakia as it crashed in Belgium near the airport in Brussels, all 72 passengers and crew members plus one farmer on the ground perishing in the tragedy.

In the moments it took for that Boeing 707 to disintegrate, so came to a dreadful and devastating end an unprecedented era of United States dominance in the sport. It had begun with Dick Button's breakthrough silver medal at the 1947 worlds, and continued on throughout the 1950s for both genders, and there seemed no end in sight. Button and the Jenkins brothers, Hayes and David, combined to win every men's Olympic gold medal from

1948 through 1960, and American men finished first and second in the worlds for eight straight years starting in 1951. On the women's side, Tenley Albright won the worlds in 1953 and 1955, and Olympic gold in 1956 at Cortina d'Ampezzo, Italy, and then Carol Heiss won every world championship from 1956-60 as well as gold at Squaw Valley.

The team was in the midst of an overhaul as most of those great champions had gone on to the Ice Follies, into coaching, or on with the rest of their lives. But with so much depth in the program, the team was re-loaded and there was no reason to believe that the United States would be surpassed in the 1960s. Laurence and Maribel Owen, the daughters of nine-time U.S. ladies champ Maribel Vinson-Owen, were both reigning U.S. champs, Maribel in pairs with Dudley Richards. The U.S. men's champ, Bradley Lord, and silver medalist Gregory Kelley, were both on track to become world champions. There was U.S. ladies' silver medalist Stephanie Westerfeld, and bronze medalist Rhode Lee Michelson, to give Laurence Owen competition. And in ice dancing there were U.S. champions Diane Sherbloom and Larry Pierce, and runners-up Dona Lee Carrier and Roger Campbell.

And then they were all gone.

The day after the crash, U.S. skating officials established a memorial fund to honor the victims and to begin rebuilding the extinct team. Fundraisers were organized in many of the country's skating hotbeds and exhibitions and shows were put on by some of the stars of the past with proceeds earmarked for rising young skaters, and one of the first gifts distributed went to Fleming, then a 12-year-old living in Northern California who had been coached by Bill Kipp, one of those who died in the crash. Fleming, who grew up with three sisters in a house where money was always tight, used the award to buy a new pair of skates, and it was apparent very early on that the skating association had invested wisely in her. She practiced four hours per day under the tutelage of her new coach, John Nicks, much of that before the sun had risen, and she dominated the California junior scene in the early 1960s before stepping up to the national level, and ultimately, the international stage.

She won a silver medal in her first U.S. Championship in 1962 in the novice ladies division, won bronze in 1963 in the junior ladies' division,
and then in 1964 won the first of five consecutive gold medals when she was 15. That year she participated in her first Olympics in Innsbruck, Austria, and she placed sixth, but was the highest finishing American. After that competition, Heiss, a television commentator for ABC, said she had no doubt Fleming would win gold at Grenoble in '68. Fleming's family moved to Colorado Springs in 1965 so she could train with Carlo Fassi, who like Nicks had been hired to help fill the U.S. coaching void. With Fassi's technical expertise, Fleming became the world champion in 1966, repeated in 1967, and then Heiss was proven prophetic when Fleming easily won Olympic gold at Le Stade de Glace.

During the tedious compulsory figures, which counted what Jack deemed a ridiculous 60 percent of the overall score, Fleming carved her figures nearly perfectly and she built an almost-insurmountable lead heading into the free skating long program. Still, this was the Olympics, and she was 19 years old, and the weight of an entire skating program was on her shoulders as she waited to take the ice.

When it was finally her turn, she leaped and spun and smiled and had the crowd mesmerized by her combination of grace and athleticism, though her performance was not without flaw. She two-footed the landing on an incomplete double Lutz and turned a double axel into a single - at least that's what Jack was told by Helen - and when she finished she skated off with puddles in her eyes because she thought she may have blown it. But in reality, she would have needed to fall three times and flip the bird to the panel of judges to lose the gold, and she did none of that.

"Boy," she told the world press in a news conference after the final scores had been tabulated, "it was all rougher than I thought. I mean, up until tonight I had figured the worst part of the whole thing came a week ago when I came out to practice. All my competitors came around and sat on the edge of the rink and just killed me with piercing looks. I got through that all right, but this was something else."

Jack had requested some one-on-one time with the new ice queen and because he was one of America's foremost sports columnists, he was granted the interview. When it was over, and he'd learned all about how her mother,

Doris, had hand-sewn her costumes, and how her nerves had almost gotten the best of her, and how one summer when she was very young and her father was out of work, the family lived at a campsite because they could not afford a home, Fleming thanked Jack, then turned to a friend and said, "How do you like my new little necklace?"

Jack had barely finished writing that cover story when it was time to begin following Killy, who did indeed win all three gold medals, capturing the downhill, giant slalom, and slalom in breathtaking and controversial fashion, the sound of his gleeful countrymen roaring in celebration reverberating throughout the foggy French hills.

Oh, the fog. If not for all the snow and ski bunnies, Jack would have sworn he was watching from the top of the Golden Gate Bridge in San Francisco rather than a press tower overlooking the finish line at Chamrousse. It wasn't too bad during Killy's first victory in the downhill, but it got progressively worse over the several days of alpine competition and when it was time to run the final race - the much-anticipated slalom when Killy, after winning giant slalom gold, would be chasing history - the course was shrouded in white soup. The spectators were lucky if they could see the person next to them, let alone who was schussing down the mountain. As for the competitors, Rick Chaffee - one of the few American racers who didn't suffer an injury during the meet as eight of the 14 men and women on the U.S. team crashed either in training runs or competition - summed it up best when he said of his slalom run, "I made every gate I could find."

Killy came into these Games as the overwhelming favorite. He'd had a spectacular 1966-67 World Cup season when he won 23 of 30 races including all five World Cup downhills. And he got off to an equally blazing start in 1967-68 as he dominated the Alps in the fall, winning races in Italy, France, Switzerland, and Austria, and then came over to the United States and in a 10-day period won seven more titles in New Hampshire and Colorado, a stretch of success unparalleled in the world of alpine.

"In a starting gate," Killy said with his ever-present titanic confidence, "it never occurs to me that I will not be first."

Why would it? Flying down a mountain, with all his flair and daring, in a diametric state of controlled chaos, he was more overpowering than baseball flamethrowers Sandy Koufax or Bob Gibson blowing fastballs past weak-hitting utility infielders. There was no one on the circuit who could keep pace with him, and generally, the few times Killy had been defeated in a slalom or giant slalom, it was his own errors of aggression that cost him, not someone like Americans Billy Kidd and Jimmie Huega, or Austria's Heini Messner and Gerhard Nenning, skiing faster.

Victory did not come as easily in Grenoble for Killy as most had predicted, though. He barely won the downhill, cruised in the giant slalom, and then was awarded the gold in the slalom only after two racers who finished ahead of him were disqualified.

The downhill was first, and heavy winds delayed the start of the race which only made Killy sit and wait with the pressure of winning on his home powder weighing on his shoulders. Also gnawing at him was the fact that the course wasn't really powdery at all, it had turned ruggedly icy, and during his training run he ground much of the wax off his skies, wax that could not be replaced in time for his championship run. Before he got positioned in the starting gate he turned to a teammate and, in a rare moment of dubiety, admitted that he did not think he could win. Thus, his strategy was simple: Go for broke, and if he fell, so be it. He didn't fall. He catapulted off the line as only he could and turned in the fastest first interval. However, as the run progressed the wax issue began shaving milliseconds off virtually every meter he covered. Sensing this, Killy masterfully took a slightly different line around the final gate near the finish and when Swiss time stopped, he was in the lead. One by one the racers descended after him, and none could overtake him, his teammate, Guy Perillat, coming the closest, just .08 seconds behind.

"My start was tremendous, and I took every risk I could find on the course," Killy said at his press conference. "I also had a little secret I knew about the finish line. Early in the practice runs, I had realized that if I cut a sharp line just at the pole on the right, I could actually gain a couple of meters. I had never taken this line during practice, because I didn't want anyone to know about it."

The giant slalom was no contest, Killy winning with ease over Willy Favre of Switzerland and bronze medalist Messner, and then came the swirling controversy that engulfed the slalom. The seeding race for the slalom was postponed due to impossible fog, and the next day, the conditions were virtually the same, but the French organizing officials - despite throaty protests from the television networks who tried to explain that the racers would be invisible on TV - refused to push it back another day because it would have then conflicted with the climactic 90-meter ski jump. So, the race went on, soon to be followed by uproar.

Before it even started, Killy and the boys were saying they could only see two gates in front of them, which, as you might imagine, was a bit unnerving. No one wanted to descend into the murkiness, but they were told to, so they did, and not surprisingly, the daring Killy had the fastest time of the first heat, 49.37 seconds. This allowed him to lead off for the second heat, an advantage on the freshly manicured course, and he posted 50.36 for a total of 1:39.73. However, things began to go askew when a Norwegian racer named Haakon Mjoen totaled 1:39.18 to surpass Killy, and then Austria's Karl Schranz - after being allowed a re-start on his second run when he claimed someone in a dark-hooded parka had wondered onto the course and distracted him - wound up posting 1:39.22.

So began a shit storm of the highest order. First, it was determined that Mjoen had missed a gate and was thus disqualified. Then, the judges went back over the video of Schranz's first attempt at a second run and found that he missed the 18th and 19th gates, a few seconds before he pulled off at the 22nd gate when the mystery man allegedly appeared.

"There was no one on the course," an official said later. "Schranz saw a solider far down below who was not on the course. The soldier had not bothered anyone else."

And so, just like that, Killy was king. Yes, it was good to be the king, not that Jack would know. He spied Miss Deneuve in the back of Killy's final press conference, and he caught her eye and smiled. Blank stare, a look away, no idea who he was. Olivia got a kick out of that.

5 - *This is Walter Cronkite, Good night*

As if Jack hadn't had enough of the gray smudge that had engulfed Grenoble for much of his time there during the Olympics, it was a similarly cold, dank, late-February day on Long Island as he sat down in his den to write a column on NBA superstar Wilt Chamberlain, who had just become the first player in history to surpass the 25,000-point career scoring plateau.

Jack smiled to himself more than a few times as he pored over the notes he had scribbled down during his conversation with the 7-foot-1 skyscraper of a man who was every bit as engaging and outspoken as he was dominant on the basketball court. Some of the things Wilt said, the off-the-record stuff, Jack would have loved to somehow weave into the piece, such as Wilt's too-numerous-to-count female conquests. But he knew those rapt paragraphs wouldn't have made it past any of *SportsWorld*'s copy editors, particularly feisty feminist Lucy Melrose and the motherly Joan Bradshaw. And really, was America ready to read about a black man having repeated sexual encounters with white women? The country was still processing the release a few weeks earlier of *Guess Who's Coming to Dinner*, a film starring Sidney Poitier, Katherine Hepburn and Spencer Tracy, which tried to positively portray the controversial subject of interracial marriage, especially in light of the June 1967 Supreme Court ruling that deemed anti-miscegenation laws unconstitutional, thus making such unions legal in all 50 states.

So, Jack stayed on topic - this latest in a long line of Wilt's basketball achievements - and taking only a slight detour to explore the rumors that this would be Wilt's last season in Philadelphia and how playing for the Lakers in Los Angeles had been ruminating in his head, words that would certainly create a furor in the City of Brotherly Love and might just lead a few of those Philadelphians to tell Wilt to shove his 25,000 points up his big black ass.

As Jack worked his way through the structure of the column, every now and then he stepped away from the beige Remington Monarch that sat atop his mahogany desk, walked out into the living room where Olivia was reading Jacqueline Susann's latest novel, and looked out the big picture window at the peaceful neighborhood where the McDonalds had settled in the mid-1950s, one of thousands of families who fled New York's boroughs and created what was now being called the suburban sprawl. He watched the occasional Chevy or Ford make its way through the slush, and he glanced up at the oaks and elms and maples that lined both sides of the street, one in front of each house, and he conjured a picture of their colorful autumn beauty before the winter had stripped them bare of all they wear.

Late in the afternoon during another break from the exploits of Wilt, Jack strolled into the kitchen where he peeled a banana and gazed out the back door into the cookie-cutter yard with the faded wooden fence, the same fence that Patrick used to throw his fastballs against when he was playing Little League and thinking he could be the next Whitey Ford, even though, unlike the Yankee great who grew up in nearby Queens, he was right-handed. There were so many good times spent in that rectangular patch of land, Jack and Olivia watching Patrick and Kathleen play freeze tag with their friends, or sitting around a fire roasting marshmallows and telling spooky stories which made the boys giggle and the girls squirm in discomfort, or was it the other way around? Now it was just the two of them, Jack and Olivia, empty nesters, finding their way in this new phase of their marriage, happy with the way their life had turned out, but still with so much to worry about because when you have kids, you never stop worrying about them.

Kathleen was nearby at Columbia, all that great work she had done in high school now manifesting itself in an Ivy League education. But there was a volatile tension permeating the campus, the Vietnam War at the epicenter, further stirred by the growing anti-government faction spewing its daily venom, and the racial unrest that was percolating over the building of the new gymnasium in Morningside Park. Jack worried about his daughter, not because she was a young woman with strong opinions on all of those issues, but that she was so full of Irish piss and vinegar and didn't always know when to back down from a debate. In these emotional times, it wasn't popular to be sensitive to the plight of the Negroes, as Kathleen was. And she couldn't always bite her tongue and walk away when members of Columbia's combative Students for a Democratic Society expressed their distaste for what they called the American killing machine in Vietnam, of which her brother Patrick was a reluctant member, there only because he had to be, doing what he was told in the name of protecting good ol' Uncle Sam from the threat of rampant Communism.

At least Kathleen was only a no-traffic 30-minute car ride away and if something were to happen, Jack could extricate her from trouble rather easily if need be. But Patrick was on the other side of the world, in grave danger every day, a danger Jack knew all too well. With the mail from Vietnam delayed days or sometimes weeks depending on where it originated from, for all Jack and Olivia knew, their son was already zipped into a body bag and headed back to Garden City for burial. It was a fear they lived with every single waking moment, that phone call from the Marines Corps where they express their deepest sympathies and tell you that your son or daughter died honorably for their country in the name of Semper Fi, as if that was going to make you feel better.

"I, Patrick McDonald, do solemnly swear that I will support and defend the constitution of the United States against all enemies, foreign and domestic; that I will bear true faith and allegiance to the same; and that I will obey the orders of the President of the United States and the Orders of the Officers appointed over me, according to the regulations and the uniform code of military justice. So help me God."

He was 20 years old when he took that oath, and Jack and Olivia could only hope and pray that he'd celebrate birthday number 21 in the coming summer. They tried not to think about it, but it was impossible, and as they were sure Patrick was doing, Jack and Olivia were counting the days until his tour was complete, praying to a new god - DEROS, which stood for Date Eligible for Return from OverSeas.

Patrick had written a letter to his parents, and one to his sister, about a week after the initial Tet attacks, and the one to Jack and Olivia arrived after Jack had flown to France for the Olympics. Patrick knew he couldn't put a happy face on his situation because his parents would know better; they were intelligent people who read the *New York Times* and watched the nightly news and were acutely aware of what was happening. So, he wrote the truth, that the men of the 3rd Battalion, 26th Marines, were in deep shit at Khe Sahn, and he was afraid that he'd never survive the relentless mortar and rocket pounding his Kilo Company had endured.

"I don't sleep, none of us really do," Patrick wrote. "I think about how I'm going to die every day. Is it going to be a VC sniper, is it going to be a fire bomb, or will a mortar round land right in the middle of my tent and blow me to smithereens?"

Khe Sahn had come under attack 10 days before Tet had been launched. On what was considered a routine morning recon mission, 3/26 India Company left its base camp to investigate the site of an ambush the day before, and just as they crested the misty ridge line of Hill 881 North, they were met by rocket-propelled grenades and automatic weapons and 20 Marines were cut down in about 30 seconds before the survivors could take cover and wait for fire support. The depleted company held on and was ready to engage later in the day, but it was called back to the combat base because a captured NVA defector had provided critical intel of the NVA's plan to overrun Khe Sahn starting later that night on Hills 881 and 861.

Sure enough, just as the soldier had warned, a heavy barrage of mortar rounds, grenades, and rockets battered the Marine outpost at 861 just after midnight, followed shortly thereafter by approximately 300 NVA who breached the defensive wire in a brazen advance that Patrick and the other men of Kilo Company turned back. It was a brutally bloody and deadly conflict, some of it resorting to old-style hand-to-hand fighting. The attack on 881 never happened, but in the wee hours of the morning, just as Patrick and the troops were regrouping, the base was bombarded by mortars, rockets, and artillery shells, one of the rockets striking the main ammunition dump and detonating 1,500 tons of ordnance, the explosions sending helicopters tumbling down the eastern end of the runway where they burned for hours.

With ammunition and supplies woefully diminished, not to mention the loss of men, Khe Sahn - a region that General Westmoreland called "the gateway to South Vietnam" and steadfastly believed had to be held, at all cost - was severely compromised. Even the grunts like Patrick knew it. A day later, the 1st Battalion, 9th Marines arrived, and a few days after that came the ARVN 37th Ranger Battalion, but that left about 6,000 allied troops to defend against an NVA force estimated to be at least 20,000 strong, and probably more.

However, Khe Sahn was merely a diversionary ploy to draw attention away from the cities that were about to be attacked in the Tet Offensive, so there were no further confrontations over the next two weeks, which is why Patrick had time to write his letters. The men spent their days fortifying their trenches, laying down rolls of barbed wire, and taking their patrols within the confines of the established perimeter, dodging the NVA's daily "we're still out here so don't get too comfortable" shellings. At night, they tried to relieve the tension by singing songs, listening to music, playing cards, and smoking pot, waiting and wondering when the gooks were going to come, and where would they be coming from.

As Jack finished his banana and tossed the peel into the garbage, Olivia entered the kitchen and shook her head, admonishing her husband as if he were a little kid who was going to spoil his appetite too close to dinner. "Pork chops, green beans, and mashed potatoes; how's that sound for tonight," Olivia said.

"Sounds great," Jack said, turning around to face Olivia before adding, "Come here and let me kiss that beautiful hand."

"Wise ass," Olivia said, recalling the grief she had given Jack over his encounter with Catherine Deneuve and Brigitte Bardot in France.

"Can we eat before Cronkite because I'd really like to sit down and hear what he has to say about his trip to

Vietnam?" Jack asked, referring to that night's much-anticipated broadcast of the *CBS Evening News* where the popular and universally-respected anchor was going to share his first-hand account and thoughts on the war.

Cronkite had been stunned by the Tet Offensive and what the CBS correspondents in country were reporting, and he had said on his broadcast the night after Tet had begun, "What the hell is going on? I thought we were winning the war?" Cronkite had put his faith in President Johnson and took him at his word when he would say that progress was being made in Vietnam and that America, indeed, was accomplishing its mission. An all-out public relations campaign had been foisted on the American public throughout 1967 to get that very message out, and Vice-President Hubert Humphrey had proclaimed in an appearance on NBC's *Today* show that, "We are on the offensive. Territory is being gained. We are making steady progress."

And then there was Tet, and Cronkite determined that he'd had enough of second-hand information. He flew to Vietnam to see for himself what was happening, and following a two-week stay during which he interviewed hundreds of troops and officers and officials, he returned to his anchor desk with a look of disillusionment on his face.

Jack and Olivia sat in their living room, just as an estimated nine million other Americans did, to hear what Cronkite had to say in his special report that was titled, "Who, What, When, Where, Why?"

"Tonight, back in more familiar surroundings in New York, we'd like to sum up our findings in Vietnam, an analysis that must be speculative, personal, subjective," Cronkite began. "Who won and who lost in the great Tet Offensive against the cities? I'm not sure. The Viet Cong did not win by a knockout, but neither did we. The referees of history may make it a draw.

"Another standoff may be coming in the big battles expected south of the Demilitarized Zone. Khe Sahn could well fall, with a terrible loss in American lives, prestige, and morale, and this is a tragedy of our stubbornness there; but the bastion no longer is a key to the rest of the northern regions, and it is doubtful that the American forces can be defeated across the breadth of the DMZ with any substantial loss of ground. Another standoff.

"On the political front, past performance gives no confidence that the Vietnamese government can cope with its problems, now compounded by the attack on the cities. It may not fall, it may hold on, but it probably won't show the dynamic qualities demanded of this young nation. Another standoff.

"We have been too often disappointed by the optimism of the American leaders, both in Vietnam and Washington, to have faith any longer in the silver linings they find in the darkest clouds. They may be right, that Hanoi's winter-spring offensive has been forced by the Communist realization that they could not win the longer war of attrition, and that the Communists hope that any success in the offensive will improve their position for eventual negotiations. It would improve their position, and it would also require our realization, that we should have had all along, that any negotiations must be that - negotiations, not the dictation of peace terms.

"For it seems now more certain than ever that the bloody experience of Vietnam is to end in a stalemate. This summer's almost certain standoff will either end in real give-and-take negotiations or terrible escalation; and for every means we have to escalate, the enemy can match us, and that applies to invasion of the North, the use of nuclear weapons, or the mere commitment of one hundred, or two hundred, or three hundred thousand more American troops to the battle. And with each escalation, the world comes closer to the brink of cosmic disaster.

"To say that we are closer to victory today is to believe, in the face of the evidence, the optimists who have been wrong in the past. To suggest we are on the edge of defeat is to yield to unreasonable pessimism. To say that we are mired in stalemate seems the only realistic, yet unsatisfactory, conclusion. On the off chance that military and political analysts are right, in the next few months we must test the enemy's intentions, in case this is indeed his last big gasp before negotiations. But it is increasingly clear to this reporter that the only rational way out then will be to negotiate, not as victors, but as an honorable people who lived up to their pledge to defend democracy, and did the best they could.

"This is Walter Cronkite, good night."

6 - The Mick

The last time Jack, and everyone else for that matter, saw
Mickey Mantle run with the remarkably blinding speed
that was the basis for his nickname "The Commerce
Comet", the speed that led baseball people to believe that
he was destined to become the greatest player who ever
was or ever would be, occurred on the afternoon of
October 5, 1951.

Jack was sitting in the Yankee Stadium press box, still on
staff at the *New York Herald-Tribune*, assigned to write a
sidebar on Game 2 of the World Series between the
dynastic Yankees and the miracle-making 'Shot Heard
Round the World' New York Giants. It was the bottom of
the first inning, and Mantle, the prized Yankee rookie,
stepped into the batters' box as the leadoff hitter and, after
being greeted by a tremendous ovation, promptly laid
down a perfect drag bunt which he easily beat out for a
single.

Because he'd only attended a few Yankee games that summer, all while Mantle was on a demotion to the minor leagues, and because Jack did not cover Game 1 of the Series, this was the first thing he had ever seen Mantle do on a baseball field. What a sight it was, those powerful legs churning down the base path, dirt flying up from his spikes, a veritable vapor trail in his wake, as more than 66,000 people in the cavernous ballpark exalted in delight.

"Wow," Jack thought to himself as he watched the play unfold, and it prompted him to recall the comment Casey Stengel had made a year earlier when he'd first laid his eyes on Mantle at a rookie camp out in Arizona. "There's never been anything like this kid," the ol' perfesser had told a gaggle of beat writers. "He has more speed than any slugger and more slug than any speedster, and nobody has ever had more of both of 'em together."

Four innings later, that was no longer true. Mantle went racing into the right-center-field gap to chase a fly ball hit by the Giants' own magnificent rookie, Willie Mays, while drifting over from center field was the aging Yankee legend, Joe DiMaggio. When the ball was hit, Mantle didn't think the once-incomparable DiMaggio, the man who he was being groomed to replace, had a chance of making the play. But what Mantle hadn't noticed was that DiMaggio had gotten a great jump, which he always did because he knew every hitter's tendencies, he knew what the pitch was and how the pitcher was throwing it, and he used this information like no outfielder ever had. When Mantle realized DiMaggio was going to make the catch, he deferred to the veteran and tried to stop his momentum to avoid plowing into him. Sadly, he slammed on the brakes precisely on the tiny spot in the outfield where a drainage cover was located. His spikes got caught, his knee buckled like someone had chopped it with a Louisville Slugger, and Mantle went down just as DiMaggio was closing his mitt. He lay there in agony as a funereal silence enveloped the ballpark, and as he was carried off the field you knew that blazing, God-given speed was gone forever.

Seventeen years later, on a warm and breezy March morning in Fort Lauderdale, Jack sat next to Mantle in the Yankee dugout at their spring training base and listened to the Mick talk about that awful day when he thought his major-league career might be over before it had really started.

"I was there," Jack said to Mantle, "and that was the story I had to write for the late great Herald-Trib. How the phenom, Mickey Mantle, had ruined his knee, and possibly his baseball career."

"Sorry I fuckin' disappointed you," Mantle teased, smiling that wide country boy smile that hadn't changed in all those years.

Jack had flown back down to Florida to write a story about Mantle who, despite the debilitating knee injury and so many other ailments along the way, not to mention his penchant for late-night carousing, had gone on to forge one of the greatest baseball careers in the sport's voluminous history. But like that day at Yankee Stadium, Jack was going to be crafting another disheartening piece about Mantle, this one detailing how that sure-fire Hall of Fame career was now sputtering to a meek end.

It was widely assumed that 1968 was going to be Mantle's major league swan song, and this was his final spring training with the Yankees. Mantle hadn't said anything publicly to that effect, but it was common knowledge that retirement was on the horizon because he was a shell of the player he once was, and the Yankees were a shell of the team they had once been.

"I don't know what the hell I'm going to do," Mantle said to Jack when Jack asked him the retirement question point blank. "It ain't the same around here, you know that. All my pals are gone, and with all these young kids here we probably ain't gonna contend. And, ya know, I just can't play like I used to."

Jack couldn't argue with any of that. These certainly were not his Yankees, the Yankees of Whitey Ford, Billy Martin, Roger Maris, Tony Kubek, Moose Skowron, Bobby Richardson, Hank Bauer, Yogi Berra, Gil McDougald, and so many other greats. No, these were the Yankees of Horace Clarke, Jake Gibbs, Joe Pepitone, Tom Tresh, Gene Michael, Fritz Peterson, and Mel Stottlemyre, compounded by the ghost of Mantle struggling to play first base, to run the bases, and to reach the short right-field porch with that once-mighty swing. These were not the Yankees who won seven World Series titles and 12 American League pennants in Mantle's first 14 years in Gotham. These were the Yankees who finished dead last in 1966, and in 1967 only managed to improve to ninth in the 10-team circuit, playing those moribund seasons in a combined 37 games under .500.

"It ain't the way it used to be," Mantle said.

Before he left home, Jack had phoned Stengel, retired and living in California, in the hope that he could remember the details of Mantle joining the team late in 1950, and the ever-sharp Stengel was more than happy to wax poetic.

As they did every year, the Yankees had invited some of their top prospects to join the club for the final two weeks of the season to give them a taste of what it was like to be a Yankee, and to be a big leaguer. They traveled with the team, sat in on the skull sessions, and took batting and infield practice. That year, Mantle played at Class C Joplin, Missouri and he'd walloped 27 home runs, driven in 136 runs, and collected 199 hits for a .383 batting average. Everyone knew he was considered DiMaggio's heir apparent, and it was just a matter of time before Mantle would be the man patrolling center field for the pinstripers. The first time he took BP, some of the Yankees were thinking it might happen that very same day. It was at Sportsman's Park in St. Louis, and the kid with the blond crew cut who weighed only 165 pounds but had forearms as thick as a blacksmith's put on quite a fireworks show.

Mantle stepped into the right side of the box after all the veteran players had taken their cuts and started hitting rockets. After a few minutes, he switched to the left side, and the barrage continued. His bat cut a wicked swath and the ball seemed to catapult off the white ash as if it was made of rubber. He hit tremendous shots into the deepest reaches of the ballpark, and while DiMaggio largely ignored what was going on, most of the other Yankees could not. They stopped what they were doing, just as all the writers traveling with the team did, to watch this kid rip blasts that rivaled those of Babe Ruth and Lou Gehrig.

"You ever hear what Joe Collins said about Mickey?" Stengel asked Jack, and before Jack could answer Casey said, "Well, I'll tell ya. He said, 'Mickey tries to hit every one like they don't count if they're under 400 feet.' That just about sums it up. No boy ever hit a baseball harder than Mickey, and I played against Ruth and Gehrig and them guys, so you can write it down."

Jack did, and then when he met with Mantle, he wrote down everything Mantle shared about his early life growing up a child of the Great Depression. He was born in Spavinaw, Oklahoma and grew up in Commerce where he went to school, worked part-time as a teen-ager in the lead and zinc mines with his father, a man they called Mutt Mantle, and played baseball in the summer on steamy, dusty fields with his old man pushing him every step of the way. His mother hand-sewed every baseball uniform he wore as a child, and she never objected to his playing ball because she always reasoned if he could get to the majors it would be a better way to make a living than working in the black holes where Mutt earned his $75 a week.

Mutt had dreamed of being a pro ballplayer, but it had never worked out for him, so he lived his dream through his son, and Mickey was fine with that. Mickey loved the game so much, he told Jack, that it never crossed his mind to rebel against having baseball forced on him from the time he was old enough to walk. He wanted to play, wanted to practice, and he never objected to the endless teaching sessions with Mutt and his grandfather, Charles, a semi-pro player of renown in Oklahoma around the turn of the century. Mickey told Jack the greatest Christmas of his youth was when he was 14 years old and Mutt bought him a full-sized baseball glove, a $22 Marty Marion model. With money as tight as it was in the Mantle stead, it was a gift of enduring love and Mickey said he cherished that mitt.

Even though Jack knew most of the details, he pressed Mantle to recount how he came to join the Yankees' organization, and he happily retold the story. Tom Greenwade was the scout who discovered him, but when he first saw Mickey playing for the Baxter Springs Whiz Kids in 1948, Mickey was only 16 and couldn't be signed. Greenwade told him he'd come back the following year when he was graduated from high school, and Greenwade kept his promise. He inked Mantle to a $1,500 bonus, and years later, Greenwade was famously quoted as saying, "That's when I knew what Paul Krichell must have felt like when he saw Lou Gehrig."

By the time spring training rolled around in 1951, Mantle was ready to make a push for the team, and with Stengel as his greatest supporter, he made it, mainly on the strength of a .400 average in Florida. He was a woefully unpolished outfielder - he'd played shortstop most of his life - but long-time Yankee standout Tommy Henrich, who had retired in the off-season, came to Fort Lauderdale at Stengel's request to teach Mantle how to play the outfield. Every day Henrich drilled Mantle on the finer points, hitting him fungoes, teaching him how to catch the ball in a ready position to throw, how to field grounders or play caroms off the fence. It was a slow go. One day, Mantle lost a battle with the sun and had a fly ball conk him right on the head. Another day he overthrew his cutoff man by a bit - the ball landed in the seats behind third base. Stengel took everything into account and decided Mantle's lethal bat needed to come north for the start of the season.

Mantle started well. Early in 1951 he was leading the American League in home runs, RBI, and average, and he was playing a passable right field, but pretty soon, the wily pitchers began to catch on to Mantle. They saw they could feed him high fastballs and he'd chase after them and catch nothing but air. Mantle's average plummeted, and his slump at the plate began to affect him in the field. He was depressed, and he even broke down and cried one day in the dugout after striking out for the fourth time.

By mid-July Stengel had no choice but to send him down to Triple-A Kansas City. Mantle was crushed, he thought he'd failed, and he couldn't help wondering what his father would think. He found out pretty quickly. After starting slowly in Kansas City, he called Mutt and said he didn't think he was good enough to play and wanted to come home. Mutt drove from Commerce to Kansas City, and laid it on the line: Either Mickey could stop being a coward and act like a man, or he would indeed drive him home where he could work in the mines.

Mickey stayed in Kansas City, caught fire, and hiked his average to .361, prompting Stengel to bring him back to New York for the stretch run. As the Yankees outdueled the White Sox and Indians, Mantle hit .284 with six home runs and 20 RBI in the final 27 games which earned him a spot in the starting lineup for the Series against the Giants.

After the Yankees polished off the Giants in the Series, DiMaggio announced his retirement and Mantle, bad knee and all, stepped right into the void in 1952, and so began his ascent to Yankee immortality and American icon.

In his first seven full seasons, Mantle batted above .300 in all but one (.295 in 1953), he topped 90 RBI in six of those years, and in 1956 and 1957 he had two of the greatest seasons in major league history, earning the AL MVP in both. In '56, he won the triple crown as he mashed 52 homers, had 130 RBI, and batted .353 while leading the Yankees to their first World Series title since their record streak of five in a row ended in 1953. And in '57, although New York lost to Milwaukee in the Series, Mantle batted a career-high .365 with 34 homers, 94 RBI, and an amazing .512 on-base percentage.

There were 42 homers in 1958 when the Yankees avenged Milwaukee in the Series, 40 in 1960, and then came the epic 1961 home run chase as he and Roger Maris pursued Babe Ruth's seemingly unassailable record of 60 home runs set in 1927. The M&M boys were neck and neck most of the way, but Mantle's career-long bugaboo - injuries - slowed him in the final month and he finished with 54 while Maris passed Babe on the last day of the season.

There was one more flash of greatness in 1964 when Mantle had 35 homers, 111 RBI, and his final .300 average in lifting New York to its last appearance in the Series, and since then he had been in steady decline at the plate, in the field, and in the trainers' room. And now, here he was, already feeling the effects of 17 major league seasons before the 18th had even started.

"I think about how I used to play, and it pisses me off that I can't do the same things anymore," Mantle said to Jack, whose right hand was nearly worn out from all the scribbling he'd done in his notebook for the previous half-hour. "How can a man retire when he's 36 years old? If I'm not doing this, what the hell else am I gonna do? I guess I'm gonna find out, but gimme this season and let's see what happens. There's a lotta crazy shit happening in this world these days, so maybe this old geezer's got something left."

7 - Democratic Discourse

Jack peered over the top of the *Daily News* that he was reading, and he cast a wary eye at the pot of stew boiling on the electric range that he was sure was going to start spilling over the edges if Olivia kept stirring it so vigorously. As she whipped the wooden spoon around the pot, mixing all those delicious vegetables with the beef, Olivia was simultaneously and animatedly speaking into the telephone to her mother, Marge DuPree.

Jack got along fine with his mother-in-law - in small doses. The woman could talk until your ears bled, and she always had an opinion which she unfailingly tried to convince everyone was the right opinion. There were times in her company when Jack considered popping a few amphetamine pills like the ones the baseball players used to give them energy - they call them "greenies" - just so that he wouldn't doze off during one of her diatribes. On second thought, maybe dozing off was the way to go!

But today, Marge couldn't get a word in edge wise because daughter was doing a fine impression of mother. Not that Jack was timing it, but he figured Olivia had been speaking non-stop now for about 10 minutes, passion oozing from every word as she offered her analysis of the recent upheaval that had occurred in her beloved Democratic Party.

Jack was back home from Florida, the Mantle column finished, and he was relaxing and recharging his batteries before heading out to Los Angeles to cover the Final Four of the NCAA basketball tournament. He spent time catching up on several days' worth of editions of the *Daily News* and *New York Times* that Olivia dutifully piled up in his den, and doing some of the manly chores that needed tending around the house. The rest of his waking hours were spent listening to his wife talking politics.

Like many Democrats in the country, Olivia had lost faith in President Johnson. Johnson won the '64 election in a record landslide over Barry Goldwater, and in the early portion of his first official full term, his approval rating continued to soar for several reasons. He introduced a slate of new reforms that he said would build a "Great Society" for all Americans. His ambitious legislative agenda created the Medicare and Medicaid programs to provide federal health insurance for the elderly and the impoverished, his "War on Poverty" as he called it. He also sought to improve education, stepped up the nation's crime prevention laws, and approved bills aimed at reducing air and water pollution. Johnson signed the historic Civil Rights Act of 1964 and Voting Rights Act of 1965, controversial legislation that in the short term fueled racial unrest which led to deadly and destructive rioting in several cities, but in the long run would help to desegregate the country. Johnson also continued to support the exploration of space and aimed to keep on track the edict of his assassinated predecessor, John F. Kennedy, to walk on the moon by the end of the decade. These accomplishments, according to analysts, improved the lives of millions and contributed to economic growth and prosperity.

But his waterloo was proving to be the war in Vietnam. Like Truman, and Kennedy, and Eisenhower before him, Johnson was determined to prevent North Vietnamese Communists from overtaking the U.S.-supported government of South Vietnam. He, like they, felt this was the key to preventing Communism from spreading around the world. However, what began as a minimalist approach to America's involvement in that process with about 16,000 troops in action when he first assumed office late in 1963, things had escalated dramatically since 1965 and the number of troops now in Vietnam numbered more than half a million, including Jack and Olivia's first-born, Patrick.

With an average of 1,000 men and women dying per month in those faraway jungles with no end to the conflict in sight, the country torn apart by anti-war demonstrations, and polls indicating that fewer and fewer Americans were in favor of being in Vietnam, Johnson's perceived mishandling of the situation had now usurped all of his domestic successes. His decline in popularity did not follow partisan lines as some Democrats were as equally disappointed as Republicans with his performance, and it was becoming increasingly clear that his chances of winning the 1968 election, against whomever the Republicans opposed him with, would be severely compromised. In fact, given what had happened in the past week, Olivia was certain that Johnson's once vise-like grip on the nomination was in serious jeopardy.

The New Hampshire Democratic primary provided stark evidence of Johnson's fallibility when Minnesota Senator Eugene McCarthy garnered 42 percent of the vote compared to 49 percent for Johnson. McCarthy had declared his candidacy in November 1967, running on an anti-Vietnam platform, saying, "I am concerned that the administration seems to have set no limit to the price it is willing to pay for a military victory."

But pundits denounced his viability and opined that he had no chance to impact the race, and Olivia, despite her growing disillusionment with the war, agreed that

McCarthy was no threat to Johnson. The Tet Offensive changed everything. Just weeks before the attacks commenced, Secretary of Defense Robert McNamara said the war was beginning to wind down because the North Vietnamese were losing their will to fight. Televisions across the country were showing that this was not the case. It was a huge setback for Johnson because Tet made it clear that America wasn't getting out of the war anytime soon. Even before Tet, Americans were growing more and more disturbed by Vietnam, and now not all of the dissenters were the rabble-rousing hippies. Yet in the face of all the fervor, Johnson was committing thousands upon thousands more troops.

Emboldened by Tet, McCarthy said before New Hampshire, "My decision to challenge the president's position and the administration's position has been strengthened by recent announcements out of the administration: The evident intention to escalate and to intensify the war in Vietnam, and on the other hand, the absence of any positive indication or suggestion for a compromise or for a negotiated political settlement."

The shocking New Hampshire vote was certainly a body blow to Johnson, but a few days later, an even more serious development occurred when New York Senator Robert F. Kennedy, sensing Johnson's vulnerability, entered the race. While many voters may not have been sure who McCarthy was, they certainly knew Kennedy, the handsome and charismatic Attorney General during his brother's tenure as president who was considered a rising star in the

Democratic Party and a likely future presidential candidate.

"I like Gene McCarthy's stance on the war, but I don't know if he can get us out of there," Olivia told her mother. "Bobby Kennedy will get us out."

Jack was certain Marge was on the other end of the phone line agreeing with Olivia's proclamation. John and Marge Dupree were both born and raised on the south side of Chicago where, if you weren't a Democrat, you were an outcast. They were introduced to each other by John's neighbor, Eleanor Guilfoyle, when they were in high school. Many years later, after John and Marge were married and Olivia had been born, Eleanor made the acquaintance of one of John's good friends from the law school at DePaul University, Richard Daley, the same Daley who, in 1968, was serving his fourth term as Chicago's ultra-powerful mayor and was the long-time steward of the Chicago political machine that played such a critical role in the policy and direction of the National Democratic Party. Eleanor eventually married Richard, and the Daley's and Dupree's had remained close friends for decades.

With Daley playing puppet master and systematically securing the Cook County vote which helped John F. Kennedy carry Illinois on his way to the White House in 1960, John and Marge had spent countless hours volunteering at his campaign office in Chicago, a campaign that had been orchestrated by Bobby Kennedy. In fact, one of Olivia's most memorable experiences was getting to shake Bobby's hand when he happened to pass through the Chicago office sometime in 1959, and by chance she was visiting her parents and volunteering some of her time. Jack didn't have proof, but he would bet just about anything that the DuPree's - Olivia included - had never voted for any Republican candidate running for any office, in their lives.

When Olivia finally said goodbye to Marge, saying, "Give daddy a kiss for me," she announced that the stew looked delicious, and Jack's reply was, "Well, it's sure stirred up pretty good."

"Very funny," Olivia said. "You have no idea how good you've got it. All right, after listening with that lovely smirk on your face, what do you think about Kennedy entering the race?"

"Liv, you know I don't think much about it at all," Jack said, eliciting an exasperated roll of Olivia's eyes.

"Sometimes I just don't understand your indifference, Jack McDonald."

Jack was not a political zealot like his wife, primarily because he'd always maintained that you can't be an expert on everything. He was an expert on all things relating to sports, a versatility and knowledge base that, in addition to his transcendent command of the English language, had elevated him to the status of being one of the most well-known sports writers/columnists in the nation. He simply didn't have enough time in his schedule to devote to following politics. Sure, he stayed marginally up to date on the key issues of a campaign, be it presidential, gubernatorial, or mayoral, and he generally knew where the various candidates stood. But if a conversation got much beyond a few minutes on, say, the corruption in New York's transportation department, he was looking for a ripcord to parachute to safety. Jack was a registered Democrat, but unlike his wife, he sometimes leaned toward the other side of the aisle. Whenever Jack entered a voting booth, he tried to keep an open mind, and if a Republican seemed like the better candidate, he voted for him. He pulled the Eisenhower lever in both 1952 and '56, but voted for JFK in '60 and LBJ in '64.

"Look," Jack said, "all I'll say is it just seems with all these Democrats jumping into the fray, the party is going to splinter and you may not have a truly strong and worthy candidate in November. The Republicans are going to have a clear-cut choice, whether it's Nixon or Reagan or maybe even Rockefeller. That type of solidarity might be their ticket back into the White House."

"Do you really believe this country would be better off with Nixon in power, let alone Reagan or Rocky?"

"I didn't say we'd be better off, I said Americans might see all the division on the left and think of it as a sign of weakness. The Republicans are going to get behind their guy, whoever it is, and I can guarantee you their guy is going to say he's going to bring our boys home."

"This country is going to go to hell in a hand basket if the Republicans get control," Olivia exclaimed. "Don't tell me I didn't warn you."

"Dear, I would never doubt your political acumen. Now, can we eat dinner? And would you like a red, or a white?"

8 - Redemption

As the clock ticked down in the Los Angeles Sports Arena, and UCLA's surgical and somewhat startling evisceration of Houston in the national semifinals of the NCAA basketball tournament was moments from completion, Jack looked over at the Houston bench where the Cougars star player, Elvin Hayes, sat with a towel draped over his head, as if he didn't want anyone to see how defeated and disappointed he was.

What a stark contrast, Jack thought, to what he had witnessed back in January at the Houston Astrodome when Hayes and the Cougars - so confident, downright brash, even - had beaten mighty UCLA and Lew Alcindor in what had been billed as the Game of the Century. Hayes had been superb that night, a fierce combination of skill and will as he scored 39 points and carried the Cougars to a well-deserved victory that enabled Houston to flip spots in the wire service polls with UCLA.

But in this mismatch of a rematch, these Cougars were not those Cougars, and these Bruins were certainly not those Bruins. And so impressive was UCLA's 101-69 beat-down of undefeated and top-ranked Houston, that its 78-55 blowout of North Carolina the next night, which gave the Bruins their fourth national championship in five years, was utterly anti-climactic.

There was so much going on that circus-like night in the Astrodome, the spectacle surpassing the actual playing of the game which was saying something because the game was pretty good. But what stayed with Jack, the image that he filed away, had nothing to do with the Texas-sized hoopla as much as what he observed in the UCLA locker room afterward, the great Alcindor sitting on a bench in front of his dressing stall muttering over and over, "Never again, never again."

Never is a long time, and perhaps Alcindor was too young and naive to understand that there would be many more disappointments to face as he moved through his life. But Jack came away with a singular thought as he filed his story that night from Houston: There was a fire burning inside Alcindor, no matter how docile the gentle 7-foot-1 giant appeared, and Jack's hunch was that if UCLA were to meet up with Houston again this year, he would be writing a vastly different story.

The day before the game, UCLA coach John Wooden - who became the first man to win back-to-back NCAA basketball titles twice - was asked about his team's desire to shove a healthy dose of payback down the throats of the voluble Cougars. "Revenge is something I don't harbor," the Wizard of Westwood said. "I believe if I don't harbor it, my boys don't harbor it." Jack respected Wooden just as much as the next guy, but that was a bunch of hooey. In reality, his players couldn't wait to take the court and beat the shit out of the Cougars. They wanted revenge almost as much as they wanted to win the championship, and their only regret was because the way the tournament draw was set up, they couldn't embarrass the Cougars this way in the title game.

"We haven't really said anything publicly, but we're a vindictive team," UCLA's Mike Warren said after the game. "We've been looking forward to this game a long time."

Of course, the Cougars were flexing their muscles and flapping their gums, too, and they were excited for the opportunity to prove that what happened two months earlier was not a fluke. Hayes, never short of confidence, nor reticent to let you know exactly what he thought, didn't see any reason why anything would be different in this game. After Houston laid waste to Louisville in the Midwest Region semifinal a week earlier, Hayes was asked about a potential rematch with UCLA, this time in Los Angeles, and Hayes couldn't have been more nonplussed by the possibility.

"We've improved I don't know how much since the UCLA game," Hayes said. "They couldn't play us as close now as they did then. If we played 'em again, we'd beat 'em worse, and it wouldn't matter if it was on their own floor."

The Final Four wasn't contested at UCLA's campus arena, Pauley Pavilion, but it might as well have been. Houston enjoyed a tremendous home-court advantage at the Astrodome and now the crowd of just over 15,000 in Los Angeles was probably 90 percent pro-Bruins. The day before, Houston coach Guy Lewis was asked about playing what amounted to a road game in the NCAA Tournament, and he remarked that the crowd didn't worry him at all, but UCLA sure did. It was pretty obvious why. Since their loss to Houston, which ended a 47-game winning streak, UCLA had won its last 12 regular-season games by an average margin of 24.7 points, and in six of those games, it surpassed the 100-point plateau. The Bruins opened the NCAA Tournament with an unimpressive 58-49 victory over New Mexico State, but then cruised to the West Regional title with an 87-66 romp over Santa Clara.

In the press lounge about an hour before the opening tip, Jack sat down with several college basketball writers and listened to what they thought might happen, and the general consensus was that UCLA was going to roll. Bill Lachey from the *Los Angeles Examiner* had no doubt that Alcindor would punish the Cougars at both ends of the floor and predicted that Hayes - who had been awarded college basketball's player of the year award nearly a month earlier - would be a non-factor. "The Big E is gonna be E-liminated," he said, revealing just a bit of homerism. Buck Watson of the *Houston Post* figured UCLA would win, but not by the one-sided nature Lachey was predicting. "These boys ain't gonna roll over and die, but I'm thinkin' 'ol coach Wooden's gonna have his boys runnin' hotter than Dixie's Barbeque down in Texarkana," Watson drawled, punctuating his statement with a spit of tobacco juice into a plastic cup.

Jack wasn't exactly sure what that meant, but 'ol Buck Watson was right. Wooden's boys were red-hot all night, and they took great delight in pummeling the Cougars.

"I feel like a dead man; that's the greatest exhibition of basketball I've ever seen," Lewis said afterward. And yet, it was a pretty routine occurrence for the Bruins.

UCLA opened a quick 12-4 lead, Houston battled back to get within 20-19, and then the Bruins stepped on the gas pedal and left the Cougars choking on their fumes. Over a stretch of about four minutes UCLA outscored Houston 17-5, and the rout was on. By the time the first half came to a merciful end, UCLA was up by 22, and the lead continued to climb in the final 20 minutes, getting as grotesque as 44 points before Wooden called off the dogs and substituted liberally.

Typically in his writing, Jack didn't like to get bogged down in the X's and O's of the games he covered. Quite frankly, most of it was boring, and he found that writers who carried on and on about the ramifications of a certain play call, or the nuances of a particular defense, or the technicalities of someone's putting stroke, were masking the fact that they weren't good enough writers to tell a real story. Writers loved to think they were smarter than everyone else, but the reality was that they usually didn't know much more than the readers they were trying to impress. The good writers, which Jack considered himself to be, were the ones who could tell the reader something they did not know or did not see while they were watching the game. The fans didn't have the opportunity to talk to players and coaches, or go in to observe what went on in the private sanctity of the locker room. It was therefore the writers' responsibility to take the reader there.

However, Jack found himself intrigued by one strategy the Bruins employed against Houston because it was such an integral part of why the outcome was so lopsided. Wooden knew his team needed to do a better job of containing Hayes because if he got hot, Houston might be able to pull off another upset. Wooden and one of his assistants, Jerry Norman, came up with something they called the "diamond and one" and it was like finding a diamond in the rough. Wooden put Warren at the top of the key, Lucius Allen and Mike Lynn on the flanks, and Alcindor in the middle of the lane under the basket as the last line of protection. Those four players guarded their specific zones while the fifth man, Lynn Shackelford, shadowed Hayes wherever he went. It was genius. Shackelford was an athletic, physical player who could man up on the imposing Hayes, and whenever Hayes was able to shake free, there was always another player in that diamond who could help out. Hayes was clearly frustrated and made only three field goals and finished with a meager 10 points as the Cougars shot a dreadful 28 percent from the floor. They'd made 52 percent of their shots in the first game. "We never saw anything like it all year," Lewis said of the new defense.

"They'd had a lot to say about us and I don't think they were correct," Alcindor said. "They were annoying and insulting. We wanted to teach those people some manners."

North Carolina was cordial enough, its manners perfectly intact. What the Tar Heels were not was a worthy opponent in the championship game, though, no one really was according to their coach, Dean Smith. Smith was asked before the UCLA-Houston game tipped off which team he'd prefer to play should his Tar Heels knock off Ohio State in the second semifinal. "Getting hit by a train or a truck, it doesn't make much difference," Smith said.

Whether it was train or truck, the 23-point margin of victory was the largest in championship game history, and Smith gushed that Alcindor, who scored 19 points against Houston and then erupted for 34 against North Carolina, was, "the greatest player who ever played the game" and UCLA was "the greatest basketball team of all time. We didn't play the perfect game and you have to play the perfect game to beat them."

Jack could not disagree with Smith's comment about UCLA's team, but it was tough for him to say Alcindor was better, at least right now, than NBA stars Wilt Chamberlain or Bill Russell. One thing he would say about Alcindor was he was certainly an interesting young man, wise beyond his years, and his upcoming summer was a good indication of this.

Alcindor was planning to go back to his native New York City to play ball in the Harlem playgrounds of his youth, and, through an initiative called Operation Sports Rescue, talk to young black children about their place in an American society that didn't seem to want to include them, and show them how sports could keep them out of trouble and set them on a path that might someday lead to the type of college education Alcindor was now receiving.

Ordinarily, no one would have taken issue with this, and Alcindor would be lauded for trying to be a role model for children who looked up to him, literally and figuratively. But not this summer. Alcindor and many other black college players were intending to boycott the Summer Olympics in Mexico City, a plan that had been in the works for several months, but was now percolating under the glare of the Final Four spotlight and had produced some angry backlash.

Several months earlier, 1967 Thanksgiving time, Harry Edwards, a 24-year-old part-time sociology instructor at San Jose State who had been a star basketball player and track athlete at the school before going to Cornell to earn his masters and Ph.D., hatched the idea of a boycott as a way to protest the ongoing treatment of Negroes in America. Edwards, though not as well-known as Dr. Martin Luther King, Jr. was becoming one of the public faces of the plight of the African-American, having led a San Jose State campus protest against alleged discrimination in housing for Negro students. "If they won't rent to us," Edwards had said, "why should we run or play for them?"

Fearing a potential outbreak of violence over this issue, San Jose State President Robert Clark cancelled the first football game of the 1967 season. That angered California Governor Ronald Reagan who reprimanded Clark for backing down to Edwards because Reagan felt it was setting a dangerous precedent. While Reagan was dressing down Clark, Edwards' stance had made him plenty of enemies, and cost him the lives of his two dogs who were butchered one night and left in pieces on his front lawn.

Edwards was undeterred, and he continued to press. He called many of the best black athletes to Los Angeles for the Black Youth Conference to discuss the boycott, and it all made sense to the sociologically aware Alcindor who was among the 50 or 60 attendees. If Negroes weren't allowed to drink from the same water fountains as white people, or stay in the same motels, or eat in the same restaurants, then they didn't need to play basketball with white people in the Olympics. In other words, if white America kept behaving as it had, then white America could win the Olympics on its own.

"For years we have participated in the Olympic Games, carrying the U.S. on our backs with our victories, and race relations are worse now than ever," Edwards had said. "Now they are even shooting people in the streets. We're not trying to lose the Olympics for the Americans. What happens to them is immaterial. If they finish first, that's beautiful. If they finish 14th, that's beautiful, too. But it's time for the black people to stand up as men and women and refuse to be utilized as performing animals for a little extra dog food. You see, this may be our last opportunity to settle this mess, short of violence."

In reality, the United States was so superior in the sport, it wasn't going to need Alcindor or any of the other top black players to win the gold medal. America had never not won the Olympic tournament, and that dominance was going to continue in Mexico City whether Alcindor played or not. However, as the best college basketball player in the country, Alcindor was squared up in the cross-hairs of this controversial issue, even more than track stars Tommie Smith, John Carlos, and Lee Evans who, if the boycott was executed, would be the most visible participants in their sport.

Alcindor typically said very little to the press, primarily because Wooden, a master micromanager, shielded him and his other players from the writers and broadcasters. But when the media got wind of the Thanksgiving meeting, Alcindor had granted an interview, and Jack remembered being impressed by the young man's conviction. "Well, if you live in a racist society and you want to express yourself about racism, there's a lot of things you can do, and a boycott is one of them," Alcindor had said. "We don't catch hell because we are Christians. We catch hell because we are black." Then, when asked how he would solve the racial chasm in the country, an irritated Alcindor replied, "Why do you ask me these questions? Why don't you ask a sociologist? I'm not a sociologist or an anthropologist or a politician. Go ask the right people. I'm not qualified to talk on this."

Naturally, the white press razed Alcindor, calling for his banishment from UCLA, and suggesting he be barred from ever earning a living playing in the NBA, all of which Jack found incredibly ludicrous.

As Alcindor left the arena after the championship game wearing a colorfully garish African robe, he was making a statement far more powerful than the one he'd made on the basketball court. People could call him an "uppity nigger" all they wanted, they could say he was a traitor because he refused to represent the United States of America in a silly basketball tournament. But he knew what was right and what was wrong, and the way people of color were treated in these United States of America was wrong.

Jack would have loved to have Alcindor share his deepest thoughts, but as he walked alongside of Big Lew as the UCLA star headed to the team bus that would transport the Bruins to their championship celebration, Alcindor responded with polite respect to Jack's request by saying, "Sir, I've said all I'm going to say about that."

9 - A Shot Rang Out

Jack and Olivia walked through the front door with their dinner companions, *Newsday* sports columnist Stan Isaacs and his wife, Bobbie, and before they could get their umbrella folded up, the gregarious owner of the establishment greeted them with the same refrain he saved for his favorite customers, of which there were many.

"Hey ya crumb bums, come on in," Toots Shor said with a cheeky smile before proceeding to give a hearty handshake and backslap to Jack and Stan, and kisses on the hands of Mrs. McDonald and Mrs. Isaacs.

"Any chance we're gonna get some peace and quiet in here tonight?" Isaacs asked of the man whose restaurant/cocktail lounge had long been one of the most popular and eclectic hangouts in New York, a place where athletes, journalists, and entertainers of varying stardom mingled together along with the everyday man and his wife, provided the everyday man and his wife didn't ask for autographs or "make nuisances of themselves" as Toots would warn.

"Well, let's see, Frank is supposed to be in sometime tonight," Shor said of Sinatra, "and the judge is over there," he said as he pointed to the Chief Justice of the Supreme Court, Earl Warren. "Other than that, just a buncha other crumb bums like the two of you. No offenses to the misses, as ya know. All this rain today, I think it keeps people away."

Jack had been coming to Toots Shor's since the mid-50s when the old place located on West 51st was still flourishing, it's nightly guest list a who's who of New York royalty. Back in those days Joe DiMaggio was still holding court at the furthest back table, the everyday man of no interest to him. Even after he'd retired from the Yankees in 1951, he was Toots' most valued patron, at least until the night when Toots made an off-color comment about Joe's new wife, Marilyn Monroe, and just like that DiMaggio never spoke to Toots again. It didn't take long for the newer Yankees like Mickey Mantle, Whitey Ford, Hank Bauer, and Billy Martin to find the place because Toots had an affinity for the Yankees, though men from the Dodgers and the baseball Giants certainly weren't barred from entering. The football Giants were always visible such as Frank Gifford, Pat Summerall, Charlie Conerly, Sam Huff, and Andy Robustelli. In fact, the first-time Jack came to Toots' joint, he had dinner with Gifford, of whom he was writing a feature story about for the New York Post.

Back in an age when athletes routinely dined and drank with sports writers, iconic scribes like Jimmy Cannon, Red Smith, and Dick Young, and now the men who were more of Jack's contemporaries like Stan, Maury Allen, Leonard Shecter, Phil Pepe, and Frank Deford, as well as broadcasters such as Walter Cronkite, Mike Wallace, and that loudmouth Howard Cosell, to name merely a few, were frequently seen imbibing at the large circular bar in the middle of the room. And of course, there were the stars of television and motion pictures and the music industry, among them Sinatra, Jackie Gleason, Bing Crosby, Bob Hope, and Sammy Davis Jr., who always seemed to have a table occupied.

It was a different time back then - women who were not accompanied by a man were not allowed entrance - and Toots was the perfect host for the testosterone-pumping crowd. But as the 1960s dawned, and Toots sold his old joint and re-opened a midtown block away on West 52nd, many of his famous pals didn't follow and the new place never quite had the same allure. And now, in 1968, with so much cultural change afoot, places like Gallagher's Steakhouse, the 21 Club, El Morocco, and others were making a more seamless transition from the Silent Generation to the Me Generation and Toots wasn't able to recapture his lost glory.

But still, this is where the McDonalds and the Isaacs chose to have dinner on the evening of April 4, before Jack would leave for Augusta National to cover The Masters, and Stan would begin to chronicle the exploits of the Yankees and the Mets in the soon-to-be-started baseball season, his prime pulpit his wildly entertaining and popular "Out of Left Field" column. Jack nursed his trademark vodka gimlet, Stan enjoyed a scotch on the rocks, the women drank red wine, and the conversation was split along gender lines as the women discussed recipes and the latest episode of *As The World Turns*, while the men talked shop, as they usually did.

"Did you hear that Shecter is going to edit some type of book by Jim Bouton next year?" Isaacs asked Jack, referring to the enigmatic Yankees pitcher who won 39 games combined in 1963 and '64, the last two times the Yankees won the American League pennant, but had fallen into steep decline, much like the team, the past few years.

"Bouton is worthy of a book?" Jack asked.

"Lenny told me he's gonna start keeping a diary and he'll have all kinds of behind-the-scenes shit. That oughta stir up a hornets' nest, don't you think?"

"Ah, the Chipmunks at their finest," Jack said, a reference to the nickname bestowed on Stan and Shecter and many of the other new breed sports writers by the legendary but now somewhat out of touch Jimmy Cannon, who didn't appreciate their bold and brash style. "Ya know, if I were a few years younger, maybe I coulda been a Chipmunk."

"Hate to tell ya," said Stan, who was eight years younger than Jack, "but if you were still in the newspaper game, you'd have your own membership card, but we can't count you as one of us because we don't accept you haughty-taughty magazine types."

After the first round of drinks had been consumed, Toots came around personally to offer menus and to recommend the broiled halibut steak and the Yankee pot roast. Jack chose the pot roast, and after the others ordered, Jack asked for a second round of drinks as he waved casually to Mark Brantley, the editor of *SportsWorld*, who was just being seated for dinner along with his wife on the other side of the room.

"So, what did you think of the president bowing out of the election?" Olivia asked the Isaacs, prompting Jack to smile to himself because he knew it was only a matter of time before his wife broached the topic.

Just a few days earlier, President Johnson had stunned the nation when he concluded a nationally-televised address by announcing that he would not run for re-election in the fall.

"Simply amazing," Bobbie Isaacs said, to which Stan added, "I didn't see that one coming. But can you really blame the guy? This damn war is not going away, and now he's sending more of our kids over there and his approval rating is falling faster than an anchor in the ocean."

Johnson had begun his speech talking, of course, about Vietnam. He made mention of the fact that even while the media was leading Americans to believe otherwise, Tet had been a failure for the North Vietnamese as they had suffered tremendous casualties, far worse than the U.S. and its allies, though he did not downplay any loss of American life. "We need to bring an end to this long and bloody war," Johnson intoned.

He then moved on to his plan for peace, sharing his intention to halt the bombing of North Vietnam, and he urged the enemy to respect the United States' restraint and implored President Ho Chi Minh to engage in meaningful talks. "We are reducing, substantially reducing, the present level of hostilities, and we are doing so unilaterally, at once," Johnson said. He'd already instructed aircraft and vessels to stop bombing the heavily-populated regions, but the caveat was that for the immediate future, bombing of the area north of the DMZ would have to continue in order to protect the forward allied positions.

And then came the jaw-dropper, a moment that would forever be part of the textbooks chronicling this country's history.

"For 37 years in the service of our nation, first as a congressman, as a senator, as vice-president, and now as your president, I have put the unity of the people first. And holding the trust that is mine, as president of all the people, I cannot disregard the peril to the progress of the American people and the hope and the prospect of peace for all peoples. What we won when all of our people united must not now be lost in suspicion, distrust, selfishness, and politics among any of our people. Believing this as I do, I have concluded that I should not permit the presidency to become involved in the partisan divisions that are developing in this political year. Accordingly, I shall not seek, and I will not accept, the nomination of my party for another term as your president."

Television viewers across the country had to stop for a second and digest what they'd just heard. Was Johnson really not going to run? Four days had passed since he signed off, and still, the rumbling was voluble as Americans tried to decide whether this was a good thing or a bad thing.

"Can you imagine Kennedy and Johnson fighting for the nomination, with all the bad blood between those two?" Stan said. "You thought the Dodgers and Giants were a rivalry?"

Everyone chuckled, and then Stan continued. "When McCarthy showed well in New Hampshire, that had to hurt Johnson, but I think when Kennedy threw his hat in the ring Johnson knew the party was splintering and he wasn't going to have the support he needs."

"Yes, I agree with that, absolutely I do," said Olivia, happy that someone else saw it exactly as she did. "We are a divided nation and I think that bothered Johnson more than anything. It's like he feels he chose to fight this war, and now it has created not only a war over there, but a war on our own soil. I give him a lot of credit for bowing out. And I think Kennedy is going to run with this, and there won't be any stopping him in Chicago. He'll get us out of this war, and Patrick and all the rest will come home."

"Have you heard from your son?" Bobbie, the mother of three young daughters, asked with a soothing tone as she touched Olivia's forearm.

"A couple weeks ago he sent a letter and said he was OK, though some of what he wrote disturbed us. It's awful over there, and I know he's trying to put up a brave facade, but he's scared. They're all scared."

There was an awkward silence then, and as if Toots was eavesdropping and recognized the mood needed to be lightened, a waiter arrived on cue with the fresh cocktails Jack had ordered. Once everyone was situated, Olivia proposed a toast to Bobby Kennedy and the belief that he would solidify and unify the Democratic Party, win the White House, and continue the work that his brother, Jack, was unable to finish.

A little while later the entrees arrived, and as the two couples ate they talked about less volatile topics; how the coming construction on the Long Island Expressway was going to make life even more miserable for commuters; what chance the New York Rangers, who were opening the NHL playoffs against Chicago that night at Madison Square Garden, had of winning the Stanley Cup for the first time since 1940; and if they were going to see the strange new movie *2001: A Space Odyssey*.

And then shortly after seven o'clock came a woman's shriek from over by the bar, and then came a gasp, and another, and then the talking stopped.

"What's happening?" Bobbie asked nervously as Toots turned off the ambient music and raised the volume on the lone black and white television above the bar.

Through the omnipresent haze of smoke that filled the room, Jack gazed toward the people who were closest to the television and the empty stares on their faces indicated to him that tragedy had struck, and of course his first thought was that it had to do with Vietnam. He and Stan dabbed their mouths with their napkins, dropped them on the table, and walked over to inquire. No one even noticed their arrival, everyone fixated on the grainy screen where Walter Cronkite, who normally would have been off the air by now, was explaining that the Dr. Martin Luther King, Jr. had been murdered in Memphis, slain by an assassin's bullet as he stood on the balcony of the Lorraine Motel in that racially-charged city where he had been trying to broker a deal for striking sanitation workers, most of whom were black.

Answering the anxious waves of their wives, Jack and Stan returned somberly to the table to share the news, and Olivia and Bobbie both put their hands to the mouths, shocked by yet another act of senseless violence in a country that seemed to be ripping apart at the seams.

Jack had the tremendous honor of interviewing Dr. King for a three-part series the magazine produced in August 1966 that examined the treatment of black athletes in American society. It had taken weeks for the *SportsWorld* legal department to arrange the meeting, but thankfully, Dr. King found time in his busy schedule to sit down with

Jack in a motel room outside Atlanta, and for two hours they discussed the issue of racism in sports. "We are being used, and when we have won them their victories, they discard us like yesterday's trash," Dr. King said. "The white man cheers the Negro when he makes his baskets and scores his touchdowns, and when the uniform comes off, and that Negro walks out of the arena, the white man calls him a nigger and tells him that he can't eat here, or drink from that water fountain."

Jack was not a racist and he abhorred those who were, but he lived in a lily-white suburb on Long Island, worked in an industry that was populated almost exclusively by white males, and admittedly did not count any Negroes among his tight circle of social friends. He had several casual acquaintances, and of course he had interviewed dozens and dozens of black athletes through the years, even had drinks with some of them, sometimes right here at Toots Shor's. But he was not as racially conscious as he should have been, so to sit down that afternoon with Dr. King - a man whose courage and leadership and decency and morality were unmatched, and whose relentless and peaceful quest for equality for his people brought them hope that someday things would change - was an epiphanic moment for Jack, as well as the highlight of his journalistic career, and one of the greatest thrills of his life.

From the day in 1955 when he took up the cause of Rosa Parks - the black seamstress from Montgomery who had the audacity to sit at the front of a city bus instead of in the back where the blacks were cordoned off - to this night when this great man, recipient of the Nobel Peace Prize, was gunned down in cold blood, he'd been one of the most influential figures in American culture. And now, Dr. King was dead. An apostle of peace he'd been called, but he died at the very hand of the violence he deplored.

Jack had no doubt that this tragedy would create explosions of violence around the country, including right here in the Harlem section of New York City.

"We should settle the bill and go home; the city's not going to be a safe place tonight," Jack said. Stan Isaacs did not disagree, and so the McDonalds and the Isaacs left their unfinished entrees, thanked Toots Shor for his hospitality, and hailed a cab that would take them to Penn Station where they'd catch the train back to Long Island. On that train ride, there was no conversation, and Jack stared into the rainy darkness, and thought about a speech Dr. King had delivered at a Baptist church in Atlanta barely two months earlier, words that had been publicized because, as were most of Dr. King's orations, they were memorable.

"Every now and then I guess we all think realistically about that day when we will be victimized with what is life's final common denominator—that something that we call death," King said in his magnificent and rhythmic voice. "We all think about it. And every now and then I think about my own death and I think about my own funeral. And I don't think of it in a morbid sense. And every now and then I ask myself, 'What is it that I would want said?'

"If any of you are around when I have to meet my day, I don't want a long funeral. And if you get somebody to

100

deliver the eulogy, tell them not to talk too long. Every now and then I wonder what I want them to say. Tell them not to mention that I have a Nobel Peace Prize, which isn't important. Tell them not to mention that I have three or four hundred other awards, that's not important. Tell them not to mention where I went to school. I'd like somebody to mention that day, that Martin Luther King, Jr. tried to give his life serving others. I'd like for somebody to say that day, that Martin Luther King, Jr. tried to love somebody. I want you to be able to say that day, that I did try to feed the hungry. And I want you to be able to say that day, that I did try, in my life, to clothe those who were naked. I want you to say, on that day, that I did try, in my life, to visit those who were in prison. I want you to say that I tried to love and serve humanity. Yes, if you want to say that I was a drum major, say that I was a drum major for justice; say that I was a drum major for righteousness. And all of the other shallow things will not matter. I won't have any money to leave behind. I won't have the fine and luxurious things of life to leave behind. But I just want to leave a committed life behind."

10 - *What A Stupid I am*

Like the rest of the press corps that over the past couple hours had been watching the drama unfold at Augusta National Golf Club, Jack was both enthralled by the play of Roberto de Vicenzo and Bob Goalby on a frenetic Sunday afternoon amidst the dogwoods and azaleas, and he was somewhat pissed off that he'd have to change his flight plans for Monday.

Goalby had just struck a majestic 2-iron from about 210 yards away that landed safely on the 18th green, setting him up for a gritty two-putt par that tied him for the lead with the already-finished de Vicenzo. Playoff on Monday.

Someday, Jack thought, maybe someone will come to their senses and have these ties decided by a sudden-death playoff. On Sunday. Seriously, was it really necessary to have everyone - fans, media, volunteers - haul themselves back on Monday so two guys could play 18 more holes to determine a winner in these major championships?

Jack had covered more than his share of golf's biggest tournaments, and there was nothing quite like the sound of that collective "Fuck!" that echoed in the media room when the writers officially knew that they'd all have to come back Monday, any chance of getting home as scheduled blown to bits.

However, as the huge gallery cheered for Goalby when he lifted his ball from the cup and held it aloft, there was another compelling drama unfolding at the scorers' table. Jack, who was standing by the 18th green with several other reporters silently cursing Goalby for making that par, was certainly wondering why de Vicenzo - who had already gone over to the television room where the green jacket is placed on the winner for the broadcast before they do the real ceremony on the 18th green - had come back outside and was seated at the table. And he was as shocked as everyone else when that question was answered.

"What a stupid I am," the affable Argentinian would later say, summing up the situation quite succinctly, if not properly grammatical, in his broken English.

A few minutes earlier, as Goalby was walking off the 18th tee, Jack saw de Vicenzo's playing partner, Tommy Aaron, talking to a Masters' official, and then he watched as that green-coated man rushed off looking like his wife had just found his dress shirt with lipstick on the collar. Jack didn't think much of it, and returned his focus to Goalby. But after Goalby's approach shot soared onto the green and skidded to rest 40 feet from the hole, Jack saw the man in the green coat escorting de Vicenzo back to the table as the crowd greeted Goalby with a prolonged roar as he walked up the steep hill that led to the putting surface, and then his reporters' antenna went up.

"Something's going on," Jack said to Furman Bisher, who was covering the tournament, as he always did, for the *Atlanta Constitution-Journal.*

"Yeah, I was wondering about that myself," said Bisher, who'd also noticed the commotion.

By the time Goalby finished off his par by making a knee-knocker from four feet, de Vicenzo was looking like a man being led to the firing squad, a distant and sorrowful look on his face. As Goalby and his playing partner, Raymond Floyd, walked over to the table to attest their scores and sign their cards, surely they were puzzled by why de Vicenzo was still sitting there, balding head in his hands.

It was then revealed that Goalby's par at 18 had not qualified him for a Monday playoff, it had won him the championship because de Vicenzo had signed an incorrect scorecard, and the penalty stroke he incurred for that mistake meant that he finished one shot behind Goalby.

"I'm very happy I won the tournament," Goalby said after he'd been fitted with the green jacket and whisked off to face a throng of reporters not only happy that there wouldn't be a playoff, but also because they now had a great story to tell their readers and viewers. "I'd be a liar if I told you I wasn't. But I'm really sorry I won it the way I did. I'd much rather have done it in a playoff. Roberto has been one of my good friends for 12 years, and there has never been a nicer fellow."

Nor a sadder one. How 'bout that for a 45th birthday present, Roberto? The equivalent of a hot poker up the ass.

Jack was a decent golfer, around a 10 handicap. He was mostly a recreational player, but he had played in several tournaments as a member at Garden City Golf Club, even made it to the championship match in his flight a few summers earlier. He'd gone through the routine of keeping someone else's score, and then making sure his own score had been properly recorded. He understood the merit of that process in amateur events, but for a professional tournament, he thought it was ridiculous to penalize, let alone disqualify, competitors who were trying to make a living because their math was wrong.

Jack had written this a couple times through the years, how pros should be unburdened of the task of keeping their official score, or anyone else's. And Jack's solution was as easy as two plus two: Each group of players in a pro tournament should have a volunteer scorer walking with them, counting the strokes. Volunteers do just about everything else at tournaments, so why not let them keep score?

Naturally, the first question raised by those who disagreed with Jack - and there were many - was what happens when the official scorer gets it wrong? Simple: Make the correction, and move on. For crying out loud, Jack would argue, if Jack Nicklaus shoots a 68 and his scorer mistakenly had him for 67, then Nicklaus' score is 68. There isn't a pro golfer on the planet playing this gentlemanly of all games who is going to try to cheat on his scorecard. If there's a mistake, it's going to come to light, and then you make the adjustment. What's the big deal?

What happened to de Vicenzo was this: On the 17th hole, he'd made a birdie three to get to 12-under-par which put him in the lead by a stroke. However, Aaron had mistakenly written a four on the card. De Vicenzo went on to bogey the 18th which dropped him back into a tie with Goalby at 11-under. Taking the erroneous four on 17 into account, Aaron's addition gave de Vicenzo a 35 on the back nine when it should have been 34, and 66 for the round, when it should have been 65. De Vicenzo didn't catch the mistake, signed the card, and once the faux pas was discovered, there was nothing the green coats could do. Tournament chairman Clifford Roberts - in consultation with Masters founder and patriarch Bobby Jones, in failing health and watching the tournament on television from his cabin - had no choice but to penalize de

Vicenzo a stroke for signing for a score higher than he actually shot. Had de Vicenzo signed for a score lower than he shot, he would have been disqualified and ineligible for the second-place money of $15,000. But never mind the money, this was the Masters, one of the crown jewels of the PGA circuit. Jack just didn't understand why a simple error in arithmetic should create a potentially career-altering outcome. Penalize a guy for shanking a tee shot out of bounds, but not for shanking his scorecard.

Ever gracious despite such a disappointing turn of events, de Vicenzo explained the mishap by saying, "I am so unhappy to make five on the last hole, and Bob, he gave me so much pressure on the last hole that I lose my brain. I play golf all over the world for 30 years, and now all I can think of is what a stupid I am to be wrong in this wonderful tournament. Never have I ever done such a thing before. Maybe I am too old to win. It's not Aaron's fault; I'm sure he feels worse about it than me. It's my fault."

The ending was far more interesting than the early rounds of the tournament had been, though there was good reason for that. When the players arrived at Augusta, the country was still getting over the shock of the assassination of Dr. Martin Luther King, Jr. His funeral was held just days before the start of the tournament, and there was no denying that even a place as lily-white as Augusta National - where the only black people at the club were employees and where no black golfer had ever stuck a tee in the ground - was affected by the tragedy.

There was a noticeable downturn in attendance, and the roars that typically reverberated back and forth between the Georgia pines just weren't as boisterous. Several competitors even remarked that it was "quiet" out there, most of the people with their coveted Augusta badges just not ready to enjoy the usual splendor of the Masters with King's death so raw, the country's political landscape in upheaval, and the war in Vietnam creating so much angst and anger.

Billy Casper's 68 gave him the solo lead after the first round, and then he blamed a bad breakfast - "I had peaches and sausage and the sausage didn't sit too well" - for his second-round 75 that knocked him from the perch. Arnold Palmer had only his own bad play to blame as he equaled his highest score ever at Augusta, a grotesque second-round 79 that caused him to miss the cut for the first time in his 14 Masters appearances, four of which had ended with him wearing a green jacket. When Friday ended, Don January and Gary Player shared the top spot at 139 and Goalby was in the group at 140 along with Nicklaus and Frank Beard.

Player surged into the lead through 54 holes with a Saturday 71 that was capped by a 30-foot double-breaking birdie putt at 18, but his grip on first was tenuous at best as six other players had been in the top spot at some point during the day, and the tight grouping of 11 men within three shots of Player promised an intriguing finish, though no one could have imagined quite how intriguing.

Easter Sunday dawned idyllically sunny and warm, and de Vicenzo gave himself an early birthday present when he holed out a 9-iron from 135 yards for eagle on the first hole, then birdied the second and third holes and added another at the eighth for an outgoing 31 that thrust him into the lead. Goalby jumped into the mix with three birdies for a front nine 33, and then, like they'd been saying at Augusta almost from the time Gene Sarazen made his famous double-eagle at the 15th hole back in 1935, the back nine on Sunday signaled the start of the tournament.

Goalby executed two deft chips to rescue pars at 11 and 12 while de Vicenzo stretched his lead to two with a birdie at the 12th. Here, Goalby struck back with a birdie at 13, another at 14, and then he reached the par-5 15th in two shots and rolled in an eight-foot eagle to vault over de Vicenzo who had merely birdied the 15th and parred 13 and 14. Of course, Goalby's lead lasted barely seconds because up ahead, de Vicenzo made his birdie at 17 to draw even, and then, as he was making his closing bogey at 18, Goalby bogeyed the 17th to theoretically remain in a tie for the lead at 11-under.

Thinking he needed a par to get to a playoff, Goalby tried to play safe at the 18th tee, opting for a 3-wood to make sure he would stay short of the fairway bunkers on the left side. Instead, he came out of the shot and pushed it right, and was quite fortunate the ball hit a tree and kicked out rather than nestle into the pine straw in the woods. Having lost so much distance, par was now going to be a struggle, and even after he executed his 2-iron shot, he was still faced with a long downhill birdie putt, always a treacherous combination at Augusta. Goalby did well to get within four feet of the cup, and then calmly swished that one for the par that, unbeknownst to him at the time, was the winning stroke.

"I regret that it happened," said Goalby, "but we all must abide by the rules, that's all there is to it."

Stupid as the rules may be, Jack thought. But hey, things worked out well for Jack and his comrades. Compelling tale to tell, and an on-time departure Monday afternoon. Jack was thinking he might even get back home in time to sneak out for his first nine holes of the spring.

11 - Chaos at Columbia

The first time Kathleen McDonald saw Mark Rudd on campus at Columbia, she thought he was an irascible loud-mouth who was just trying to cause trouble, a rebel with way too many causes, though his favorite was Vietnam.

This guy was pissed off all the time, and his was a distinct voice that resonated up and down College Walk, his bullhorn louder than all the others at the Sundial rallies that were becoming a weekly occurrence. Rudd was the leader of Columbia's chapter of Students for a Democratic Society, and he and his sycophants were constantly pushing their SDS agenda on anyone who walked by their daily literature table on the Walk. Kathleen, then a meek and unknowing freshman, wanted nothing to do with any of it and she made it a point to rush past the table, or avoid it altogether.

Her brother Patrick, knowing he would eventually get drafted because his grades weren't up to snuff for college, had enlisted in the Marines straight out of high school. He figured that the sooner he did his time, the sooner it would end, and if he didn't return home from Vietnam in a pine box, then he could start figuring out what he was going to do with the rest of his life. So, the thought of Rudd and these other radical assholes spending every waking hour of their free time denouncing the war and America's role in it, Patrick's role in it, had been abhorrent to her.

Thus, for her to be sitting in a jail cell, arrested along with Rudd and more than 700 other students for taking part in the week-long building occupations at Columbia that had been organized by Rudd and the SDS as well as the Student African-American Society (SAS), was more surprising than a Grateful Dead concert without marijuana.

"Are you OK? Where are you? Have they posted bond for you?" Jack asked in rapid-fire fashion when Kathleen made her allotted phone call.

"Thank God you're OK, honey," a frantic Olivia said on the bedroom extension. "We've been worried sick watching all of this. On the news, they showed a lot of people getting beaten and hurt."

"Mom, mom, I'm OK, my group went peacefully; we didn't fight the police, but yeah, there's a lot of bloody people here. It was awful. I can't believe the way they came in and started beating up people."

"Can't believe it?" Jack said incredulously. "What did you think they were going to do? Kathleen, what the hell were you thinking getting involved in all of this?"

"Daddy, don't judge me. And don't be like them."

"Like who, young lady? Like the cops? Like the rational-thinking people? Jesus Christ, Kathleen, you could have been seriously hurt. And for what? What did all this get you besides a criminal record?"

Jack was furious with his daughter, and he was furious with all the god-damned radicals and their protests. These fucking kids would protest rain just to say they stood for something. But what did they really stand for? They wanted America to pull out of Vietnam. Well, it wasn't that simple. As a veteran of war, Jack knew this. Yes, this particular war was troublesome, Jack understood that, but for these kids, and even worse the adults who should know better, to be turning the country upside down was simply irresponsible as far as he was concerned. They didn't give a shit about anyone over in Vietnam. He wanted to tell them all to trade in their fucking bullhorns and placards for an M-16 and get their pot-smoking, hippie asses over there and help the other kids who were fighting for the very freedom these rabble rousers were abusing. It made Jack sick, and now his own daughter was riding shotgun on that bandwagon with the other disrespectful louts.

"Jack, stop it," said Olivia, admonishing her husband. "We'll talk about this when she gets home."

"Oh, we damn well will," Jack said. "What precinct are you in?"

"The 26th, right by the university," Kathleen spat.

"Yes, I know where it is," Jack said. "I just never thought I'd be driving there to bail you out."

For the past couple years, Columbia had become a beacon for protesters, and the agendas ran the gamut: anti-war, race relations, empowerment, women's rights, on-campus military recruitment, freedom of speech, and the university's ongoing affiliation with the Institute of Defense Analysis, just to scratch the surface. University President Grayson Kirk, in an effort to minimize media attention and present a facade that made it seem like he had things under control, opted to let the protesters have their pulpits without interference, as long as the rallies remained peaceful, which in large part they had. But the turning point came in the spring of 1967 when CIA and Marine Corps recruiters came to John Jay Hall, where Kathleen now lived, and were met by anti-war vigilance. And soon thereafter, a clash between more than a thousand students either opposed to, or favoring, the recruitment policies prompted Kirk to ban all indoor protests for the 1967-68 academic year. All this did was spill fuel into the gathering fire.

With Rudd and some of his SDS lieutenants stirring the embers on a daily basis, it became obvious that Columbia was going to erupt, and the only question was how violent might it become. The confluence of the rising anger over the war, the university's refusal to end its relationship with the IDA, and the increased racial tension regarding the controversial building of the Morningside gym on the edge of the campus bordered by Harlem, had led to a detonation of emotion and there was no escaping the storm.

The flashpoint for the week-long campus uprising occurred in late March when Rudd brought to President Kirk's office a petition signed by approximately 1,500 students demanding that Columbia disengage from the IDA. When Kirk ignored the petition, Rudd and five others (who became known as the IDA Six) conducted an anti-IDA protest in Low Library. Of course, this gathering violated Kirk's ban on indoor protests, and a month later, the six were placed on probation by the university.

A day after that disciplinary hearing, on the afternoon of April 23, the SDS held a rally in support of the IDA Six, and they joined forces with the SAS on the Morningside gym issue. At noon, hundreds of students that included members of SDS, SAS, and another radical student group, the Columbia Citizenship Council, as well as unaffiliated left wing liberals, gathered at the Sundial in front of Low Library where Rudd outlined three non-negotiable demands that would be presented to Kirk: Ceasing gym construction, Columbia's withdrawal from the IDA, and dropping any punishment of the IDA Six. If the terms were not met, the students would revolt.

Several speeches were made, including one by an African-American male named Cicero who was the leader of SAS, and when everyone was talked out, the assemblage proceeded to the steps of the library where it planned to confront Kirk, and take over the building. But the doors were blocked by Columbia security officers and right wing counter-protesters including the anti-SDS group Students for a Free Campus. So, Rudd led a charge down past St. Paul's Chapel and across 116th Street to the gym construction site, chanting "Jim Crow Gym, Must Go!" That proved to be unwise as New York City police were on guard, and one student who tried to breach the barrier was arrested. So back they marched to the Sundial where the decision was made to take the main classroom building, Hamilton Hall, and procure a hostage, which turned out be Dean Henry Coleman. And so began eight days of history-making chaos.

Kathleen had been in Low Plaza earlier in the day, curious about what was being said, but she did not join the mob that rushed the library, the gym site, and finally, Hamilton Hall. She went back to John Jay and sat with several suite mates discussing what had transpired, and sharing opinions on what they thought might happen next. She then called home to tell her parents she was safe, and after her mother implored her to stay in her room, Kathleen said that was her plan, but thanks mother.

The next day, classes were cancelled due to the uprising, so Kathleen tried to catch up on school work, but it was tough to concentrate because her burgeoning journalistic gene drew her out to the plaza where she met up with several friends who had been equally intrigued. They learned that overnight, the SAS had decided to split from SDS, saying the gym issue should be theirs alone and Rudd, though surprised by that change of philosophy, agreed to lead SDS out of Hamilton and left it in the capable stranglehold of the better-organized and more resolute SAS. Inside Hamilton, the black students and Harlem residents fortified the building in preparation for a possible police action, but there was no violence. Literally kicked out of Hamilton, the SDS did what it had intended to do originally - it stormed into Low Library, this time without resistance, and marched up to President's Kirk's vacant office to conduct its sit-in.

Over the next several days, there was a strange pall hanging over the campus. It was obvious things weren't normal, but it wasn't overly obvious that there was a siege underway, either. Students came and went as they pleased, and the security presence wasn't overbearing or confrontational. Kathleen read the leaflets that were being distributed by SDS members, she listened to their impromptu diatribes, and she participated in several group discussions amongst non-SDS students who collectively were trying to wrap their heads around the importance of the issues SDS was fighting for. And the more she learned, the more she felt compelled to do her part to support them in this imbroglio with the university. It was a place Kathleen never thought she would get to, and while she disagreed with the way SDS was going about trying to enact change, she had started to grasp the magnitude and the ideology of the fight.

Kathleen loved being at Columbia because the journalism school was one of the finest in the country, and she knew that all the hard work she put in to earn entry into an Ivy League institution, and the greatness she hoped to achieve during her time at Columbia, was going to pay tremendous dividends throughout her life. But it was now apparent to her that the administration of the school had run amok, and she stood in firm disagreement with its policies regarding the building of the gym, the allowance of military and CIA recruitment on campus, and the fact that Columbia was a hub for IDA research.

Rudd, though an irrational ruffian with a volatile and vociferous agenda, had opened her eyes to these things, and also had helped her crystalize her conflicted feelings on Vietnam. She loved her brother, and would support him to the ends of the earth. Too, she would never sway from her familial belief that the American way of life was worth fighting for. Generations of her relatives had stepped up when duty called, and she believed that future generations of the McDonald lineage - maybe even her own children - would do the same if need be. But she was now convinced that Vietnam was unjust. Her brother had been sent thousands of miles away and dropped into a jungle where no American boy should be, and if these protests at Columbia and dozens of colleges and universities across the country could impact the United States' policy in any way, then they were worth it.

So, as the third day of the revolt dawned, Kathleen made the decision to march into Mathematics Hall with a faction of SDS-led students to participate in the taking of the building. Her phone call that night to her parents was one of the most difficult she had ever made because she knew two things would come of it: Her father would be angry and would demand her to get the hell out of there, if for no other reason, out of respect for her brother; and her mother, even though she was harboring similar feelings about the war, would be scared to death and would back her father's wishes. Sure enough, it played out exactly as she'd thought, and finally, she had to hang up because the conversation spun into a tornado of disagreement.

As soon as the line clicked, Jack went to the hall closet to get his coat for the drive over to Columbia, but Olivia - gathering herself and putting aside her fear for her daughter's safety only because there had been no real signs of violence - talked him out of it. If Jack dragged her home, Olivia feared it would drive a potentially irreparable wedge between the stern father and the strong-minded and somewhat rebellious daughter. Jack's coat was on, and the car keys were in his hand, but he ceded to his wife's wishes with a warning that at the first sign of trouble, he was going to get her.

But then it was too late. The Bible tells us that on the seventh day, God rested. On the seventh day of the Columbia revolt, the school administration - unwilling to give in to the demands foisted upon it, and fearing that residents from neighboring Harlem would enter the fray - asked Mayor John Lindsay to send in the New York City police to bring an end to it all by removing students, quietly if possible, but by force if need be. Lindsay sought advice from Yale University President Kingman Brewster, who had experience with anti-war protests on the New Haven, Connecticut campus and had deftly prevented an uprising such as the one that gripped Columbia. Brewster told him, "The very future of the American university depended on punishing the strikers." And so Lindsay, knowing that a bloody riot could ensue, still gave the order and scheduled it to be executed in the early morning hours of April 30.

A couple days before the police marched in with their billy clubs and shields, Kathleen and several friends had abandoned Mathematics Hall because there were just too many unstable people holed up there, including Rudd. They had begun to fight amongst themselves and Rudd, frustrated by President Kirk's refusal to meet the demands of the SDS, was growing increasingly unpredictable. Kathleen was smart enough to know that the rebellion wasn't going to go on forever; at some point the police would show up, and this militant group she was aligned with was not going to leave without a fight. So, Kathleen walked out and took up residence in Avery Hall, and it was there, at 2 a.m., where she was awakened by the sound of sirens and the sight of nearly 1,000 officers streaming onto campus to begin the systematic removal of the protesters.

Hamilton Hall was first, and the black students surrendered without incident, leaving through the front door. Low Library inhabitants put up only passive resistance, but resistance of any type was not tolerated and a tone was set when several students were clubbed and suffered minor injuries. Kathleen was one of 42 students inside Avery, and the bulk of them had agreed to walk out peacefully before the cops got there, but a few hard-liners refused to let anyone leave. At approximately 2:30 a.m., the locked front door was broken open, and with Kathleen and several of the women screaming in fear, a brief skirmish broke out that resulted in injuries to both protesters and policemen, though Kathleen was not harmed. And then at Fayerweather and Mathematics halls, the evacuation got out of hand. Police were briefly derailed by barricades in stairwells and inside the rooms where the students were located, and then had to ward off aerial assaults of batteries, bottles, and anything else that could be thrown. Fights broke out, clothes were torn, blood was drawn, and all Kathleen could think of was the irony of the situation. These demonstrators did not believe in war, but they had become engaged in one on this terrible night.

While all this was taking place, a huge crowd had gathered on South Field, and when they began to taunt the police and hurl rocks, the police charged and more fighting erupted. By the time the largest police action at an American university in history was over, more than 700 had been arrested, and nearly 150 had been injured.

Kathleen was one of dozens booked at the 26th, and she sat in a holding cell clasping hands with fellow students, all just as scared as she, waiting for her father to collect her.

It was two hours after first arriving before Jack finally had custody of his daughter, and not a word was spoken as he escorted her to the car. Not until Jack had worked his way back to the Long Island Expressway did Kathleen break the silence.

"Daddy, I know you're mad at me, and I know you don't want to hear it, but I did what I felt I needed to do. I don't agree with all of the politics, and I didn't think things would get as crazy as they did, but we made a statement that people will talk about for a long time. The war is wrong, and Patrick shouldn't be there; no American should be there."

"That's not your decision to make, and it's not a decision for those lawless hippies to make either," Jack responded.

"I'm disappointed in you. I've always admired your spirit and your spunk and how you're passionate about the things you believe in, but what you did tonight spit right in the face of your brother, and me, and your grandmother, and all the people who have served this country and died fighting for its freedom."

Kathleen said nothing. What could she say? She knew her father would feel this way, and she was sorry for hurting him, but she wasn't sorry for what she had done. Maybe someday, her father would come to understand, and she only hoped that it wouldn't take burying his only son for him to recognize that the United States had to get out of this fucking war as soon as possible.

12 - Sacre Blues

Selfishly, Jack was excited to be flying to St. Louis for the start of the Stanley Cup Finals between the expansion Blues and the powerhouse Montreal Canadiens; it provided a well-timed respite from the stress that had gripped his home.

It had been a difficult couple of days; father, mother, and daughter engaging in hours of tedious discussion regarding what had happened at Columbia. Kathleen spent much of the time defending her decision to join the revolt and she was not going to change her mind about the unjustness of the United States' involvement in the war.

She tried to educate Jack on the issues that the students were railing against, and while he did gain a deeper understanding of what really had happened - especially the controversy over the gym construction - Jack refused to alter his position on the fact that these kids had no business turning the university upside down, and forcing a police action that put everyone involved, most importantly his daughter, in danger. He found the act of protesting to be a waste of time, and the protests at Columbia were particularly disappointing because they were fueled by an abject disregard for authority which ultimately resulted in a violent conclusion.

"Daddy, it was the only way we were going to be heard," Kathleen said during one exchange.

"And who exactly heard you, Kathleen?" Jack responded. "I know the cops heard you loud and clear. But who else really heard you? I'll say this, I hope Patrick didn't hear you, because if he did, I'm guessing he's pretty damned disappointed in you. He's in danger of being killed every second he's over there, fighting for all of us, and you and those loud-mouthed hooligans are taking a giant shit on him and every other kid there."

"Jack, watch your mouth," Olivia spat as she shot him a glare, which he returned in kind.

"This country is being ripped apart and it should scare the hell out of you," Jack continued. "The war, Johnson refusing to run for re-election, Dr. King being killed. God knows what else is coming. We didn't need college kids with apparently too much time on their hands causing a national scene. Like the cops don't have enough to deal with in the city."

"Will things get better if we sit on our hands and don't demand change?" Kathleen asked. "Will everything be OK if we ignore our unalienable right to freedom of speech and just let the government get away with everything it does, the same government that sent Patrick to that awful place?"

On and on it went until Kathleen retreated to her room and hardly came out the last day she was home. Classes were scheduled to re-start the day Jack was leaving to catch his flight to St. Louis, so after Olivia talked Kathleen out of taking the train back to school, father and daughter drove back to campus in peace, the cool silence broken only when Jack pulled up to the entrance at 116th Street and Broadway.

"I'm sorry you're upset daddy. I didn't mean to hurt you, and I would never disrespect what Patrick is doing. I just felt like this is what I needed to do, my little part in trying to make a difference. I hope you can understand that someday."

Jack looked at her beautiful but sad face, reached over and wiped a tear from her eye, and said, "I love you very much. Get your work done, finish the year strong, and be careful."

With that, she exited the vehicle, passed through the main gate that was now guarded warily by police, and made her way toward her dorm on the other side of campus as Jack watched her walk as long as she remained in sight.

The next day, Jack was at the morning pre-game skate of the Canadiens, refocused on work while watching the fabulous Frenchmen whirling around the ice like a finely choreographed dance troupe. As these skillful stars named Jean Beliveau, Yvan Cournoyer, Henri Richard, Duck Duff, Jacques Laperriere and J.C. Tremblay were put through their paces by legendary coach Toe Blake, Jack wasn't sure how the Blues were going to compete in this championship series. So, he asked Red Fisher, the noted hockey writer of the *Montreal Star.*

"People are going to be surprised when I write this, but this will be a tough series for the Canadiens," Fisher said.

"Why is that, Red?" Jack asked, somewhat surprised by the response.

"Look, the Blues are a first-year team, but they have a bunch of proud veteran guys who aren't gonna just roll over. Toe said as much last night when I saw him at the hotel. He's a little worried. All the pressure is on his team because if it doesn't win, it will be considered one of the all-time flops. The whole country will gasp if the Canadiens don't win. And Toe also knows that Scotty Bowman can coach. He might be a rookie in this league, but I'm tellin' you right now, this guy is a star in the making. And Toe knows it. Hell, he taught him half of what he knows."

Just like that, Jack was on the phone back to New York to tell the bosses that he was changing tack and rather than write about the Canadiens, he was going to write about this fella Bowman, assuming Bowman was willing to give him some time after the Blues' game-day skate. Jack's editor, Mark Brantley, wasn't sure if the unknown Bowman was worthy of the lead story in the magazine, but he trusted Jack's judgment and finally said, "OK, make the fucker sing."

Using a piece of information relayed to him by Fisher, Jack began the conversation with Bowman saying, "So, Scotty, tell me a little about that plate in your head." And for the next 45 minutes, as they sat in the cramped office of the NHL's youngest head coach, Jack learned all there was to know about this man who Red Fisher believed would be the next big thing in the world of coaching.

Bowman grew up in the hockey-crazed Montreal suburb of Verdun on a crowded street lined by tenement buildings, 26 in all, 13 on each side, six families per building, and if you were a young boy, you played hockey. Well, except for the two youngsters who learned how to crack safes, became armed bank robbers, and ended up in prison - one out in Vancouver, one in Boston - before Bowman reached the NHL. "Those two were a couple of characters," Bowman said with a laugh.

Bowman's father was a blacksmith, and he loved hockey. In Bowman's youth Montreal had two NHL teams - the Canadiens who were beloved by the French-speaking citizens, and the Maroons who were the favorite of the

English-speakers. Bowman's father was a Maroons fan, and Scotty remembered how his father would stand in line behind the Forum - where both teams played - to get 50-cent tickets. Interestingly, Scotty wasn't really a fan of either hometown team. He preferred Boston, and he was able to follow the Bruins because the broadcast signal from Beantown extended into Canada. "I used to have to go to bed at the end of the first or second period, so my father would always write the score before he went to work the next day," Bowman said.

There were dozens of rinks scattered around Verdun, and there were days when it was tough to get into a game because there were so many kids playing. But this was never a problem for Bowman because he was one of the best players. He first strapped on skates when he was seven, was on an organized team by the age of 10, and by the time he was a teenager Bowman had designs on a pro career, and no one doubted that he'd make it. "A player was all I wanted to be."

But Bowman never realized that dream. In March 1952, when he was just 18 years old, Bowman - playing for the Montreal Junior Canadiens - was skating in on a breakaway during a playoff game at the Forum. A Trois-Rivieres defenseman named Jean-Guy Talbot, angered because his team was losing and about to be eliminated from the Junior A series, chased down Bowman from behind and took a manic swing with his stick. He struck Bowman on the head, knocking him unconscious and opening a five-inch wide gash. "It was like being scalped," Bowman remembered, not too fondly. Bowman later underwent surgery and had a metal plate inserted into his fractured skull, and while he went on to play a couple more years in Junior A, he was not the same pro prospect-level player he'd been. "I just didn't have the same confidence and I had a lot of headaches and blurred vision," he recalled.

Hockey was all he knew. So, naturally, if he couldn't play, he was going to coach. He started in the youth leagues, and in order to augment the pittance he earned coaching, he sold paint for Sherwin-Williams. On his lunch hour, he'd make the five-minute walk over to the Forum to sit in the stands and watch Dick Irvin put the fabulous Canadiens through practice, taking fastidious notes as players such as Rocket Richard flew up and down the ice making the game look so impossibly easy.

His first big break came in 1956 when the Junior Canadiens moved from Montreal to Ottawa, and the team's coach and general manager, Sam Pollock, asked the 23-year-old Bowman to be his assistant coach. Together they led the Junior Canadiens to the 1958 Memorial Cup championship - the Stanley Cup of junior hockey - and that led to Bowman becoming head coach of the Junior A team in Peterborough, Ontario. He spent three years with the Petes, then tried his hand at scouting for the NHL Canadiens, but missed coaching and landed the head job with the Junior Canadiens - now based back in Montreal - in 1964. Blake had taken over from Irvin as coach of the Canadiens in 1955 and had become one of the most successful in NHL history by the time Bowman returned to

Montreal. Blake saw something in Bowman and took it upon himself to serve as a mentor.

"I used to go into his office a lot," Bowman said. "He knew how each of his players did against everyone else. Certain guys do well against one team but not another. He was a good strategist and a good matchup man and wasn't afraid to sit guys out to change his ammunition." Blake would often design strategies for Bowman to employ in big games, and they almost always produced the desired effect. It was during this period when Bowman learned that keeping your opponent off balance by utilizing the element of surprise was a valuable tool. And Blake also made him aware that being able to adapt to the ebb and flow of a particular game was paramount to success.

For two decades the NHL had been a quaint six-team enterprise with Montreal, Toronto, New York, Boston, Detroit and Chicago making up the footprint, the Original Six as they became known. But as the sport had begun to gain popularity, there was a voluble movement to expand into new markets, led by Rangers owner William Jennings who argued that the league needed more teams to procure a television deal in the United States. Jennings had begun preaching in the early 60s, but his fellow owners kept putting it off, particularly the Montreal and Toronto franchises who were making plenty of money on their Canadian broadcasting contract and didn't want to share the proceeds with another Canadian club, Vancouver being a leading candidate to join the NHL if expansion was approved. Finally, in 1965, NHL president Clarence Campbell was told that a major TV contract in the U.S.

would never happen until the league expanded and this, coupled with the fear that the Western Hockey League was starting to make inroads on the talent pool, pushed the idea through.

Rather than do it gradually, the NHL jumped in with both feet and decided to double the size of the league. The Original Six remained together in the East, and six new cities comprised the new West Division - St. Louis, Philadelphia, Pittsburgh, Minneapolis, San Francisco-Oakland, and Los Angeles. Vancouver, much to the joy of Montreal and Toronto, was left out because its bid was among the weakest presented. And while cities like Buffalo and Baltimore seemed better prepared, St. Louis made the cut mainly because Chicago Blackhawks owner William Wirtz insisted on a Midwest neighbor, and also because he owned the St. Louis Arena where the Blues would play.

One of Bowman's players with the Junior Canadiens was a kid named Craig Patrick, whose father, Lynn, was a long-time NHL coach. Lynn was named coach and general manager of the Blues, and after hearing Craig rave about playing for Bowman, Lynn decided to offer Bowman the chance to serve in the dual role of assistant coach and scout for the Blues.

"I moved to St. Louis in early July of 1967, and when I got there, they were doing a major cleanup of the arena," Bowman told Jack. "And I remember walking through the building with Lynn Patrick and thinking to myself, 'My God, what have I gotten myself into?' But the arena became some place to be."

That's because Patrick and Bowman pieced together a decent roster. Using the expansion draft they procured the services of players such as surefire future Hall of Fame goaltender Glenn Hall, defensemen Jim Roberts, Noel Picard, Al Arbour, and Rod Seiling and forwards Ron Schock, Terry Crisp, Darryl Edestrand and Larry Keenan. And then they picked up defensemen and brothers Bob and Barclay Plager, and forwards Red Berenson, Frank St. Marseille and Gary Sabourin.

However, the team got off to a dreadful start winning just four of its first 15 games. Patrick decided it would be best if he concentrate on his general manager duties and turned the coaching reins over to Bowman, who was all of 34 years old. The players, some of whom were as old as Bowman, weren't sure it was going to work out. And during one week around the mid-point of the season, they were ready to revolt. Bowman needed to get their attention, so he scheduled two practices a day, one at eight in the morning, one at four in the afternoon.

"Why would you do that in the middle of the season?" Jack inquired. "Weren't they a little tired?"

Bowman nodded, then explained that what he wanted to convey to the team was that they were damn lucky they were playing in the NHL, and that they didn't have to deal with the every-day problems that regular folks did. "They were ready to play hockey at the end of that week," Bowman said.

And they were also ready to play once the playoffs began. The Blues came to life under Bowman and went 23-21-14 to finish third in the new Western Division, securing their spot in the postseason on the second-to-last night of the regular season. They then dispatched Philadelphia and Minnesota in a pair of thrilling seven-game playoff series to qualify for the Stanley Cup Finals against Blake's Canadiens.

This didn't move many of the writers covering the Finals. One of them wrote that, "Montreal may be the first team in history to win the Stanley Cup in three games." Said another: "The Blues had better dress warm, or they'll catch cold in the draft as the Canadiens go past." Jack chuckled at both quips and wished he'd come up with them, but after talking to Bowman, he was as convinced as Fisher that this series wasn't going to be nearly as one-sided as most thought.

And it wasn't, even though the Canadiens went on to sweep the Blues in four games. All four were one-goal margins, two went to overtime, and as the Canadiens chugged champagne in their locker room at the Forum when it was over, they all knew they'd been in one heck of a fight.

"At least we gave them a struggle," Bowman said. "We played a better series against the Canadiens than Boston did."

Blake congratulated his former protégé, Bowman, and moments after announcing that he was retiring from coaching, ending an iconic career during which he won the Stanley Cup a record eight times, he said, "The Blues showed a lot of pride. They deserve a lot of credit. They made us work for what we got. But I'd expect that of any team with as many former Canadiens as St. Louis has."

One of those players being Jean Guy Talbot, the same Jean Guy Talbot who had literally scalped Bowman so many years earlier. After playing 12 years in Montreal, winning seven Cups and playing in six All-Star games, Talbot was left unprotected in the expansion draft and was selected by Minnesota. Shortly after the start of the season he was traded to Detroit, but the Red Wings waived him in January and the Blues picked him up. Bowman didn't care about what had happened in 1952. He knew Talbot could help the Blues, so he was all in when Lynn Patrick put in the claim. It impressed Jack that Bowman could so easily let bygones be bygones in the name of winning.

"There were only 30 seconds left in the game," Bowman had told Jack in their meeting before the series began. "I think about that sometimes. What if the game had been 30 seconds shorter? Jean just lost control. He wrote me a long letter explaining it, pouring his heart out. I figure he just started me on my career 15 years earlier than planned."

Following the post-game handshakes with the Canadiens, Bowman walked gingerly off the ice, gazing into the seats where the Forum faithful were on their feet respectfully applauding both clubs. The look on his face was not one of disappointment, it was a steely, cold-eyed, emotionless mask of determination that left Jack with the feeling that

Red Fisher was right about Bowman: This very well could be the boy wonder of hockey coaches, and Jack surmised that somewhere down the road, Bowman was going to be on the other side of this result, and he'd be planting a kiss on that majestic Stanley Cup in a victorious locker room.

13 - California Dreaming

Kathleen was barely off the plane when she spotted her cousin, Daisy, standing by the check-in counter at the gate, on her tip-toes, head swaying from side to side, trying to see above the other people who were there to greet the arriving travelers at San Francisco International.

The moment their eyes met, both girls let out a giddy yelp that turned a few heads, and within a few more seconds they were locked in a full-on embrace that brought a gleeful end to a two-year separation.

"Oh my God, your hair is so long!" Daisy exclaimed as she gave Kathleen a thorough once over. "And you have boobies!"

Same old Daisy. The wild child, mouth always one step ahead of her brain, no filter whatsoever. Oh how she'd missed her favorite cousin who had been whisked away to California by her Uncle Carl and Aunt Mary, Jack's sister. Daisy was a year older than Kathleen, but growing up they'd been inseparable, two peas in a pod as their parents used to say. They'd celebrated birthdays and holidays together, enjoyed pajama parties at each other's houses half a dozen or so times a year, and vowed that they would someday live on the same street, marry handsome men, and have lots of babies.

But Uncle Carl left his job with Proctor and Gamble and pursued a sales opportunity with Carnation, the manufacturers of evaporated milk, coffee creamer, instant breakfast drinks, and other dairy-related products. With Uncle Carl's transfer to the company's base in Southern California, Daisy hadn't had a choice but to leave Manhasset and say goodbye to her friends and Kathleen. The Heller's settled in Anaheim, barely two miles from Disneyland, on a beautiful, quiet street lined with mission tile-roofed homes on small plots, each fronted by a Eucalyptus tree, though Daisy had hardly spent any time there. She transferred the two semesters of art history credits she had earned attending Rutgers and enrolled at the University of San Francisco where she continued to study the works of Van Gogh, Rembrandt, Monet, and many other long-ago deceased geniuses while immersing herself in the growing counterculture lifestyle that had taken root literally before her eyes.

As sad as her departure from New York had been, Daisy found a fascinating new world on the other side of the country, and her weekly letters had enthralled Kathleen. There were poetry readings and comedy shows in the coffee shops of the Haight-Ashbury district; performance artists on the streets around the University of California-Berkeley and USF; concerts at the Fillmore and Winter land; and the open experimentation with LSD that at once worried and intrigued Kathleen who had resisted the temptation to alter her state of mind at Columbia beyond the buzz attained from smoking a little weed. Daisy was a free spirit, and after years of living in "the most boring neighborhood in the world" she had come into full bloom on the left coast.

"I can't believe I'm here," Kathleen said of her first trip to the other side of the country.

"I know, and it's about damn time," Daisy replied as they walked through the terminal toward the baggage carousels. "We're gonna have the greatest summer ever."

In the weeks after the uprising at Columbia, Kathleen had wrapped her head around her classwork and had done what her father had instructed her to do: She finished the semester strong and kept her grade point average in the 3.5 range, right where she'd been before her attention had been diverted by the tumult on campus. It had been an arduous task getting through finals, and when they concluded, she knew she needed to escape New York. She couldn't fathom spending the summer at home with Jack and Olivia. She loved them dearly, but the tension between her and Jack hadn't really dissipated, and she also wanted to get away from the ever-present worry over Patrick's safety. She understood the angst, and often shared it. She thought of her brother every day and prayed for his continued well-being, but watching her mother scour the *Times* each day for any sliver of information, and sitting down after dinner each night to watch Cronkite's broadcast was too much for Kathleen. She needed to go away, and California, with Daisy, was where she wanted to be.

Daisy had spent the summer of 1967 in San Francisco, taking classes to get back on track after her transfer from Rutgers, and willingly soaking in the psychedelic sights and sounds of the Haight-Ashbury scene during what the media had already come to refer to as the Summer of Love. In the morning she attended school. In the afternoon, she worked as a waitress at the Magnolia Thunderpussy, a restaurant right on Haight Street owned and operated by the former Bay Area burlesque star of the same name. And in the evening she wore flowers in her hair and acted like every other inquisitive and apolitical 20-year-old who was caught in the centripetal force of the hippie lifestyle preaching "Make love, not war."

After going home to Anaheim for a two-week visit following her third-year finals, Daisy had headed right back up the Pacific Coast Highway to San Francisco to do the same thing this summer. And when Kathleen had called to inquire about coming out for a few months, she could barely contain her merriment over her favorite cousin joining her for a summer adventure. Daisy had asked Ms. Magnolia if she'd hire Kathleen and she said, "Any cousin of yours is welcome here, sweetie," so the plan was hatched.

Olivia, not knowing of Daisy's diligent pursuit of the counterculture's holy grail - sex, drugs, and rock and roll - thought it was a good idea. Jack, also oblivious to what he would have called Daisy's miscreant behavior, of course balked. He had already made a phone call to the city desk editor at the *New York Post* to grease the skids to get Kathleen some summertime newspaper experience, something Kathleen had asked him to do months before the imbroglio at school. In the world of journalism, nothing was more important than in-the-field training. Jack had no doubt whatever they were teaching in J-

School was surely useful, but the only way to hone your writing skills was to write, preferably real news, on deadline. Kathleen would have had that opportunity, but now she was opting to spend the summer waitressing and sleeping on the couch in her cousin's tiny apartment. He just didn't understand it.

It took some convincing by mother and daughter, but Jack relented and had allowed her to go. He bought an open-ended round-trip airline ticket - "I expect you back here no later than a week before classes start again," he'd said - and slipped a couple C-notes into an envelope to tide her over until she started working.

Within a week of her arrival, Kathleen had fallen in love with the Bay Area and wondered whether she'd ever go back to the grime and commotion of New York City. She listened intently to the political activists who reminded her so much of Mark Rudd and his fellow SDS radicals. She watched the hippies float around in a state of chemical bemusement in their daily search for psychological healing and spiritual transcendence. The Magnolia Thunderpussy was sheer wonderment, a bustling establishment populated by a melting pot of personalities, from tie-clad local businessmen to tie-dyed, long-haired, fully-bearded beatniks. And of course there was the music. Kathleen did not live on the West Coast, but she was fully aware of the rock and roll revolution that was taking place there, and San Francisco was at the epicenter of it all with bands like the Grateful Dead, Jefferson Airplane, Frank Zappa's Mothers of Invention, and Big Brother and the Holding Company fronted by Janis Joplin.

On any given day, Grace Slick and her Airplane band mates might come strolling out of their house on Fulton Street across from Golden Gate Park, meet up with Jerry Garcia and Bob Weir of the Dead who would have come from their place on Ashbury Street, and wander into the heart of Haight. They might even stop in at the Thunderpussy for one of Magnolia's phallic-shaped banana splits or another of the erotically-themed desserts.

Kathleen had barely unpacked her bags at Daisy's tiny apartment on Crayton Street, a block west of Ashbury, when Daisy informed her they were taking a road trip for the weekend.

"I just took a road trip, all the way across the country," Kathleen said with an exasperated bent.

"Sweetie, life is a never-ending road trip," Daisy said as she thrust a promotional poster at Kathleen. "We're going down to San Jose for a music festival. If it's anything like last year at Monterey, it's gonna be amazing."

The previous summer, Daisy had traveled down with several USF classmates to the picturesque oceanside town of Monterey for what was then the largest and most widely-promoted concert ever staged in the United States. Over a historic three-day period, an estimated 200,000 people bore witness to the career launchings of Jimi Hendrix, Janis Joplin, and Otis Redding, as well as performances by Simon and Garfunkel, The Who, the Byrds, the Mamas and the Papas, and Ravi Shankar, among others. Pete Townshend smashed his guitar to bits and drummer Keith Moon kicked over his kit as The Who closed their energetic set with the song *My Generation*; Hendrix did Townshend one better, first lighting his guitar on fire before sledgehammering it to the floor at the end of *Wild Thing*; and Joplin strained her vocal chords to their breaking point with a soulful set that enraptured the masses. For those who didn't overdose on LSD, it was a never-to-be-forgotten experience.

If this event, being called the Northern California Folk Rock Festival, came anywhere close to that, Daisy promised that Kathleen would be transformed.

Early on a Saturday morning, the girls packed up Daisy's sky blue '62 Dodge Dart and as they made their way down the 101 to San Jose, Kathleen was struck by the beauty of San Francisco Bay to the east of the freeway as they passed through San Bruno, San Mateo, and Palo Alto. With the window rolled down and the fresh breeze blowing through her hair, Kathleen's senses were alive, the sights and the smells allowing her to drift away and forget all that had happened back home, not to mention the unrest in the country during the first four history-changing months of 1968. The radio was tuned to KSAN, a station pioneering the presentation of freeform rock, and the airwaves pulsated with the music of some of the bands who would be performing at the festival such as The Doors, The Dead, and the Steve Miller Band. The music lifted her soul, but being the writer that she was, the lyrics were what she found so soothing as these revolutionary poets seemed to be speaking to her.

"Strange days have found us,
Strange days have tracked us down,
They're going to destroy,
Our casual joys,
We shall go on playing,
Or find a new town" ...

Jim Morrison's subversive passion oozed from every syllable, and by the time Daisy wheeled into the parking area at the Santa Clara County Fairgrounds, Kathleen was ready to drop her guard and go with the flow, any pretense she had when she'd gotten into that Dodge Dart a couple hours earlier completely washed away. What a scene it was that greeted them - people for as far as the eye could see, wild hair, tie-dye shirts, topless men, topless women, hippies, beatniks, bohemians, suburban kids trying to find the meaning of life, marijuana smoke billowing into the warm but overcast sky, and a distinctive rhythm and groove to the river of bodies as they celebrated the music.

"Come on, we're gonna go to the front," Daisy said after they had entered the main stage area.

"How do you suppose we're gonna do that?" Kathleen asked just as Daisy provided the answer, taking hold of her hand and bobbing and weaving and pushing her way through the congestion. It was an exhausting excursion, and it took a good portion of the set authored by People, but they made it all the way to the barrier separating the elevated stage from the sea of humanity, the last few feet cleared out when a girl started tripping on acid and had to be carried out by her friends.

"This will do," Daisy said happily as she took a hit off a joint offered by a guy wearing cut-off jeans, a white tank top, leather sandals, and a red bandana around his bald head whose name, she learned, was Cosmic. "Peace, brother," Daisy said as she handed the joint to Kathleen who reluctantly took a drag before passing it back to Cosmic. The bands came on one after another, all offering a unique sound and vibe, and Kathleen was mesmerized by it all. She was also intrigued by a handsome guy almost directly in their line of sight to the stage who was tinkering with what looked like a tripod for a camera. Finally, when there was a break in the music as Steve Miller wrapped up his set and the roadies began preparing for The Dead, Kathleen asked the man what he was doing.

He turned around to see where the query had come from, saw Kathleen and Daisy staring back at him, and decided they were too pretty to ignore, so he told them.

"I'm part of a film crew," he said. "We're shooting footage tomorrow of The Doors for a documentary."

"Really?" Daisy said. "Totally groovy, man. Are you famous or something?"

"Me? Nah, just helping a buddy. Making a little bread, ya know. Starving actor. Gotta eat."

"Actor? Have you been in any movies?" Kathleen inquired.

"Nothing you've ever heard of," he said as he moved the tripod a few feet to the left of where it was. "Just need to catch a break."

"So if we can get back here tomorrow, can we be in your Doors movie?" Daisy asked. "I love them. Morrison's kind of fucked up, but I love the keyboard player, Ray Manzarek."

"Maybe. I'm not sure how much of the crowd we're supposed to be filming. The doc is about the band, right."

"What's your name," Kathleen asked.

"Harrison. Harrison Ford. But you can call me Harry."

"Cool, Harry," said Daisy, introducing herself and Kathleen. "Look, we'll make sure we get back here to this same spot tomorrow, so see what you can do, OK. We'll do anything you want. Anything."

"Well, not anything," Kathleen said, giving her cousin the evil eye, which made Harry Ford smile a hypnotic smile.

Minutes later Harry finished his task, waved to the girls, and headed backstage where they could see him talking to someone who seemed kind of important, maybe the director. And then their attention was diverted when the crowd erupted in unison as Jerry Garcia, Bob Weir and the rest of The Dead strode onto the stage.

By nightfall the girls, like everyone in the crowd, were completely spent. The Dead, Janis Joplin and her band Big Brother and the Holding Company, and Jefferson Airplane, had provided a remarkable conclusion to the first day of the festival. All three had ripped through their hour-long sets with ferocity, and Kathleen was astonished by the raw power and emotion with which Joplin and Grace Slick sang, and how the people responded to their every move.

Slick, with her shiny brown hair flowing down past her shoulders, her bangs masking her eyes, and her airy gown rippled by a soft breeze, was such a commanding yet feminine presence as she sashayed in and out among the rest of the band singing *Somebody to Love.*

"When the truth is found, to be lies,
and all the joy within you dies,
don't you want somebody to love,
don't you need somebody to love,
wouldn't you love somebody to love,
you better find somebody to love ..."

Joplin, not nearly as pretty as Slick, her unruly blondish-brown hair sometimes looking like a tangled net in front of her cherubic face as she belted out Ball and Chain in a voice so sultry, even husky, punctuating the lyrics with guttural screams that emanated from deep in her diaphragm and audible probably all the way back to Haight-Ashbury more than 60 miles to the north.

"Sittin' down by my window,
Honey, lookin' out at the rain,
Lord, Lord, Lord, sittin' down by my window,
Baby, lookin' out at the rain,
Somethin' came along, grabbed ahold of me,
And it felt just like a ball and chain,
Honey, that's exactly what it felt like,
Honey, just draggin' me down ... "

Kathleen couldn't take her eyes off these goddesses of rock and roll. It made her wonder if she'd ever be able to captivate people with her writing the way these women did with their singing. Oddly, it made her think of her father. He was a nationally-recognized columnist, the face of America's premier weekly sports magazine, and though she didn't have exact figures, she estimated that *SportsWorld*'s subscription and newsstand base had to be close to a million, maybe less, maybe more. That was quite an audience, something she really hadn't ever thought about until this moment. Her father traveled around the country and even the world to sporting events and shared his thoughts and insight with all those readers. If she could ever land a job with *Time* or *Newsweek*, or maybe the new music/culture/political glossy that printed its first edition right in San Francisco just last year and was already a huge hit, *Rolling Stone* magazine, could she build up a similar following?

Heady stuff, indeed, but soon vacuumed from her mind when she saw Harry Ford by the far left side of the stage trying to get her attention.

"Hey, Harry Ford, how are ya?" Daisy greeted him after she and Kathleen fought through the exiting crowd.

He smiled, then asked if they'd like to come over to the film crew's tent for a little post-concert hang, and the girls jumped at the chance, their fatigue overcome by a rush of excitement. For the next two hours, well past midnight, as the moon cast a dim pall over the ever-quieting fairgrounds where thousands of worn out or spaced out festival-goers would spend the night sleeping in their cars or in sleeping bags on the ground, Daisy and Kathleen swapped life stories with Harry Ford.

Kathleen was sad to find out that Harry was married and he and his wife, Mary, had a son named Ben born a year earlier, but once this disappointment passed, she was fascinated by his story. He was 25, born in Chicago, to which Kathleen quickly chimed in that her mother was born there and her grandparents still lived there. He'd gone to Ripon College in Wisconsin and was studying philosophy and English, but then decided to take a drama course and he fell in love with acting. He wound up flunking out of school, but he didn't really care because he was working in theater, doing everything from acting to building sets, and was convinced that he would go to Hollywood and become a star.

He and Mary packed their belongings into her Volkswagen Bug, made it to Southern California late in 1964, and so began what had thus far been a frustrating period in his life. He said he signed a contract with Columbia Studios that paid him about one-hundred-fifty bucks a week, but only when he was working, and even that was barely enough to live on, so he took jobs as a carpenter to make ends meet.

"Have you ever heard of James Coburn?" Harry asked. After the girls nodded that they had, he said, "That was my first movie, came out a couple years ago; James starred in *Dead Heat on a Merry-Go-Round*. I was a bellhop, I had two lines. 'Paging Mr. Ellis... Paging Mr. Ellis...' and then I said to James, 'No, sir, Charles Ellis, Room 607.'"

"Sorry Harry, I didn't see that one," Daisy said with her typical frankness.

Harry said that Columbia had dropped him not long after that, but Universal Studios then signed him for a little more money, and he'd had bit parts in a couple of television shows, *The Virginian*, and *Kung-Fu*, but he was still a nobody in the industry.

"So what the hell are you doing here?" Daisy asked.

Harry explained that his friend, Paul Ferrera, who had gone to UCLA to study film direction, had asked him for help on this project that would be titled *Feast Of Friends*. Ferrera wanted to capture what life on the road with one of America's fast-rising rock bands was like, and to perhaps get into the mind of Jim Morrison, a mind that certainly warranted exploration. Harry had gotten Ferrera some carpentry work when he was short on cash, so Ferrera offered him this opportunity to return the favor. Harry, with nothing on his plate at the time, thought it would be an interesting experience.

They had done some initial shooting a couple weeks earlier at the Renaissance Pleasure Faire in Agoura, and after this festival they were heading to Bakersfield, and then down to Los Angeles for the band's much-hyped show at the Hollywood Bowl in July.

"Jim Morrison is gorgeous," Daisy said.

"He's fucking nuts," Harry said with a smile.

When the girls got up to leave, Harry said, "If you're in that same spot tomorrow, I'll make sure I pan out to get you on film. I can't guarantee it'll make the final cut, that's Paul's call, but you'll have a chance."

They smiled, then wandered off into the darkness to go find Daisy's Dart and try to get some sleep.

The next day, they made sure they worked their way back to their spot by the barrier to the left of center, and after several hours of music by bands neither of them had heard of, Harry appeared just before Country Joe and The Fish took the stage to get his tripod and camera situated, and he gave the girls a thumbs up. Once Joe and The Fish were done, it was time for The Doors to close the festival, and as soon as Morrison took the stage, sporting a new short haircut which he had given to himself on the Hells Angels-escorted limo ride to the venue, a wave of excitement flowed through the wearying crowd.

They opened with *Break On Through*, moved right into *Alabama Song*, and eventually played *When The Music's Over, Moonlight Drive, Light My Fire, The Unknown Soldier,* and *The End*, a disturbing and haunting song replete with improvised lyrics that made Kathleen flinch. Harry stood sentry behind his lens, capturing everything, and when he turned for crowd footage, he did as he promised and started the shot where Kathleen and Daisy were, then slowly panned from his right to left, eventually ending up back on Morrison who was flailing around in his theatrical style which only served to whip the crowd into further frenzy.

When the show ended, the girls stayed where they were until Harry had dismantled the camera from the tripod, and before he hustled backstage, he bid them farewell and said he hoped they didn't end up on the cutting room floor.

"Good luck, Harry," Kathleen said. "I hope you make it big someday."

14 – Zeroes

A few months back when Jack had gone to Florida and spent spring training time with Mickey Mantle, he asked the great slugger who was the meanest pitcher he'd ever faced. Interestingly, no one who he'd batted regularly against in the American League came to mind. Instead, he referenced two "nasty sons of bitches" from the National League who he'd met through the years in the World Series. Bob Gibson of the Cardinals, and Don Drysdale of the Dodgers.

"I hated to bat against Drysdale," said Mantle, who'd only stood in the box against the big right-hander five times, one at-bat in Game 4 of the 1956 World Series, and four in Game 3 of the '63 Fall Classic. Mantle's only hit was a harmless single, and he struck out twice.

"After he hit you he'd come around, look at the bruise on your arm and say, 'Do you want me to sign it?'" Mantle said with a laugh, which prompted Jack to laugh. "You heard about the time in St. Louis when Gene Oliver hit a homer off him?" When Jack said he hadn't, Mantle continued. "So Oliver gets him, and he's standing there admiring it, and then he yells to the kid in the dugout, 'Hey batboy, come get the bat.' Drysdale hears that and he's got smoke firin' outta his ass. Next time up, he puts one right in Oliver's ribs and he's on the ground rollin' around and Drysdale says, 'Hey batboy, come get Oliver.' Mean motherfucker, that one."

Two months into the baseball season, major league hitters were apparently swinging with toothpicks, if batting averages and earned run averages were any indication. The year of the pitcher was in full swing, Drysdale was the poster boy for the dominance the hurlers were enjoying, and with Drysdale standing on the precipice of history, Jack made another trip out to Los Angeles the first week of June to see if the "mean motherfucker" could set an all-time record for consecutive scoreless innings.

Drysdale blanked the New York Mets 4-0 in his first outing of the season, then went six starts in a row without a victory before emerging from that drought with a two-hit shutout of the Cubs. Unbeknownst to anyone on that mid-May night at Dodger Stadium, Drysdale began a streak well-nigh unrivaled in the near century that baseball had been played in the National League. Drysdale proceeded to shutout Houston, St. Louis, Houston again, and San Francisco. Five consecutive white-washings, 45 straight scoreless innings. So, when he took the mound in Chavez Ravine on the evening of June 4 against Pittsburgh, Jack was in the press box to chronicle whether Drysdale could get through the first two innings to break Carl Hubbell's NL record for uninterrupted scoreless innings, and to see if he could get through the other seven and pitch a major-league record sixth straight shutout.

Through the end of May, there had already been 51 shutouts in the National League, 50 in the American League, including a perfect game by Oakland's Catfish Hunter three weeks earlier, just the 10th in major league history and the first in the junior circuit since 1922. More than half the games played in both leagues combined had ended with one or both teams scoring one run or less. They were startling numbers, and many in the game's hierarchy were growing concerned that the lack of offense was driving away the younger generation of fans who craved offense and wanted to see home runs. There was talk of lowering the mound from 15 inches to 10, or of moving the rubber back anywhere from six inches to two feet to give batters a fraction of a second longer to see pitches. Tony Kubek, the former All-Star Yankee shortstop who was now a broadcaster, suggested limiting pitching staffs to eight men to stop the proliferation of relief pitchers entering games with their fresh arms. "Every time you look up there's a new pitcher in the game," Kubek said. "A good hitter studies the pitcher and his pattern of pitches, and they'll get to him around the third time through the order. However, if it comes to the third time around and there's a new pitcher, then the batter is right back where he started."

Dick Groat, who played the majority of his 14-year big league career in Pittsburgh and retired at the end of the 1967 season with a lifetime batting average of .286, added another layer to Kubek's argument by pointing out that the depth of pitching staffs had also improved. "When I came up, you looked at two good pitchers and two so-so's you could pick your batting average up on," he said. "You can't do this today. Look at the New York Mets. They may be down in the standings but they have four good young arms that make it tough on everybody."

When Jack sat down with Drysdale a couple days before his start against the Pirates, the veteran of 13 major league seasons had no sympathy for the hitters. In fact, he blamed them for the dearth in hitting and scoring. "They're stupid if they keep swinging for the fences," Drysdale said. "When they do that they're helping me as well as the rest of the pitchers. They're just not thinking right, but I'm glad they're doing it."

Drysdale grew up in Van Nuys, California and didn't even pitch in high school until his senior year, 1954. But that was all the Dodgers needed to see and they signed him to a $4,000 bonus contract right after graduation. He played half a year at Class C Bakersfield in the California League,

155

leaped all the way to triple-A Montreal of the International League in 1955, and by 1956 he was in Brooklyn where he went 5-5 as a rookie with a 2.64 ERA. In Brooklyn's seven-game World Series loss to the Yankees, he made one brief relief appearance and gave up a two-run homer to Hank Bauer, but later induced Mantle, the most feared slugger in the game who that year achieved the triple crown and won the AL MVP award, to ground weakly to second.

By 1957 Drysdale was a regular in the Dodgers rotation, and for the next 11 years he never started less than 29 games. From 1962-66, with the team relocated to Los Angeles, he surpassed 40 starts all five years and produced a record of 98-70 while winning the 1962 Cy Young and helping the Dodgers capture three NL pennants and two World Series championships.

And if the Cardinals' Gibson wasn't the most menacing pitcher in the game, it was Drysdale. His philosophy was simple: "Sooner or later you have to say it's my ball and half the plate is mine," said Drysdale, who led the NL five times in hit batsmen, most recently in 1965. "Only I never let on which half of the plate I wanted."

Therefore, if you dared to lean over looking for an outside pitch, you might pay a painful price unless you had Houdini-like ability to escape his wrath. One other thing - if your pitcher brushed back or hit a Dodger, watch out. "My little rule is one for two. If one of my teammates gets knocked down, then I'm knocking down two on the other team."

Groat once said, "Batting against Don Drysdale is the same as making a date with a dentist." And Mike Shannon of the Cardinals, recalling Drysdale's notorious reputation for pitching inside and plunking batters, said, "Don Drysdale would consider an intentional walk a waste of three pitches. If he wants to put you on base, he can hit you with one pitch."

Jack said to him, "You realize you could kill somebody if you hit them in the head."

"I never hit anybody in the head in my life," said the man they called **Big D**. "But you have to move them off the plate; you have to get them out of there. I don't throw at their head, but every other part of their anatomy is in play."

What wasn't in play against the Pirates, at least not very often, was the ball. Drysdale, spurred on by a voluble crowd of more than 30,000 eager to see history, mowed Pittsburgh down with ease. He yielded only three hits, did not walk a batter, struck out eight, and only one out was recorded in the outfield. Drysdale matched Hubbell's NL record of 46 1/3 consecutive scoreless innings when he retired Roberto Clemente on a grounder to second in the top of the second inning. After hitting Manny Mota, he struck out Bill Mazeroski to erase Hubbell's 35-year-old standard. The next seven Pirates went down before Donn Clendenon broke up Drysdale's no-hit bid with a single leading off the fifth. By then, Drysdale had the only runs he would need to win as the offensively-challenged

Dodgers scratched out three singles and a walk to score twice off Jim Bunning in the fourth.

"I think I was stronger than in some of the previous games," Drysdale told a throng of reporters, including Jack, who stood behind the pack of primary beat guys and jotted down some notes while watching the confident pitcher hold court. "My control was pretty good and I know I didn't throw as many pitches as I have before. And yes, there was a lessening of tension after the first few innings."

Gary Kolb blooped a double to left with one out in the Pirates' sixth but was stranded when second baseman Paul Popovich made a nice play on a slow grounder to get the speedy ex-Dodger, Maury Wills. And then Pittsburgh's final baserunner was Wills, who singled with two out in the ninth, only to see slugger Willie Stargell ground out to Popovich to wrap up Los Angeles' 5-0 victory, and the historic sixth straight shutout.

In the six games, 54 scoreless innings, Drysdale had given up just 27 hits, 24 of those singles, and only 11 men had reached third base. The opponents batted .145 against him, and he struck out 42 while walking only nine. Absolute dominance.

When Jack talked afterward with Dodger manager Walter Alston, he asked him to compare this performance to the five previous shutouts. "This was one of his better shutouts," said Alston, whose smile indicated to Jack that he was kidding because a shutout, after all, is a shutout.

"I can't believe I have six shutouts in a row," Drysdale told Jack long after the local reporters had moved on to talk to his teammates, leaving Jack alone in front of Drysdale's locker as he knotted his solid blue tie. "Luck is a big factor in those things and luck has been on my side."

For instance, Drysdale offered, look at what had happened in his previous outing against the rival San Francisco Giants when his shutout streak was in serious jeopardy in the ninth inning at Dodger Stadium. He walked Willie McCovey on a 3-2 pitch, yielded a single to Jim Ray Hart, and then walked Dave Marshall to load the bases with no outs. Up came rugged catcher Dick Dietz who worked the count to 2-2, then took a fastball on his left elbow which would have forced in the shutout-ending run if not for a rather interesting decision by home plate umpire Harry Wendelstedt. It was his interpretation that Dietz made no effort to avoid the pitch, and actually leaned into it, so he called ball three, touching off a baseball rhubarb of epic proportion. Dietz went ballistic, and so did Giants manager Herman Franks who came out of the dugout screaming epithets. When order was restored, Dietz hit a shallow fly to left that wasn't deep enough to score pinch runner Nate Oliver from third. Pinch hitter Ty Cline then grounded to first baseman Wes Parker who threw home to force Oliver for the second out. When Jack Hiatt popped out to Parker for the final out, Drysdale's concurrent streaks were intact. "Wendelstedt said I stuck my arm out on purpose," Dietz said. "What am I? Crazy? I'm not going to let him hit me—not Drysdale. He'll cut you in two out there. I just couldn't move."

Next up for Drysdale would be the Philadelphia Phillies in four days, where he would need three more scoreless innings to surpass the legendary Walter Johnson's all-time major league record of 56 2/3 innings without allowing a run, set back in 1913. Jack had set up his trip to be in Southern California with built-in down time to visit his sister Mary, and her husband Carl, at their new place in Anaheim, and perhaps attend the potentially historic game. But first, he jumped into his rental car and drove over to the Ambassador Hotel on Wilshire Boulevard to say hello to an old friend, and hopefully shake hands with the man who might very well become the next president of the United States.

15 - The Mindless Menace of Violence

Jack's first year covering the New York Giants for the New York Post was 1955, and one of the earliest acquaintances he made on his new beat was with a gentle giant of a man named Roosevelt Grier, a rookie third-round draft pick out of Penn State.

That year, the team held its training camp on the other side of the country at Willamette University in Salem, Oregon. "Less distractions out there," coach Jim Lee Howell said, which was true, but more importantly, there was also money to be made for owner Wellington Mara by playing a couple of preseason games on the West Coast where pro football was still a novelty. One day, Jack was looking to do a human interest piece rather than another nuts and bolts football story, and Rosey seemed like a suitable candidate, if for no other reason than they were two rookies, so-to-speak, getting the hang of their new jobs in faraway Oregon. So, Jack sidled up to Rosey following the afternoon practice and he asked the 6-foot-5, 250-pound defensive lineman if he'd like to grab a beer off campus after team meetings were finished for the evening.

"Sir, I'd be happy to do that, but I can't break curfew," Grier said. Jack assured him that he'd be back well before Howell sent defensive coordinator Tom Landry around the dorm for bed check, and Grier smiled and asked, "Where would you like to go?"

They sat down in a quiet saloon a few miles away from the university, and Jack hoped the gawking from some of the patrons was rooted in the fact that Rosey was just such a huge human being, and not because they found it odd that an average-sized white man was having drinks with an over-grown black man. Never having been to this part of the country, Jack wasn't sure what race relations were like, but his thought was that it was a little less volatile than the deep South, where in fact, Rosey was born.

Jack ordered his usual vodka gimlet, Rosey asked for a Budweiser, and before the waitress returned, Rosey was in full flight recounting to Jack his upbringing in rural Georgia, talking in such rich detail which had Jack furiously scribbling in his notebook. Named for Franklin Delano Roosevelt - the governor of New York at the time of Rosey's birth in July 1932 who became president of the United States four months later - Rosey was one of 11 children born in the tiny town of Cuthbert to Joseph and Ruth Grier. The family lived on rented government farmland, and by the time he was five years old, Rosey was consumed by the hard life of farming, and he knew the only way he was going to make a better life for himself was to get an education. Schooling wasn't a priority for black people in those parts in the late 1930s, so if Rosey wanted to attend, it was fine with his parents, but before he went he had to complete his chores on the farm. So, each day Rosey would rise before the sun and milk the cows, slop the hogs, and work the peanut and cotton fields if need be, and then he'd walk 10 miles to school, and 10 miles back home. Day after day after day. "I wanted to go to school, and I knew I had to go to school," he said.

His life changed when he was 11 and the family moved north and settled in Roselle, New Jersey, which sat about 25 miles south of where Jack had grown up in Englewood. They lived with an aunt, and Rosey's father took a job with a pharmaceutical company, though his wage barely covered the cost of living. It was difficult, but at least Rosey's peanut-picking days and 20-mile round-trip hikes were over. He thrived in school, and on the way to becoming the first member of his family to earn a high school diploma, he became the star athlete at Abraham Clark High School where, unlike in Georgia, the color of his skin did not preclude him from pursuing athletic glory. Rosey drew interest from several colleges before accepting a track scholarship from Penn State where he would throw the discus, shot put, and javelin, but with the provision that he would also be allowed to play football as a walk-on for coach Rip Engle. With the help of assistant coach Joe Paterno, Grier became one of Penn State's best players. He played both ways on the offensive and defensive lines and earned All-America honors while helping to turn around the sagging Nittany Lion football fortunes. Off the field, he held a leadership position in the first intercollegiate Greek-letter fraternity for African-Americans, Alpha Phi Alpha, and he wooed the coeds by singing in a chorus named the Midnight Cavaliers.

Jack was enchanted by the young man's story, and he turned it into a tremendous Sunday feature that not only sold a few extra copies of the *Post* at the newsstand, but, according to Rosey, helped him gain early acceptance from the often-harsh New York sports fans. From that first meeting in Salem, a friendship was formed that remained tight all these years later, even after Rosey had been traded by the Giants to the Rams where he was part of Los Angeles's famed Fearsome Foursome defensive line until an Achilles' injury ended his career in 1967.

Since hanging up his cleats, Rosey had become involved with several endeavors including singing, acting, and social activism, though everything was currently on hold as he had been asked by his friend, Robert Kennedy, to assist with security during the New York senator's presidential campaign.

Knowing he would be in Los Angeles to chronicle the exploits of Don Drysdale, and that Rosey would be in his home city because the California Democratic Primary was held the same night that Drysdale was chasing the shutout streak record, Jack phoned Rosey to see if he might be able to come to the Ambassador Hotel where Kennedy was headquartered for a possible meet-and-greet at what was expected to be a late-night victory celebration. Kennedy, an avid sports fan, knew of Jack through his work for *SportsWorld*, so Rosey had no trouble getting Jack on the guest list, and Jack looked forward to meeting the man many felt was going to be the next president, as well as catching up with his old friend.

"He can't wait to meet you," Rosey told Jack on the phone a couple days earlier when the plan to meet at the Ambassador was formulated. "I told him you'd be interviewing Drysdale and he already said he wants your opinion on why no one can hit in the major leagues anymore."

"Tell him my wife wants to know if he'll marry her," Jack said with a laugh, knowing left-wing-liberal Olivia was seething back home because Jack had little interest in politics, yet he would be meeting the man whom she believed was going to save the country.

When Jack arrived at the hotel it was just past 11:30 p.m. and the main ballroom was jammed with nearly 2,000 well-wishers eager to listen to Kennedy's victory speech. The polls had been closed for more than three hours, and the returns indicated that while it was a tight race with Eugene McCarthy, Kennedy was going to carry the state, thus cutting into the delegate deficit he faced against Vice President Hubert Humphrey who had opted not to compete in the primaries. Jack knew the importance of Kennedy's victory in California, but he also knew the senator had a long road to hoe if he was going to wrest the nomination from Humphrey when the Democratic Convention commenced in Chicago two months later.

But that was tomorrow's concern. This night was one to celebrate the weeks of stumping in the ghettos and barrios that helped deliver the victory, campaigning that was clearly augmented by the presence of Rosey and Olympic champion Rafer Johnson. The two popular African-American ex-athletes had been brought onto Kennedy's team because they were friends of the Kennedy family, and they would provide help to former FBI agent William Barry who was in charge of security at a time when the

Secret Service was not assigned to presidential candidates. But also, Kennedy's strategists recognized that Rosey and Rafer could be valuable assets in trying to secure the minority vote. Both men understood this, and did not feel they were being used because in their hearts, they believed in Kennedy and knew his intentions were genuine. Kennedy had a built-in advantage with minorities because his brother, Jack, had been sympathetic to the civil rights movement and the calls for equality during his brief tenure as president earlier in the decade. Still, the senator realized that he could not rest on those laurels, especially given that he'd only entered the race in mid-March and had plenty of catching up to do on the campaign trail. Every vote was going to matter.

Jack managed to work his way through the crowd to a spot that was perhaps 30 feet from the stage, on which a lectern had been set up for Kennedy. Jack struck up casual conversations with people in his midst, he noticed the singer, Rosemary Clooney, there with two children he assumed were hers, and then around midnight there was a stirring in the chandelier-lit room, and then raucous cheers when Kennedy and his entourage appeared. Kennedy stepped to the microphone, Rosey standing about three feet behind him, just over Kennedy's right shoulder, and smiling that impossibly perfect Kennedy smile, the handsome victor soaked in the chants of "We want Kennedy, we want Kennedy." He thanked everyone three times before finally waving his right hand in a request for quiet. After an awkward few seconds of trying to figure out if the two microphones were working, he opened his remarks by saying that he wanted to express his "High regard to Don Drysdale" for pitching his record-breaking sixth consecutive shutout earlier in the evening, a comment that made Jack instantly think two things: This guy's a good politician, and maybe he really does want to talk about baseball at the party later. Kennedy then said in regards to Drysdale's achievement, "I hope we have as much good fortune in our campaign."

During a lengthy list of thank yous to individuals who had helped him in California, Kennedy acknowledged the support of the black community, and at that point he introduced Rafer and Rosey, thanked them for their work, and added jokingly, "Rosey said he'd take care of anybody who didn't vote for me; in a kind way" which elicited laughter from the crowd, as well as the big man.

Kennedy then spoke of his dual triumphs on this night in both the California and South Dakota primaries, and what, in his mind, that potentially meant to the country. "I think it indicates quite clearly what we can do here in the United States. The vote here in the state of California, the vote in the state of South Dakota; here is the most urban state of any of the states in our union, South Dakota the most rural of any of our states in the union, and we were able to win them both. I think we can end the divisions within the United States. What I think is quite clear is that we can work together in the last analysis, and that what has been going on in the United States over the period of the last three years - the divisions, the violence, the disenchantment with our society, the divisions whether between blacks and whites, the poor and the more affluent, of between age groups, or the war in Vietnam, we can start

167

to work together. We are a great country, an unselfish country, and a compassionate country, and I intend to make that my basis for running over the next few months."

Kennedy began to wind down, and he concluded his speech by saying, "And now it's on to Chicago, and let's win there." The crowd erupted with spirited glee, began chanting his name again, and there was a pulsation in that ballroom, reflected in the faces young and old, that this was the man who was going to make it all better in a nation that, in just the first five-plus months of 1968, had endured too much strife and was desperate for a new beginning. Jack was caught up in the jingoism, and he clapped appreciatively and thought of his wife who had probably been sleeping three hours by now, but would surely be thrilled when she learned of the poll results in the *Times* and would call her parents to discuss Kennedy's remarks because they, of course, would understand.

Kennedy waved a few more times, then turned to his right and was going to exit the stage and make his way to the Embassy Room where the after-party was being held, but he reversed his course on the orders of someone Jack did not recognize and came back to his left, the side where Jack was standing. Jack would learn later that Kennedy had been asked to go to another suite, the Colonial Room, where the press was waiting to ask questions, so the revised plan was to cut through the kitchen pantry to get there, and once the newsmen were placated, Kennedy would then join the party. As he slowly maneuvered through the phalanx of staffers and guests who had been on stage with him, Jack watched Roscy in the hope that their eyes would meet, and they did. Jack gave him a wave, Rosey smiled and winked, and then with Ethel Kennedy on his arm he disappeared through a door, behind which the unthinkable was about to happen.

Maybe 40 seconds after Jack and Rosey had exchanged glances, Jack heard a succession of loud pops, but he was unsure from which direction they came. At first he thought people were just popping balloons and he thought nothing of it. But then he noticed a commotion by the doorway Kennedy had exited through, followed by shouting, and then screams, and it occurred to him that something had gone wrong. He wasn't alone. Within a minute, someone shouted that Kennedy had been shot, and looks of gasping disbelief washed over the room. In the frantic next few seconds, Jack wasn't sure what to do and he just stood in place, somewhat paralyzed by the moment. His trance was broken when two men approached the lectern and excitedly asked for a doctor to come forward. A third man, who looked concerned but calm, took the microphone and implored everyone to leave the room in an orderly fashion, and soon thereafter, a fourth man stepped up and announced, "Ladies and gentlemen, we have a doctor. Can you please clear the room, and offer your prayers at this hour?"

That was the moment when Jack knew that Bobby Kennedy would not be talking baseball with him; not this night, not any night.

A 24-year-old Jerusalem-born Palestinian immigrant named Sirhan Sirhan was hiding in the kitchen pantry, and when Kennedy appeared, he approached from behind and fired three shots at the senator with a .22 caliber pistol, one which entered just under his right ear, and two more that hit him near his right armpit, one exiting from his chest, the other lodging into the back of his neck. The assassin fired off the remaining five shots in the chamber and every bullet did damage as they wounded William Weisel of ABC News, Paul Schrade of the United Auto Workers union, Democratic Party activist Elizabeth Evans, Ira Goldstein of the Continental News Service, and Kennedy campaign volunteer Irwin Stroll. He was finally subdued by Rosey, Rafer Johnson, and George Plimpton, an esteemed writer and passing acquaintance of Jack's.

In the chaos, Johnson managed to wrest the gun from Sirhan and put it in his pocket, while Rosey pinned Sirhan down on a metal table and draped his big body over the killer as several men were kicking and punching, seemingly intent on killing him right there, just as Jack Ruby had done to Lee Harvey Oswald. Sirhan was eventually taken into custody by two Los Angeles police officers who then transported him in a patrol car to Rampart Station.

Jack did what had been asked and exited the ballroom. With morbid curiosity, he stood outside the hotel with hundreds of others trying to catch a glimpse of Kennedy being loaded into the ambulance that had arrived on site. Jack saw the stretcher wheeled out, saw Rosey escorting Ethel as she held her husband's hand, and once they were safely in the emergency vehicle, he rushed off to find his own transportation to Central Receiving Hospital where Kennedy was going to be brought.

Jack watched the ambulance pull away, and he was gripped with sadness. Less than a half hour ago, a vibrant man stood before him representing potential hope and healing for a country that was coming unglued, and now he was being whisked away, bleeding and dying, perhaps the last sounds he would ever hear being the screaming siren that cut through the mild Los Angeles night.

When Jack arrived at his hotel about 10 minutes from the Ambassador, he sat on the bed, turned on the television, and watched the coverage from the police station and the hotel. He could not possibly sleep, and when he realized it was 7:30 in the morning back home on Long Island, he called Olivia who was probably just waking up.

"What are you doing awake at this hour out there?" was Olivia's groggy response when she answered the phone.

"Liv, turn on the news," Jack said.

As she peeled off the sheet and blanket and walked over to the television in their bedroom, Jack said, "Kennedy was shot tonight."

Olivia screamed, and the first tears welled almost as soon as the screen came to life and a newsman was there, in front of Good Samaritan Hospital where Kennedy had been transferred for surgery, providing the latest available information.

As Jack recounted what had happened, how the shots had been fired no more than 100 feet from where he had been standing, Olivia stared blankly at the television, dabbing at her eyes, thankful that Jack was OK, but overcome with grief, almost as if she had lost a loved one.

Kennedy remained in grave condition throughout the day and night, but finally, 26 hours after he had been wounded, at 1:44 in the morning on June 6, he died, his three-months-pregnant wife, his brother Ted, his sister-in-law Jackie Kennedy, and several other members of the family, but none of the couple's 10 children, by his side.

Two months earlier, Kennedy was in Cleveland on the campaign trail the day after Dr. Martin Luther King, Jr. had been murdered, and though he'd only joined the primary race three weeks before, Kennedy observed a day of mourning for his friend. He made one appearance, at the Cleveland City Club, where he delivered a speech that would hauntingly foretell his fate.

"This is a time of shame and sorrow. It is not a day for politics. I have saved this one opportunity, my only event of today, to speak briefly to you about the mindless menace of violence in America which again stains our land and every one of our lives.

"It is not the concern of any one race. The victims of the violence are black and white, rich and poor, young and old, famous and unknown. They are, most important of all, human beings whom other human beings loved and needed. No one - no matter where he lives or what he docs

- can be certain who will suffer from some senseless act of bloodshed. And yet it goes on and on and on in this country of ours.

"Why? What has violence ever accomplished? What has it ever created? No martyr's cause has ever been stilled by an assassin's bullet. No wrongs have ever been righted by riots and civil disorders. A sniper is only a coward, not a hero; and an uncontrolled, uncontrollable mob is only the voice of madness, not the voice of reason.

"Whenever any American's life is taken by another American unnecessarily - whether it is done in the name of the law or in the defiance of the law, by one man or a gang, in cold blood or in passion, in an attack of violence or in response to violence - whenever we tear at the fabric of the life which another man has painfully and clumsily woven for himself and his children, the whole nation is degraded. 'Among free men,' said Abraham Lincoln, 'there can be no successful appeal from the ballot to the bullet; and those who take such appeal are sure to lose their cause and pay the costs.'

"Yet we seemingly tolerate a rising level of violence that ignores our common humanity and our claims to civilization alike. We calmly accept newspaper reports of civilian slaughter in far-off lands. We glorify killing on movie and television screens and call it entertainment. We make it easy for men of all shades of sanity to acquire whatever weapons and ammunition they desire.

"Too often we honor swagger and bluster and wielders of force; too often we excuse those who are willing to build their own lives on the shattered dreams of others. Some Americans who preach non-violence abroad fail to practice it here at home. Some who accuse others of inciting riots have by their own conduct invited them. Some look for scapegoats, others look for conspiracies, but this much is clear: violence breeds violence, repression brings retaliation, and only a cleansing of our whole society can remove this sickness from our soul.

"For there is another kind of violence, slower but just as deadly destructive as the shot or the bomb in the night. This is the violence of institutions; indifference and inaction and slow decay. This is the violence that afflicts the poor, that poisons relations between men because their skin has different colors. This is the slow destruction of a child by hunger, and schools without books and homes without heat in the winter. This is the breaking of a man's spirit by denying him the chance to stand as a father and as a man among other men. And this too afflicts us all.

"I have not come here to propose a set of specific remedies nor is there a single set. For a broad and adequate outline, we know what must be done. When you teach a man to hate and fear his brother, when you teach that he is a lesser man because of his color or his beliefs or the policies he pursues, when you teach that those who differ from you threaten your freedom or your job or your family, then you also learn to confront others not as fellow citizens but as enemies, to be met not with cooperation but with conquest; to be subjugated and mastered.

"We learn, at the last, to look at our brothers as aliens, men with whom we share a city, but not a community; men bound to us in common dwelling, but not in common effort. We learn to share only a common fear, only a common desire to retreat from each other, only a common impulse to meet disagreement with force. For all this, there are no final answers.

"Yet we know what we must do. It is to achieve true justice among our fellow citizens. The question is not what programs we should seek to enact. The question is whether we can find in our own midst and in our own hearts that leadership of humane purpose that will recognize the terrible truths of our existence.

"We must admit the vanity of our false distinctions among men and learn to find our own advancement in the search for the advancement of others. We must admit in ourselves that our own children's future cannot be built on the misfortunes of others. We must recognize that this short life can neither be ennobled or enriched by hatred or revenge. Our lives on this planet are too short and the work to be done too great to let this spirit flourish any longer in our land. Of course we cannot vanquish it with a program, nor with a resolution.

"But we can perhaps remember, if only for a time, that those who live with us are our brothers, that they share with us the same short moment of life; that they seek, as do we, nothing but the chance to live out their lives in purpose and in happiness, winning what satisfaction and fulfillment they can. Surely, this bond of common faith, this bond of common goal, can begin to teach us something. Surely, we can learn, at least, to look at those around us as fellow men, and surely we can begin to work a little harder to bind up the wounds among us and to become in our own hearts brothers and countrymen once again."

16 - The Merry Mex

Jack stayed out in Los Angeles for almost a week after the death of Robert Kennedy, spending time with his sister, Mary, and her husband, Carl. They stayed up late several nights in the Heller's living room in Anaheim discussing the tragedy and all that was happening in America. Jack was still shaken by the fact that he'd witnessed the final moments of Kennedy's life, and had watched the vibrant senator walk through a door not 50 feet from where Jack had been standing where, on the other side, he would be shot three times while a couple thousand of his unknowing supporters were still celebrating his California Democratic Primary victory.

The column about Don Drysdale's historic pitching feat had been difficult to write through wavering concentration, the words simply not flowing like they usually did. During the past few tumultuous months, writing about sports had seemed so trivial to Jack, but what pushed him through the darkness was that he knew how important sports were to the people of this country. So important, in fact, that a man who was trying to become the next president of the United States had taken time to pay homage to a slice of baseball history. That's what ultimately helped Jack finish off the piece. Referencing Kennedy's acknowledgement of Drysdale's sixth consecutive shutout in his victory speech energized Jack. Recalling Kennedy's words, his smile, and the accompanying cheer his congratulatory message produced, Jack's typewriter began singing a familiar tune, and when he filed to the magazine, he was satisfied with what he'd written.

When Jack phoned the office to make sure the column landed safely, he told his editor, Mark Brantley, that he was taking a few personal days. Ever mindful of the bottom line, Brantley made sure Jack wouldn't be charging his extended hotel bill to the company, and Jack, irritated that this even came up, explained that he'd already checked out and would be staying at his sister's house before flying to Rochester, New York to cover the U.S. Open golf tournament at Oak Hill Country Club. "I won't even bill you for a cup of coffee, Mark," Jack said as he hung up.

The time off in California, which Olivia wholeheartedly endorsed, was therapeutic in many ways. Jack needed to unwind after the maelstrom of Kathleen's involvement with the student uprising at Columbia, on top of the never-ending worry for Patrick's safety in Vietnam, and the frightening unraveling of the country. Jack and his brother-in-law played golf a couple times, and Jack also lounged by the pool with his sister and talked about how the girls were doing up in San Francisco. On the night Kennedy's body was being transported from his funeral at St. Patrick's Cathedral in New York City to Washington, D.C. for burial at Arlington National Cemetery, the same night where, at London's Heathrow Airport, James Earl Ray, the man suspected of murdering Dr. Martin Luther King, Jr., was arrested by Scotland Yard, Drysdale was back on the mound. Jack pulled a few strings and procured tickets for he and Carl to go to Dodger Stadium to see if Dandy Don could break Walter Johnson's all-time record for consecutive shutout innings.

It was a welcome departure for Jack to be an ordinary fan sitting along the first-base line when Drysdale did indeed surpass Johnson before finally giving up a run after 58 innings when Philadelphia's Tony Taylor singled and scored on a sacrifice fly in the top of the fifth. The Phillies would score twice more before Drysdale exited to a standing ovation in the seventh inning, and the Dodgers hung on for a 5-3 victory, Drysdale's eighth win in 11 decisions to date in 1968.

After a couple more days of relaxation, Mary drove Jack to LAX so he could "rejoin the real world." Mary smiled and said, "You know, you could live wherever you want with your job. You choose to live in New York, but you could move out here."

"If I lived out here I wouldn't get a damn thing done," Jack replied. "How does anyone work here when the sun's shining every single damn day?"

"Well, give it a try; you might like it."

He kissed his sister on the cheek, then headed inside the terminal to catch his Pan-Am flight back East, back to his life, back to his job.

But first, a little more play. Buoyed by the 77 he'd shot at Rancho Park the second time he played with Carl, Jack's first priority upon arriving in Rochester was to go to Oak Hill to get his credentials to the media tent, and then ask around for suggestions on where to play 18 before settling in to cover the tournament. One of the volunteers was a man named Paul Kircher who was a member at Monroe Golf Club which, like Oak Hill was a private, Donald Ross-designed gem located in the upscale suburb of Pittsford. Kircher said he'd be happy to host Jack for a round, so the day before the Open began, Jack met Kircher and two of his pals in the grill room for lunch and a cocktail, and after Jack was regaled with some local golfing lore, the men headed to the first tee for a 2 o'clock start. As they loosened up and waited for the group in the fairway to clear, Kircher asked Jack what he thought Lee Trevino's chances were of winning.

"Well, I've heard of Trevino, but I don't know much about him," said Jack, an avid player and a somewhat keen observer of the PGA Tour, not only as a sports columnist who covered the four major championships for *SportsWorld*, but also as a fan of the game. "I remember he was in contention last year at Baltusrol, and then Nicklaus shot 65 the last day and that was the end of that. And I remember hearing that he was a talkative guy. Some of the writers who cover the Tour say he's a great interview."

"Lee's staying at our house this week," Kircher announced proudly, "and I can tell you that he is a talker. He's been like the pied piper with my young ones. He has them out in the backyard looking for lucky four-leaf clovers. A business associate of mine from Dallas - that's where Lee's based - called a couple months ago asking if we'd host the young man, and my wife and I agreed. Figured that would be a good way to get a little closer to the tournament."

"Then you probably know more about him than I do, Paul," Jack said.

As Kircher steered the electric cart in the direction of where Jack's first tee shot had come to rest in the right rough, he told Jack that a friend of his, a member at Oak Hill named Gerry Liebel, a fine amateur player who'd won the Rochester district championship a few years earlier, saw Trevino play his first practice round and came away greatly impressed. "Gerry knows a lot more about golf than I do," Kircher said. "I told him Lee was staying at our house, but he'd probably be gone by Friday when they make the cut. Gerry said, 'Don't count on that. This fella's got the shots. He can make himself known this week.'"

"Paul, I don't root for players, or teams, I root for the story, and it sounds like Trevino would be a hell of a story if he wins," said Jack. "Tell you what, if he happens to win it, I'm coming to your house for a glass of champagne."

"Let me say right now you are cordially invited," Kircher said.

Five days later, Jack took Kircher up on that invitation, and it added terrific color to his story as he recounted Trevino's historic week when he became the first man in the 68-year history of the U.S. Open to shoot four rounds below 70 to beat Jack Nicklaus by four strokes.

As Jack guessed, Trevino was a great story. Born out of wedlock, he and his two sisters were raised by his mother, Juanita, and his maternal grandfather, Joe Trevino, an immigrant from Mexico. They lived in what could only be called a shack on the outskirts of Dallas, located in a vacant field near Glen Lakes golf course, devoid of indoor plumbing and electricity. Joe was a gravedigger and a legendary drinker who Trevino said, "was the only man I ever knew who could sit in a bar from nine in the morning to nine at night, then get up and drive away." When he was a kid he had an old 5-iron of Joe's and he'd swing away at apples or balls that golfers at Glen Lakes had lost, the early beginnings of a flat but useful swing.

He quit school in the eighth grade to go to work because food was a necessity. "The closest we ever came to real meat was Texas hash and baloney," he said. "And we'd drink Kool-Aid." His first job was at Glen Lakes, and then he moved on to a pitch and putt course in North Dallas owned by a man named Hardy Greenwood who became, in effect, a father-like figure to Trevino. Young Lee did a little bit of everything - picked up balls on the range, shined shoes, worked the pro shop, mowed the greens, caddied - and he divided his other waking hours by playing golf, hitting hundreds of balls on the range, bowling, drinking, playing cards, and chasing skirts.

He quickly became a scratch player, and he played in more than his share of money matches, hustling whatever mark he could find. "You don't know what pressure is until you've played for five dollars a hole with only two dollars in your pocket," he once said. Unsure of what his future held, he enlisted in the Marines and was a machine gunner in the Far East, and when his tour was up, he re-enlisted and was sent to Okinawa for a special services assignment where he mostly taught classes on a rifle range and played golf with officers.

When he returned home, he was again rudderless. He got married, fathered a son, then was divorced within two years. He and Greenwood had a falling out when his former boss disapproved of how he was living his life, but shortly after he had re-married, Trevino was taken under the wing of a wealthy cotton farmer named Martin Lettunich who brought him to El Paso so that he could practice, make some money in games around town, and work as an assistant pro at Horizon Hills Country Club. Trevino borrowed money to qualify for the 1966 U.S. Open at Olympic Club in San Francisco, and he finished 54th. Then in '67 he earned playing privileges on the PGA Tour, but after a middling start he had decided against trying to qualify for the Open at Baltusrol. His wife, Claudia, would have none of that and she sent in the twenty-dollar fee. Trevino shot the lowest score in the qualifier, went on to finish fifth in the tournament, and the money he won enabled him to secure his playing privileges for 1968.

A couple weeks before teeing it up at Oak Hill, Trevino had nearly earned his first pro victory in Houston, but he lost a late lead and Roberto de Vicenzo, recovered from his Masters disaster, stole the tournament. "I had been playing well," Trevino told Jack as they stood on the lawn of Kircher's front yard. "I blew the tournament. On the way to Rochester, I stopped in Utica and watched some Little League baseball. Then I stopped at McDonald's, then I got a six-pack of beer, found a motel room and stayed overnight."

Trevino said that little detour cleared his mind, and when he showed up at the Kircher house, he was ready to go. Jack laughed when Trevino told him how he met Mrs. Kircher. She had just returned from the club pool and was still wearing her bathing suit when he rang the doorbell. "Now, this is an attractive lady, and I had never stayed with anyone before," Trevino said. "She was unpacking groceries and she had all these cans of Mexican food. So I asked her, 'Do you like Mexican food?' And she said, 'No, I bought it for you.' I said, 'I don't eat that stuff.' That's how my week started."

Trevino played his practice rounds with veteran pro Doug Sanders, and right away surmised the course suited his game. Each day he got more comfortable with the holes and how they played, and he said, "I just fell in love with the course." And then Oak Hill and Rochester fell in love with him.

Trevino started with a 69 on a cool, drizzly day, and was sitting two strokes behind Bert Yancey. "Oh, believe me,"

184

Trevino said, "I just wish I could have three more of those 69s the rest of the way." Yancey continued his solid play in the second round and he stayed two strokes ahead of Trevino as they each shot 68, prompting Yancey to boldly proclaim, "Trevino's got to catch me." Trevino was wondering how he'd do it, especially after the way he played that second day, even though that was his best score of the week.

Nicklaus said he wasn't discouraged after a 70 dropped him seven strokes behind Yancey, but the same could not be said for Arnold Palmer. He followed his 73 with a sloppy 74, prompting one of the Arnie's Army faithful to declare, "He stinks." To a certain extent, Palmer agreed, saying, "It was a simple case of atrocious putting. Tomorrow I may leave the putter in the bag and use my finger to roll the ball up." It wouldn't have mattered what Palmer used to putt with in the third round. He played abysmally, signing for an embarrassing 79 which sent him plummeting to near the bottom of the pack.

Meanwhile, Yancey and Trevino further separated themselves from the field with a 70 and 69, respectively, leaving Trevino one shot in arrears heading into the last 18. Seven strokes behind Yancey, Nicklaus conceded that, "I'd have to shoot 65 or so in order to catch him."

Paul Kircher did not doubt Nicklaus could shoot 65, but it was his opinion that even if he did, he wasn't going to catch Trevino. He was also pretty sure that Yancey was not going to be able to hold on, so on the eve of the final round, Kircher began confidently preparing for a Trevino celebration by purchasing champagne.

As expected, Nicklaus made an early final-round charge with birdies at Nos. 3 and 4 and was within three shots of the lead when, also as expected, Yancey began to fade with bogeys at Nos. 1 and 3. Trevino started with a bogey at the first, then parred eight in a row to take a one-stroke lead over Yancey. Trevino then dusted everyone on the back as he made two long birdie putts at Nos. 11 and 12, and parred the last six.

"I never even thought about winning the tournament until I left the 15th hole where I hit the flag with an 8-iron," Trevino said. "Then I realized I had a shot at winning the Open because I had a five-stroke lead with three holes to go. And that's when I went into my bad play. I was so nervous, I couldn't get my shots airborne. I was coughing and leaking oil. I'm certainly glad I didn't think about winning the thing beforehand, I might have had a heart attack."

His 5-under-par total of 275 tied the Open scoring record set just a year earlier by Nicklaus. Soon, he was holding aloft a winner's check worth $30,000, and calling back to his home club in Dallas to inform the members that the drinks were on him that night.

Just before Jack left the party, Trevino took a pull on a Budweiser and said, "One of the best things was that no one knew me. I sat in a golf cart one night drinking beer and not one person asked for an autograph. They thought

186

I was the cart boy or something. Rochester will always have a special place in my memory."

17 - No Happiness in this Valley

Rain was pouring down into the Song Lo Dong Valley, making this day like just about every other day in the jungles of Vietnam. Fucking miserable. Patrick had grown used to the constant barrage from the skies, walking around in a uniform that was either soaked by rain, soaked by sweat, or soaked by traversing through swampy water. He couldn't imagine what he smelled like, but then he'd catch a whiff of the guy next to him and he'd get an idea. Patrick was convinced that animals were more hygienic than he and the rest of the grunts.

What he hadn't grown used to is watching comrades die, but if he was being perfectly honest with himself, it was better them than him, which is what any other Marine would say. If that made him a selfish prick, an asshole in a foxhole, so be it, but it certainly didn't make him different. If there's one thing Patrick had come to learn during his tour of duty, it was that there's nothing noble about dying. All that bullshit you hear about dying for your country fighting the good fight, protecting the American way of life? Patrick would lie in his bunk at base camp some nights, or under the stars if the men of the 3rd Battalion 26th Marines Kilo Company were out on patrol, and he'd think about what that meant as he tried in vain to fall asleep. His conclusion was always the same: Dying means

188

you're dead, and you don't get to partake in the American way of life. Dying means they give your parents or your wife a folded flag, proclaim you some kind of hero, then toss your carcass into a hole and pretty soon all that's left is a pile of worthless bones.

There was one goal, and one goal only, for the men and women serving in Vietnam: To not die. Fuck this war, fuck whatever it is we're fighting for. No one on the front lines, at least no one Patrick had come across during his eight months in country, had a strong political position regarding the war. And most of their attitudes were described quite accurately by the acronym '4U' or 'UUUU.' Patrick had seen both variations written on helmets, tattooed on arms, and carved into wooden tables at the barracks or in the mess hall. It stood for "The Unwilling, led by the Unqualified, doing the Unnecessary, for the Ungrateful." Fighting the commies, or saving the South Vietnamese people, didn't mean much of anything to the grunts. All that mattered was surviving this nightmare so you could go back home and get on with your life, whatever life that was. But on this day, as the incessant rain pelted down from an angry gray-black sky into the Song Lo Dong Valley, five more Marines would never get on with their lives because they met a gruesome demise, the only kind that ever happened in war.

The men of Kilo Company had been walking almost non-stop for two days, doing their part in what was called Operation Mameluke Thrust, an objective designed to preempt further enemy attacks against the port city of Da Nang. Along the way, as they expected, they had

189

encountered their toughest challenges since they'd left Khe Sahn, though nothing could match that prolonged daily dodging of death. Early on they ran into a North Vietnamese Army squad entrenched in fighting holes and bunkers, but were fortunate to ward off that attack without any casualties because Sergeant Major Hound Dog Harriman caught a reflection of a rifle scope out of the corner of his eye and the men were able to take cover just as the automatic killing machines began firing. Air support was called in, and within 10 minutes, the NVA were showered with napalm and the lucky bastards who survived were retreating into the 10-foot high elephant grass.

Later that first day, Kilo came upon a village littered with fresh graves and destroyed huts. Once it was confirmed that the village was deserted, and it was swept for Bouncing Betty's - the three-pronged mines cleverly set in the ground that blow your legs off if you step on one - Hound Dog decided this was as good a place as any to stop and rest for the night. But the confluence of stifling heat and humidity, the voracious bugs, and the sound of troops throwing up or shitting as they battled dysentery and dehydration made it impossible to sleep. They were a weary bunch when they disembarked before sunrise, back on the trail that was leading them to where? They never really knew.

About an hour into the morning, just as the sun was cresting on the horizon, they discovered what appeared to be an abandoned NVA medical complex, but upon further inspection, they found a mother lode of weaponry including a 122mm rocket launcher, dozens of AK-47 rifles, and pallets of ammunition. Also, there were medical supplies, maps, documents, and several hundred pounds of rice. They threw everything they could into their M-818 truck, dumped all the rice and mixed it into the mud, and continued on their way.

"These fuckers are gonna be pissed when they get back here and this shit's all gone," Patrick said to his pal, Rollie McAvoy from Baton Rouge, Louisiana.

They were feeling pretty good about themselves, but that satisfaction was tempered a couple hours later when Hound Dog raised his right fist, signaling a halt to their march. Hound Dog was a soldier's soldier, a natural-born leader, the latest in a long line of war-tested Harriman's that extended back to the Civil War. He was from Asbury Park, New Jersey, so as a fellow New Jerseyite Patrick always felt a connection with him, and despite being scared shitless most of the time, Patrick took comfort being with Hound Dog because guys like him always seemed to find a way to stay alive.

As part of Mameluke Thrust, several companies of the 3rd Battalion 26th Marines were tasked with searching for and destroying enemy positions in the tactical area that extended south to An Hoa, and Kilo Company was currently kicking ass in that initiative. It hadn't been an easy road so far, but now it was about to become potentially far more difficult and dangerous. They had reached a point in their journey where they would have to maneuver between the hills overlooking the eastern end of

Song Lo Dong Valley, a place the Marines derisively referred to as "Happy Valley" because in actuality, there was nothing happy about this shit hole of a place.

Happy Valley was home to a major Vietcong/NVA base camp, storage area, and supply infiltration route. They would move troops and weapons from NVA base areas near the border of Laos down Route 614, to units operating near Song Tuy Loan or other positions overlooking Da Nang City, Da Nang Air Base, Force Logistics Command, port facilities, and the Marble Mountain Air Facility. This was a particularly dangerous region because it left American troops perilously exposed to NVA attacks from the surrounding camouflaged peaks, "like shooting fish in a barrel" Harriman had said. Just after New Year's Day, nearly a month before the Tet Offensive was launched, nearly 100 soldiers died there when Marine positions were overrun in a surprise assault, and there had been several other bloody battles in the months that followed. This is why this operation was so important; this region had to be rid of the enemy and secured.

"No fucking around, no talking, no smoking, no stopping to take a shit," Hound Dog said, warning them of what they could potentially encounter as the rain - which had started pouring down about a half hour earlier - cascaded down his hard, concerned face. "Stay awake, keep your eyes and ears open. The fuckin' gooks could be anywhere in here."

The men stared back at Hound Dog, and they knew this was serious. If this crazy dude was worried, Patrick thought to himself, this shit couldn't be good, and it brought to mind something he'd heard a few months back, a fellow Marine who'd said, "If I had a farm in Vietnam and a home in hell, I'd sell the farm and go home." That pretty much summed up Vietnam. Still, there was a mission to complete so they pressed forward, slogging through the mud, wide open eyes glazed by a mix of fear and awareness. They walked double file behind the cargo truck, each man scoping out the landscape on his side of the formation, watching and listening while at the same time hoping and praying that nothing was out there.

But of course, they were out there, and virtually out of nowhere, just as Hound Dog had expected, the attack came fast and it came furious. And had this officer with the keen instincts and military smarts not spotted out of the corner of his eye the movement up on the hill from the northwest flank, the body count would have been much higher. "Cover, cover!" Harriman screamed as the 82mm rounds began exploding all around his diving men. In the recently concluded month of May, more than 2,000 Americans had died in Vietnam, the highest single-month toll since the war began. Before the echo of Hound Dog's warning had reverberated, three men of Kilo were hit, and private first class Joey Gattis of Kansas City never felt a thing, killed instantly with a direct shot through his left ear not five feet from where Patrick had hit the muddy deck. As Patrick and the rest of the men fumbled with their M-16s, they indeed were "fish in a barrel" and within seconds

193

six more were wounded, four fatally, before Kilo Company even returned fire.

Patrick's first instinct was to bury his head in the brush and hope that the bullets would miss him, but he knew he had to engage to help ward off the ambush. So, he shouldered his rifle and began spraying rounds into the hills as did the others who were still capable of fighting. He had no idea if he was picking anyone off because you really couldn't tell in a situation like this. The enemy was invisible, hidden in the foliage, and your only point of reference were the flashes from their guns as they tried to kill you. Hound Dog was about 30 feet in front of Patrick and from a crouched position behind the truck, he screamed orders and pointed to the spots where his men needed to concentrate on. He then grabbed the PRC-25 radio and called for air support, barking out the grid coordinates on his map over the din of exploding mortars and grenades, and wondering if Kilo could hold on until the B-52s could sweep in and napalm the shit out of these sneaky fucks.

The company medic, Navy hospital corpsman Dan Lamorello, crawled on his belly to see who was alive. Tyrone Washington of Louisville was the first man he reached, but he was gone, a hole in his chest still spewing blood. Right next to him was Billy O'Bannon from Chatham, Massachusetts, bleeding profusely from a neck wound, also dead almost instantaneously. Lamorello moved on and found Chris Harrison from Rye, New York screaming in pain with a round in his right shoulder. "OK, hold on, hold on," Lamorello said as he reached into his bag for a morphine syrette. He plunged the needle into

Harrison, squeezed the tube, then tossed it away and tried to stanch the bleeding, eventually leaving the kid with only the simple advice to "keep pressure on it. I'll get back when I can."

A few yards away, Lamorello could see that Gattis' head was ripped open and there was nothing he could do, so he made his way toward Scooter Zrkemski of Raleigh, North Carolina. "I'm OK, got one in the thigh, go get Robby, he's fucked up," Scooter yelled as he pressed on his own leg, the pain grotesquely twisting his face. "Lemme tie that off," Lamorello said, but Scooter waved him away. Scooter was right, Robby Peterson of Roanoke, Virginia was fucked up, gasping for air, as he tried to keep his intestines inside his blown-up belly.

"McDonald, get over here!" Lamorello yelled at Patrick who was only a few yards away. "Get over here, I need help!" Patrick crawled on his elbows and knees, trying to keep his ass down as low as he could. When he arrived, he almost puked when he saw the hole in Peterson's stomach. "You gotta hold this gauze in his mouth so he doesn't bite his tongue off," Lamorello said. "And keep his head steady, he's bucking like a bronco." Patrick did what he was told, but had to avert his eyes as Lamorello stuck his hands into Peterson's stomach trying to put things back in place before wrapping him up. Peterson was in agony, and even though Patrick was telling him it was going to be OK, he knew it wasn't, and Patrick could literally see the life draining from his friend's face. Lamorello kept wrapping, but it was doing no good. Peterson was beyond repair, and less than a minute after Patrick stuck that gauze in his mouth, Peterson's eyes closed for good. Another dead Marine. The worst kind.

Lamorello grabbed Patrick and moved on to find Eddie Kravitz of Milwaukee lifeless, one right through his heart, so he tried to help Johnny Temple from Tupelo, Mississippi. Johnny took a bullet in his right bicep and another in his right hip and he was in a bad way, but he was still alive and Lamorello thought he could be saved. The medic worked on the hip with morphine and a gauze wrap, and he told Patrick to tie a tourniquet around Johnny's arm and then wrap the torn muscle. If Patrick felt totally out of place in war, he felt even more helpless trying to play doctor, but he did what Lamorello told as best he could, and the bleeding from the bicep slowed down.

"You good, Johnny, you good?" Patrick said to his fallen buddy who seemed to be slipping into shock. "Look at me, you good? Stay with me."

Johnny looked up and blinked, and then nodded his head. "It hurts man," he said, tears rolling down his cheeks, his left hand vise-gripped onto Patrick's right leg.

"I know, but the doc's here, he's gonna fix you up. You're gonna make it, just hang on."

The noise of war was deafening, and explosions of gunfire and grenades and mortar shells continued, but Kilo Company was obviously having some success because the rapidity of the NVA attack was slowing. Some of that was due to reloading, but some of it was the sharpshooting of the Marines dwindling the enemy's numbers. Hound Dog had plotted his response well and his guys had effectively hunkered down, gained their wits, and fought back gallantly. They were still in grave danger, but at least now they had figured out where the attack was coming from, and all they had to do was keep pumping lead up there and hang on until the planes showed up. And once the bombs were dropped and the NVA were either dead, dying, or retreating, the Huey helicopters would arrive to transport the wasted and wounded members of Kilo to the nearest M*A*S*H facility.

Lamorello thanked Patrick and told him to get back to his position, and while the corpsman wasn't his superior, he did what he was told and returned to the waning firefight. Only a few more minutes passed before the beautiful roar of the B-52s could be heard in the distance, and once the napalm was dropped and the planes departed the scene, the only sound you could hear was the screaming of the surviving NVA as they tried to flee with their flesh sizzling.

When it was over, Hound Dog ran down to where Lamorello was still attending to Johnny Temple, and he asked for a killed in action and wounded in action count. "Looks like five dead, four wounded; we need to get Temple outta here quick, he's hit twice."

"Fuck!" Hound Dog screamed when he learned the news. Five of his men dead, four others injured. It could have been much worse, but one casualty was too many on Hound Dog's watch. He ran back to the front, grabbed the radio and demanded the Hueys get in there ASAP, then slammed the handset back into the cradle and gathered the troops.

"We got five men wasted, we got four more WIA," he announced. "Get them bodies up here to the truck while we wait for the choppers. Check your ammo, who knows what else is out there. Stay alert. We're gonna load these guys up and then get the fuck outta here."

Later that night, Lamorello sat down with Patrick and thanked him for his help. "You did good out there," he said. "Johnny's gonna be OK, and you helped save him." He then pulled out a piece of paper from his bag, and shared with Patrick a poem that was entitled The Corpsman's Prayer:

"Grant me, oh Lord, for the coming events;
Enough knowledge to cope and some plain common sense.
Be at our side on those nightly patrols;
And be merciful judging our vulnerable souls.
Make my hands steady and as sure as a rock;
when the others go down with a wound or in shock.
Let me be close, when they bleed in the mud;
With a tourniquet handy to save precious blood.
Here in the jungle, the enemy near;
Even the corpsman can't offer much lightness and cheer.
Just help me, oh Lord, to save lives when I can;
Because even out there is merit in man.
If it's Your will, make casualties light;
And don't let any die in the murderous night.
These are my friends I'm trying to save;
They are frightened at times, but You know they are brave.

Let me not fail when they need so much;
But to help me serve with a compassionate touch.
Lord, I'm no hero -- my job is to heal;
And I want You to know Just how helpless I feel.
Bring us back safely to camp with dawn;
For too many of us are already gone.
Lord bless my friends If that's part of your plan;
And go with us tonight, when we go out again."

Patrick wasn't a religious man, but those words hit home on this night. His only thought when he gave the piece of paper back to Lamorello is that he'd lived to see another day.

18 - The Ugly Bear

Sonny Liston, erstwhile heavyweight champion of the world, was once asked what he would do if he was granted a mulligan for his life. "I'd like being a doctor or a lawyer," he replied. "The doctor and the lawyer still get paid, no matter what. A doctor can kill you, he still gets paid. A lawyer can let you get put in jail for 20 years, he still gets paid. There's no way those guys can lose."

Liston got paid on the night of February 25, 1964, but the prize money was no consolation for what he lost in that ring in Miami when a young loudmouth from Louisville named Cassius Clay took away his heavyweight title with a shocking display of skill and power which prevented Liston - heretofore considered the baddest man on the planet - to answer the bell for the start of the seventh round.

And then 15 months later, May 25, 1965, Liston got paid again, but even worse than losing the rematch to that same loudmouth who now called himself Muhammad Ali, Liston lost any remaining aura of invincibility, and perhaps most importantly, he lost his dignity. That incredible night in Lewiston, Maine, he went down in the first round, floored by what many believed was a phantom punch, immediately raising the question of whether Liston had been paid by the mob to take a dive.

"We'd like you to fly out to San Francisco to do a story on Sonny Liston," Jack heard his editor, Mark Brantley, say on the telephone.

"Sonny Liston?" Jack replied. "Why would we want to do a story on Sonny Liston?"

"He's on the comeback trail, Jack. He's trying to resurrect his career and with Ali out of the way he's trying to take a shot at winning back the title. He's fighting at the Cow Palace next week. Some guy named Henry Clark."

"You gotta be kidding, right?"

"Not kidding, Jack, this is coming straight from the top. Abrams wants the story done, and he wants Jack Mac to do it. Says he played golf with some guys in Vegas who are connected to Liston and they said he's gonna win that championship back."

Jack had no doubt that *SportsWorld*'s managing editor, Martin Abrams, was playing golf in Las Vegas recently. Abrams played golf everywhere he went. And then he'd bore you to tears if he ever bumped into you in a hallway or a men's room, giving you a shot-by-shot account of his round. Jack also had no doubt the guys Abrams was playing with in Vegas were mobsters, which would explain the connection to boxing, especially Liston since he was known to have been mobbed up back in the day when he was beating the shit out of every guy they threw him in the ring with.

"So what should I do with this plane ticket to Houston? Remember, I was supposed to be going there to cover the All-Star Game and write a story about why pitchers are dominating this season."

"You've already been to the Astrodome this year, and you just wrote about Drysdale last month."

"Yeah, two stories that you also assigned me to, if I'm not mistaken. Seriously, Mark, do you really think writing about a washed up and disgraced fighter trying to make a comeback against a bunch of tomato cans is worth our time?"

"Look, I'm just telling you what the boss is telling me. Besides, you'd really rather watch a bunch of guys striking out in a game that doesn't count for anything, in a domed baseball stadium, of all the crazy things? And isn't your daughter out there in San Fran? You can visit her on the company dime."

Well, that was the first thing coming out of Brantley's mouth that made any sense. He hadn't seen Kathleen since he dropped her off at LaGuardia Airport a couple months back, and now *SportsWorld* would essentially be paying him to go see her. And once he swallowed his pride and put aside the fact that it was inherent to his personality to always disagree with his editor, Jack had to concede that a story on Sonny Liston might be pretty interesting. Whether his so-called comeback was to be taken seriously or not, there was certainly plenty to write about with that guy, and in the next couple days, as Jack dug a little deeper into his research before flying out to San Francisco, he had to grudgingly admit that this wasn't a bad idea. Jack was not all that interested in boxing, at least not since Rocky Marciano retired as the undefeated heavyweight champion of the world in 1955. He peripherally knew of Liston, and of course he was aware of what had happened in the two fights with Ali, but he came to learn that the story of Charles "Sonny" Liston was indeed fascinating.

He was one of 25 children who came from the fertile seed of Tobey Liston, 15 from his first wife, and 10 more from his second wife, Sonny's mother, Helen Baskin. Tobey Liston was a sharecropper in Arkansas, a mean son of a bitch who cared little for Charles. Jack unearthed a quote from Liston regarding his father: "The only thing my father gave me was a beating." Helen left her husband in the mid-1940s and fled to St. Louis, and Charles went with her. He did not attend school, he worked menial jobs, and he could not stay out of trouble. He was arrested for the first time at the age of 16 and was given probation, but a repeated series of misdeeds eventually led to an arrest and conviction on two counts each of robbery and larceny and he was sent to the Missouri state penitentiary to serve a five-year sentence. While in prison, a fellow inmate branded him as Sonny, and it was while he was behind bars that Liston took up boxing, a pursuit that set his troubled life on a new course.

He was paroled in 1952 after serving less than half his sentence, and with the help of the prison chaplain, Liston hooked up with a trainer named Monroe Harrison, who was a one-time sparring partner of the heavyweight champ, Joe Louis. Harrison lined up a man named Frank Mitchell to be his manager. With their help, Liston became one of the top amateur fighters in the Midwest, winning several titles. He turned pro in 1953, lost only once in his first three years - and he beat that opponent, Marty Marshall, in a rematch - before trouble came knocking again in 1956. Reputed St. Louis mobster John Vitale had taken an interest in Liston's career, and in return for helping with some of Sonny's expenses, he used Liston as an "enforcer" for labor disputes. The cops knew of Liston, and they constantly harassed him. He would leave the gym and they'd stop and search him, just because they could. Finally, in May of 1956, Liston was pushed past the brink; he assaulted a police officer and was sent back to prison, serving nine months.

When he got out, Mitchell sent him to Chicago because he felt it would be better for his boxing career, and another mobster, Blinky Palermo, took a stake in Liston. Over the next few years, Liston moved on to Philadelphia, but no matter where he was, two things remained static: He battered everyone who faced him, knocking out almost all of his opponents, and he kept getting into trouble outside the ring. Rap sheet aside, by the end of 1961, there was no denying he was the No. 1 contender for the heavyweight belt owned by Floyd Patterson. Because of Liston's alleged mafia ties and prison record, Patterson's manager, Cus D'Amato, did not believe Liston deserved a shot at the title. Still, even after Liston testified before a U.S. Senate committee investigating the connections between organized crime and boxing, and it was clear that mobsters owned Liston, the two camps finally settled on a match. And on the night of September 25, 1962 at Comiskey Park in Chicago, Liston pummeled Patterson without mercy and knocked him out in the first round to win the championship. Less than a year later in Las Vegas, Patterson was given a rematch and the same thing happened, a savage first-round knockout which improved Liston's career record to 35-1.

Liston was a menacing figure, widely considered the scariest man in the world. He seemed indomitable in the ring, his massive 14-inch fists resembling weapons of destruction, and no one wanted to fight him. The Patterson bouts were his only activity in 1962 and 1963, so when he gave the brash Cassius Clay a shot at the title in 1964, Liston had fought less than two live rounds in the previous two and a half years. Further, he thought Clay - who'd won an Olympic gold medal in Rome in 1960 - was far too much of a pretty boy finesse fighter to stand a chance with him, and he did not train as seriously as he should have.

No one outside of Clay's camp could believe what happened that night in Miami, but the uproar paled in comparison to the reaction following the second fight when everyone in attendance, and everyone watching on closed-circuit television, screamed of a fix.

When Jack met Liston at his hotel for their interview a couple days before the fight with Henry Clark, he found the man Ali had nicknamed "The Ugly Bear" a surprisingly engaging fellow. Jack had heard he was illiterate, often sullen and uncommunicative, wary of the white man for sure, but also non-trusting of his own race. Liston's rise in the boxing world coincided with the ratcheting up of the Civil Rights movement in the early 1960s, and it had been conveyed to Liston that many blacks felt his "angry black man" persona would irreparably damage the cause. He was a symbol of what white America feared, exactly the type of man the Ku Klux Klan felt needed to be eradicated.

In the black community, the perception was that the pursuit of equality stood a better chance of succeeding if Liston dissolved into the background, and that the faces attached to the movement were those of Rosa Parks sitting at the front of the bus; of the nine Arkansas high school students - the Little Rock Nine as they were called - integrating an all-white high school; of James Meredith becoming the first black student to enroll at the University of Mississippi; of Daryl Hill becoming the first black to play football in the lily-white Southeastern Conference for the University of Maryland; and of Dr. Martin Luther King, Jr. speaking to the masses in his scholarly and eloquent way. Liston, the convicted felon, was the stereotypical black man, not only to the racists, but to those who just didn't know any better.

Jack started slowly with Liston, asking him first about his comeback. Liston's contention was that he still had what it took to become champion, and with Ali currently banned from the sport and stripped of the heavyweight title because he refused to go fight in Vietnam, the division was up for grabs. In the year since the decision regarding Ali, the World Boxing Association had conducted an eight-man elimination tournament - which did not include Liston - to determine the new champ. In April 1968, Jimmy Ellis won a 15-round decision over Jerry Quarry to claim the belt. Following a year in seclusion after the second Ali fight, Liston had quietly gone to Sweden for a four-fight package bridging 1966 and 1967 where he spent a total of 16 rounds in the ring, winning by knockout each time. He took another 11 months off, then resumed his resurrection tour in March by knocking out Bill McMurray in Reno, Nevada, and stopping Bill Joiner in the seventh round in a bout in May in Los Angeles. Now Clark was on the agenda, and Liston told Jack that if he continued to whip these guys, he'd be positioned for a title shot, whether it was against Ellis, perhaps Joe Frazier, or whoever else might possess the belt sometime in 1969.

Jack then steered the interview into the murky territory of Liston's brushes with the law, the Ali fights, and his alleged connections to the mafia. Jack wasn't sure whether the man would offer explanations for any of it, or haul off and cave his face in with one of those anvil-like fists. He was pleasantly surprised by Sonny's willingness to talk, but not surprised that he continued to deny, deny, deny.

"Clay caught me cold," Liston said. "Anybody can get caught in the first round, before you work up a sweat. Clay stood over me. I never blacked out. But I wasn't gonna get up, either, not with him standing over me. See, you can't get up without putting one hand on the floor, and so I couldn't protect myself. I was never counted out. I coulda got up right after I was hit."

Which was true. What happened is that when Liston went down, Ali stood over him, taunting him, screaming, "Get up and fight sucker, get up and fight!" By the time the referee, the old heavyweight champ Jersey Joe Walcott, escorted Ali to a neutral corner, Liston was back on his feet, and Walcott allowed the fight to continue. That's when a reporter at ringside yelled to Walcott that Liston had been down 17 seconds and the fight should be over. Incredibly, Walcott stepped between the two fighters and ended the bout, proclaiming Ali the winner, and chaos ensued.

Jack pressed Liston on the rumors that circulated after the fight. Ali had converted to the Muslim faith right after he'd beaten Liston the first time, and some said Liston threw the second fight because he feared he would be murdered by the Muslims. There was even a claim that he was approached a few days before the fight in Maine by two Muslims who said, "You get killed if you win." Others chalked it up to the mafia paying him to lose. Liston said it was all a bunch of bullshit.

The Clark fight, Jack was surprised to find out, was being televised live on ABC's *Wide World of Sports*. Howard Cosell was doing the play-by-play, and Ali's trainer, Angelo Dundee, provided color. The outcome was never in doubt. Clark had talked a pretty good game beforehand. He regaled the press with stories of how he'd go up to San Quentin to fight the inmates, and he intimated that Liston had nothing on the murderers and the rapists. "You talk about tough fights, those guys got to try and kill you or they'll catch all kinds of hell from the rest of the guys," he said with a laugh. "Liston thinks he's a big, bad man. And he wants everybody to think he's a big, bad man. He wants everybody to be afraid of him. He sees me and right away he starts to scowl. All I see is a fool."

Well, all he saw in the ring was leather pounding into his face. Liston controlled the fight from start to finish and Clark barely had a response. However, as Dundee pointed out, Liston's punches lacked the power that once defined him. With some of the blows he absorbed, Clark should have fallen like a tree. Instead, the challenger stood there and was able to take it until right near the end of the seventh round when he was completely defenseless, so the referee stepped in and ended it.

"If I missed any punches it wasn't anybody's fault but mine," said Liston. "He sure as hell didn't duck any."

In his story, Jack devoted exactly three paragraphs to the fight itself. All it did was muddy up the real story of a man who'd lived a hard life, who'd endured more than his share of trouble and heartache and controversy, who'd survived an association with the mafia, who'd been brow beaten not only by racist white people but by folks of his own color who wanted him to fail, and who was now trying to rise above it all and get back to doing the one thing he always did so well: Beat other guys up.

Whether he'd ever get another shot at the title was anybody's guess. Whether he could even be competitive with the top-rated fighters, men like Jimmy Ellis and Joe Frazier since it had taken him seven rounds to dispatch Henry Clark, was yet another guess. But Sonny Liston was at long last happy with where he was, and there was something to be said for that.

19 - The Streets of Berkeley Ablaze

Jack had traveled to virtually every major city in the United States, and he'd made several trips overseas, most recently to France for the Winter Olympics, but none of that prepared him for his first visit to San Francisco's Haight-Ashbury district where his daughter Kathleen had been living and working and, Jack was now wondering, who knows what else, for the last two months.

As Jack pulled his rented Buick to the curb in front of his niece Daisy's apartment on Crayton Street - a block away from Ashbury Street which Jack had heard all too much about - it seemed as if he was in a make-believe land. On the front porch of the house to the left of Daisy's place, there were four women and two men sitting in a circle, holding hands - were they praying? - as they passed a bong around to each other. On the front porch of the house on the right, there were three guys and a girl singing a folk song - probably something by Bob Dylan, or maybe Joan Baez, Jack surmised - as they passed their own bong amongst each other.

It was 2 o'clock in the afternoon on a Sunday, but Jack figured this scene would have been the same had it been Monday, Tuesday, or any other day that ended with a 'Y.' Do any of these people work for a living, Jack thought to himself? All of the males had long hair, bushy beards, ripped jeans, and grungy-looking t-shirts. Jack wondered if they were auditioning for some new movie about Jesus

Christ, but none of them were carrying a cross on the way up to Hollywood's version of Golgotha, so he ruled out that possibility. The females all had long hair, and if it wasn't adorned with flowers, their manes were wrapped in bandanas or scarves. As for their wardrobe, the two dominant looks were too short shorts crawling up their crotches with halter tops that revealed way too much cleavage, or, long, airy summer dresses held up by spaghetti straps that also revealed too much cleavage.

Jack had seen more than enough free spirits roaming the streets of New York City, but this was an all-out freak show. This was a segment of America Jack had no interest in, and as he made his way up the creaky wooden steps toward the paint-chipped six-panel front door, he wasn't sure what to expect when Kathleen came out to greet him, but the thought did cross his mind to grab her by the hand, throw her in the car, and fly her back home right that very minute.

"Hey dad!" Kathleen said with a big, excited smile as she opened the door on which her father had just knocked because the doorbell didn't work. As Kathleen kissed him on the cheek and gave him an elongated tight hug, he was relieved to see that she hadn't morphed into a beatnik. And in those few seconds of embrace, it felt like all the angst that had built up before he put her on the plane to come out here had been seemingly washed away. She looked happy, in relation to some of her neighbors she looked coherent, and she was dressed normally in jean shorts and a t-shirt with her hair tied up in a ponytail.

"I feel like I'm in a different world out here," Jack said as he entered the house. "Do these people contribute to society in any way?"

"Gee, dad, it took you all of 10 seconds to make that sweeping generalization," Kathleen said with a frown.

Just then, Daisy came bouncing out from the kitchen to say hello to her uncle Jack, and Jack's eyes were immediately drawn to the stitched gash on his niece's forehead.

"Hi uncle Jack, how are ya?" the ever-upbeat Daisy said as she rushed over to give him a kiss and a hug.

"I'm fine, but the better question is, how are you? What happened?"

"Oh, just a little boo-boo; no biggie," Daisy said as she winked at Kathleen.

"What happened?" Jack said, a little more sternly than his first inquiry.

Rather than subject Daisy to her father's interrogation, Kathleen explained how Daisy wound up in the emergency room getting 22 stitches to close a wound caused by her head getting in the way of a flying bottle during an uprising near the University of California-Berkeley campus a few nights earlier.

There was always a cause to fight for in Haight-Ashbury, and on the night in question, Daisy, Kathleen, and a few thousand others took over the streets to show their support for their fellow rabble-rousing brothers and sisters in France who had been embroiled in massive political and social unrest for several months.

The root of the turmoil in France dated to February, right around the time of the Olympics in Grenoble, and in the intervening months, the protests against President Charles de Gaulle reached such a volatility and scope that he feared civil war or revolution would tear apart a country that was less than 25 years removed from the horror of World War II. At issue was de Gaulle's heavy-handed governmental rule, the sub-standard wage structure and working conditions for those toiling in the factories, the fact that women had almost no say in the country's political sphere, and the perception that de Gaulle's monopoly on broadcast media allowed him to bias the news to further his policies.

De Gaulle's reign was initially thrust into peril when the French Communists and French Socialists formed an electoral alliance in an attempt to oust him from power. In support of this union, a series of student protests fueled the fire, and the unrest in the country began to burn out of control as they railed about de Gaulle's capitalism and consumerism; how he was strangling the French culture with his conservative, Catholic beliefs; charging him with class discrimination; and pointing out how political bureaucracy was unfairly controlling the university's funding. The police were called, and once they surrounded the university the students left without incident, though a precedent had been set. Conflicts between students and administration continued until the universities at both Nanterre and Sorbonne were shut down on May 2, and that only ratcheted up the tension. A march attended by more than 20,000 students, teachers and supporters to protest the university closures and the announcement of the expulsion from school of several students was met by police opposition and a near riot ensued as the students threw rocks while the police answered with baton beatings, tear gas canisters, and several hundred arrests.

Days later, with the universities still closed, another riot broke out on the Rive Gauche with hundreds of students injured and/or arrested as they tried to cross the bridge over the Seine River. This perceived police brutality brought on a wave of sympathy for the students, and the movement grew exponentially. On May 13, more than one million people trudged through Paris without police interference, and Prime Minister Georges Pompidou announced the release of the arrested students and the reopening of the universities, yet this did not dissuade further protests. In fact, this prompted France's adults to join in lockstep with the kids by striking en masse in an effort to procure higher wages. At its zenith, more than 11 million workers - about one-fifth of France's total population and about two-thirds of its total workforce - had walked out, nearly crippling the economy for a two-week period.

De Gaulle secretly left the country for half a day without anyone knowing where he'd gone, prompting some to believe he had fled. Actually, he went to meet with his military leaders to discuss how to handle the revolution he feared was imminent. With the full support of his military, the emboldened president returned with fresh resolve, even as half a million people marched in Paris that day chanting "farewell de Gaulle." In a radio address to the country, he said he would not back down to the demands of the students and strikers, but would agree to reform. In doing so, he dissolved parliament, and announced that a new election would be conducted in June. In the meantime, he ordered the strikers to return to work to avoid his instituting a state of emergency that would be carried out by the military, now stationed just outside Paris and ready to mobilize.

At the conclusion of his speech, about a million de Gaulle supporters marched through the Champs-Elysees waving the French flag, and further violence was avoided. This action doused the enthusiasm of the student protesters and the striking workers, and when it struck them what devastation a civil war would do to the country, the cause wilted. In the re-election, de Gaulle earned a monumental victory and regained control of the country, even though polls showed the country felt he was old, self-centered, authoritarian, and out of touch with the average Frenchman because he was too focused on military and foreign affairs as opposed to the obvious domestic issues at hand.

Throughout these tense months, activists in Berkeley had kept a close eye on France, and in late June, Peter Camejo of the Young Socialist Alliance - a shit disturber of the highest order - organized a rally in support of the French people to be held in front of Cody's Bookstore on the corner of Telegraph Avenue and Haste Street. The Berkeley City Council had voted down the organizers' request to shut down a short stretch of the street next to the Berkeley campus for the event, but the attendees would be allowed to gather on the sidewalks. Daisy and Kathleen were among the roughly 2,000 people who showed up, and when the crowd spilled into the street and choked traffic, the Berkeley police department tried to get the throng to disperse. They were met with resistance, and reacted by firing tear gas canisters. That sent the girls and most of the gathering home, but several hundred militants reconvened at the corner of Telegraph and Bancroft and built a barricade in the street, then set it on fire before vacating.

The next night, another demonstration was held, and it quickly escalated into violence. Store windows were smashed, more street fires were set, and in the melee with not only the Berkeley police but the supporting Oakland police, Daisy was hit in the head by a bottle and was briefly unconscious as Kathleen knelt next to her screaming for help. Daisy came around fairly quickly, was helped to her feet by two men, and after taking off her t-shirt to wrap Daisy's bleeding head, Kathleen managed to get the attention of a police officer who called for an ambulance, and told Kathleen to "cover those things up."

This continued for another two nights, with increased police presence and intervention, and the city of Berkeley instituted a night-time curfew, which of course was ignored. Finally, the city backed down and allowed the protesters to gather on Telegraph for one day, without threat of police retaliation.

Jack was beside himself as he listened to Kathleen recreate the story. First Columbia, and now this. It was as if trouble was following his daughter from one side of the country to the next, but the reality was that trouble was everywhere in this deeply troubled time, and it was difficult to avoid.

On the one hand, Jack could not fault Kathleen for her awareness of what was happening in the world, her inquisitiveness relating to the changing culture and times, and her willingness to lend her voice to causes she believed in, even if they weren't the causes that Jack would have supported. This was the world she was going to live in, and it was a far different world than the one Jack grew up in. On the other hand, he feared for her well-being, and it drove him batty knowing that he really couldn't protect her. Sure, he could haul her back to New York, demand that she live at home in seemingly safe suburbia while she finished out her days at Columbia, but what would that solve? Nothing, and she'd hate him for it.

This was life in 1968, societal and cultural mores changing quicker and more explosively than Bob Gibson's fastball. It was a time filled with uproar and historic coming of age moments, and to be young and vibrant and intelligent and aware and engaged were gifts that Kathleen possessed which could not be ignored, nor muted. It had been different for Jack with Patrick. When he was home Jack had allowed Patrick a longer leash, and he did not worry as much when he stayed out too late or got himself into an untoward situation, chalking it up to a boy being a boy and needing to flex his muscle and make his mark. Whether that was fair or not, so be it. Kathleen was his baby girl, and to see her spreading her wings and growing into a woman was a difficult adjustment.

But he owed it to her to try, so Jack listened to Kathleen recount the story of the Berkeley uprising, and hard as it was, he held his tongue, did not furrow his brow, did not flinch upon hearing the dangerous details, and he did not reprimand her, not even for taking off her shirt in public to stanch Daisy's bleeding.

"Anybody up for lunch? My treat," Jack said when Kathleen was finished.

And off they went, to the Magnolia Thunderpussy, of course, so the girls could enjoy the look on Jack's face when they introduced him to their boss and owner of the establishment who so represented the spirit of the times, and the spirit of Haight-Ashbury.

20 - Ode to Dandy Don

Don Meredith made Tom Landry cry. Twice.

"Bullshit," Jack said to the fun-loving quarterback of the Dallas Cowboys.

"Jack, you known me how many years?" Meredith said in his Texas twang. "You think I'd bullshit you? Y'all sayin' you shot 82 at Pebble Beach is bullshit, but this ain't no bullshit, I'll tell ya."

Having watched Landry, the head coach of the Dallas Cowboys standing stoically on the sideline on Sunday afternoons at the Cotton Bowl, his face perpetually set in consternation, a seemingly bloodless, emotionless robot in his suit and tie and omnipresent Stetson fedora looking more like a Xerox executive than a football genius, Jack found this proclamation hard to fathom, but utterly delectable as a journalist.

So, as Jack sat across from the unfiltered Meredith at a table in the quarterback meeting room at the Cowboys training camp on the campus of California Lutheran College, he eagerly scribbled these juicy Landry details in his notebook. True, the crux of the NFL preview issue cover story Jack was crafting would be centered on the personable Dallas quarterback who entered the 1968 season feeling like it was time he and the Cowboys finally dethroned Vince Lombardi's Packers for NFL supremacy. But Tom Landry crying? Twice?

"You gonna use that?" Meredith asked, knowing full well what Jack's answer would be. "Aw, fuck it. What's he gonna do, cut me?"

Jack had flown into San Francisco on this latest trip out West, and after a week in the Bay Area covering the Sonny Liston fight, visiting with Kathleen and Daisy, and playing a round of golf at the fabulous Pebble Beach Golf Links, he rented a car and headed south toward Los Angeles on the Pacific Coast Highway, first to his sister Mary's house, and then to meet Meredith. Jack had made this drive from San Fran to LA before, and though it took about eight hours, Jack couldn't get enough of the majestic scenery, the ocean waves pounding into the jagged left edge of the country, and the quaint little seaside towns where life just seemed to move at a slower pace.

With the car window open and the salty air tingling his nose, Jack chuckled to himself thinking about how happy the evil keepers of the *SportsWorld* expense accounts must have been when they learned he was driving and not flying, as if the money saved was going directly into their pockets. And then he thought how pissed they were going to be when that lesser line item would be offset by the sure-to-be exorbitant bill he'd be submitting for treating Meredith to dinner and drinks.

Jack's light mood was altered once he became engulfed in the congestive nightmare that was Los Angeles' freeway system, traffic that was even worse than anything he'd encountered on the Long Island or Deegan expressways back home. When he finally arrived at Carl and Mary's home in Anaheim for his second visit there in two months, there was much-needed food and wine, a dip in the pool, and conversation long into the night about their daughters and what they were doing in hippie land USA. Jack, per Daisy's request, did not share with her parents the story of her stitched up head. "They're fine," Jack said.

The next day, he weaved his way back through the snarl and the smog to Thousand Oaks, a posh town about 50 miles northwest of Los Angeles where the Cowboys had been training since 1963. He watched Landry, dressed in his standard issue training camp attire - white t-shirt, gym shorts, whistle around his neck, baseball cap covering his balding pate - put the Cowboys through a two-hour workout under a penetrating sun yielding temperatures that peaked in the high 80's. When it was through, and Meredith had showered off the stench of practice, he greeted Jack with a hearty Texas handshake and led him to the meeting room where they would talk for nearly an hour.

"I did shoot 82, and I could have broken 80 if I hadn't dunked two into the ocean at seven," Jack said, knowing that Dandy Don had played Pebble before.

"That itty-bitty hole? That's barely a hundred yards, ain't it?" Meredith said of the short par-3 hole that juts out into the Pacific.

"Wind got me, both times," Jack said. "So, enough about that. When exactly did you make the Teflon man cry?"

It happened in 1965. The Cowboys were in their sixth year of existence, all of them with Landry as coach and Dandy Don as quarterback, and they were barely making headway in their pursuit of an elusive playoff berth. Meredith had slipped and fallen in a training camp dormitory in the summer and suffered injuries to his throwing shoulder and elbow, and while he played through the discomfort - as he had his entire career - his preseason passes were more erratic than a meteor shower.

The problem carried into the start of the regular season, and though the Cowboys won two of their first three games, Landry benched Meredith in favor of rookie Craig Morton. That move proved disastrous as Dallas lost three in a row, so in Week 7, Landry turned back to Meredith when Dallas traveled to Pittsburgh to take on the Steelers.

"The worst game I ever played in my life," Meredith said recalling a grisly 22-13 loss during which he completed only 12 of 34 passes for 187 yards with two touchdowns and one interception. "After the game I saw Tom Landry cry. He wasn't crying so much about the game as he was crying about me. He had been fair, more than fair, to his mind, and he wanted so much for me to do well, and I was awful. I'm no good at pep talks, but I got up in the locker room, that dismal locker room at Pittsburgh. The players had their heads down, couldn't do anything, couldn't remember how to take off their uniforms. I told them I was going to work harder and we were going to win."

Landry was at a crossroads. The pressure was on in Big D. Never mind the fact that the franchise was only six years old; Cowboy fans had grown tired of losing, and they were starting to wonder if it was ever going to end with Landry calling the plays for Meredith. Landry had to decide whether to push forward with Meredith or move on to Morton or another rookie, Jerry Rhome. He thought about it Sunday night on the flight from the Steel City back to Texas, and all day Monday, before coming to the conclusion that it wasn't time to scrap more than five years of investment in Dandy Don. He called Meredith into his office Tuesday, told him, "You're my quarterback." And then Landry cried again, and so did Meredith, and from that point, the Cowboys' fortunes turned.

They earned a place in the consolation Playoff Bowl in 1965, then advanced to the NFL championship game in 1966 and 1967, losing both times to the Packers in a pair of classic, down-to-the-last-minute games, crushing defeats that lingered in Meredith's craw like a bad batch of Red Man chaw.

Jack asked Meredith about those games, and he could tell they were still a sore spot, even now in the shadow of the start of a new, promising season. The emotion was almost as palpable as it was a few months back when Meredith had agreed to fly out to Los Angeles to appear on Johnny Carson's *Tonight Show* with Green Bay quarterback Bart Starr, by now a five-time NFL champ and two-time Super Bowl winner. Carson asked Starr about the most recent title game and his dramatic, game-winning quarterback sneak where he lunged over the frozen goal line behind a perfect block by guard Jerry Kramer. Would the Packers, who were out of timeouts with 16 seconds to go, have had time for another play if Starr hadn't scored. Starr, never a man to gloat or brag, said he wasn't sure, but Meredith chimed in, "You sure wouldn't have."

That defeat at Lambeau Field, on a day only a polar bear could love, the coldest game in NFL history - "I can't describe how cold it was; all I can say is it hurt just to breathe," Meredith said - had come almost one year to the day after Green Bay's first title game conquest of the Cowboys, a far different 34-27 victory at the balmy Cotton Bowl. Meredith passed for 238 yards, including a 68-yard touchdown pass late in the fourth quarter to Frank Clarke that pulled Dallas within seven points. The Cowboys got the ball back at the Green Bay 47 with 2:12 remaining, and Meredith marched them to the 2, but on fourth-and-goal, he rolled out to his right and was quickly pressured by Packers linebacker Dave Robinson. He managed to get a pass away in the general direction of Bob Hayes, but safety Tom Brown intercepted it.

225

Dallas thought it was the better team in both games, but especially in 1967 when it was clear the Packers were aging, and their dynasty was nearing its end. However, Dallas' 9-5 regular-season record, partly due to Meredith missing three games early in the year with pneumonia, wasn't good enough to secure home-field advantage in the championship game, so it had to trek into the arctic, and that wreaked havoc with Landry's dynamic offense which relied on skill and precision rather than brute strength like Lombardi's power running game.

"That field was so bad," Meredith said. "We thought we had an advantage in our speed, our quickness, our multiple formations. We had studied hard and knew what to do. Suddenly we couldn't do anything we had done all season. Our game plan was gone down the ice."

In an interview with another national magazine, Cowboys general manager Tex Schramm had been somewhat critical of his long-time quarterback's work habits in the offseason. "When you've got your future riding on one guy, a quarterback, you like to have him be a little serious," Schramm was quoted as saying. "You say be dedicated, pay the price, and he says 'I'm not Bart Starr, I'm Don Meredith.' Well, we know we'll never make Don Meredith into Bart Starr. They're different personalities. Starr is the epitome of a hardworking, dedicated athlete. Meredith is like a Babe Ruth or a Bobby Layne. If Starr is Stan Musial, Meredith is Mickey Mantle. I understand that, but sometimes I get annoyed at his flippancy. Last spring I told him he had to join the adult world. He got mad and stormed out of my office. The next day he came back and said, 'I'm not gonna join your adult world. I'll live in my world and you live in yours.'"

Meredith laughed when he recalled the exchange, and then said to Jack, "Don't tell ol' Tex, but I've been acting like an adult this year."

It was true. Meredith wasn't at the Cowboys facility throwing passes every day in the epoch between the Ice Bowl and training camp. He'd still spent plenty of time flying around the country making appearances, making commercials, checking on some of his business holdings including his new restaurant in Dallas called Dandy's, and playing in pro-am golf tournaments. But the loss to the Packers hurt almost as much as his frozen limbs that day. So he spent more time working out, watching his diet, staying in tune with the playbook, and, yes, throwing passes. He even quit smoking.

Meredith admitted there were times when he wondered why he was still playing football, taking the punishment. "Sometimes when I'm lying on the ground at Yankee Stadium or someplace, and some guy like Sam Huff is pounding my poor thin body, I tell myself, 'Dandy, why did you ever take this up as a career? Why don't you get a decent job? You're too nice a person for this to be happening to, Dandy. Why don't you go back to East Texas where you belong? Let the other fellows play football. You don't need it.'"

But as the 1968 season was approaching, those two losses to the Packers still festering, and every masculine bone in his body craving to prove his detractors wrong and lead the Cowboys to glory, Meredith knew that playing football is exactly what he should be doing. The commercials, the business deals, the possibility of acting on television or in movies, maybe going into broadcasting, would all be there in a year, or two, or three, when his new contract would expire. For now, he was a football player, a quarterback, still the big man on campus in Big D.

"Do you think you should be considered the equal of Bart Starr, or Johnny Unitas?" Jack asked Dandy Don.

"I don't feel a Starr or Unitas could do a better job with the Cowboys than I can," he said. "I mean this simply because I've been with Landry for eight years and I know his system and therefore I'm more adaptable. I know how he thinks and how he wants things done. And I think we'll all agree Landry has proved his is a pretty good way to think."

Jack had spoken to a few of the Cowboys after practice before he sat down with Meredith, and he gathered that like Unitas, like Starr, Meredith was the most respected man on the team, especially given the way he had come back to work ready to eviscerate, once and for all, the heartbreak of the championship game losses.

"Meredith is setting the example," said offensive tackle Ralph Neely. "He nearly ran my legs off the first week we were out here, before camp started. Some days I'll be dragging and tired, and I see him working hard. That makes me think if he can do it, I can do it. So, I work hard, too. If we are going to win the championship this year, he's the man who will do it for us. He's the leader."

In closing, Jack asked Dandy Don if he'd know when to quit, or did he think he would keep pushing forward, much the way Unitas had the last couple years, even though his once prodigious skills had begun to erode with age.

Meredith said, "Pardner, when my time is right ..." before crooning in a melodic, country voice that he used to put on display back in the old days when he was performing in one-act plays or, on a whim, cutting an album, "Turn out the lights, the party's over. They say all good things, must end ... "

21 - The Chicago Police Riot

John Dupree always liked to say that Eleanor Guilfoyle was the prettiest girl in Canaryville, at least until Marge Fitzpatrick moved into the neighborhood.

John and Sis, the nickname which Eleanor went by, grew up four houses apart on South Throop Street on the south side of Chicago, hard by the Union Stock Yards where both their fathers walked to work each day, Patrick Guilfoyle as a butcher, and Edward Dupree as a freight handler for one of the railroad companies that shipped the cattle in for slaughter. Sis was the eighth of 11 staunchly Irish-Catholic Guilfoyle children, John was the third of four equally staunchly Irish-Catholic Dupree kids. John was two years older than Sis, but there was always something that drew the two of them together, and usually when John would go to the Guilfoyle house, it was to spend time with Sis, under the guise of wanting to meet up with her brother, Lloyd, who was his age.

Lloyd figured this out sometime around their freshman year in high school and he never really had a problem with it. In fact, he often told John that when Sis reached high school age - not a god-damned day before - he wouldn't play the protective big brother card if John ever wanted to ask Sis out to a dance or a Charlie Chaplin movie. But it was never that way for John. Sis was his best friend, and that's always how he and she wanted it.

And so, it was that Sis did what any best friend would do when Marge Fitzpatrick's family moved into Mrs. Mulberry's house across the street from the Guilfoyle's, and Sis saw the look in John's eyes the first time he met the new neighbor. She made the introduction, and helped facilitate a union that was still going strong some 48 years later.

John and Marge officially became a couple when John was a senior, and the moment Marge graduated St. Mary's in 1923, she took his hand in marriage and the newlyweds moved into a bungalow a few blocks away from where their families lived right there in Canaryville. They were South side through and through. Within a year, they were the parents of a beautiful green-eyed, dark-haired bundle of joy whom they named Olivia Grace.

The young family went through some tough times, especially with Marge unable to work as she cared for the baby. John toiled days at the Martin Senour Co. paint factory to pay the bills as well as the cost of evening classes at Northwestern, where his goal was to earn a degree in political science which he hoped would help him gain entry into the law program at DePaul.

Along the way, John befriended a charismatic and energetic man named Richard Daley, at once an aspiring law student at DePaul who had begun to dip his toes in the roiling waters of Chicago politics while earning a wage to defray his tuition by working in the rough-and-tumble meatpacking district pushing cattle through the stock yard pens, as well as serving as the manager at the Hamburg Athletic Club.

Daley spent some of the scant free time he had perched next to John on bar stools at South side joints that generally ignored Prohibition like the The Pump on Halstead Street, or Babe Connelly's Bar on 37th Street, tipping a few cold beers and solving the country's problems. The topics of discussion were wildly diverse, ranging from the cases they were studying in law school, to the turbulent political climate in Chicago, to the blood on the hands of Chicago crime boss Al Capone, to whether their beloved White Sox would ever recover from the devastating Black Sox World Series scandal of 1919. They were men of similar upbringings and religious beliefs, men of education, men of ambition, and they had well-formulated designs on how they were going to make their city better - John becoming an attorney who would represent the poor and disenfranchised, Richard fixated on a career in government.

One of their mutual friends happened to be Lloyd Guilfoyle, Sis' brother, who occasionally played softball with them, or joined them for poker games at the Hamburg AC. One summer night in 1930, Sis - who by then was working as a secretary at the same paint factory where John was employed - took John up on his request to come watch he and Lloyd play ball at Mark White Square Park. Little did John know that that invitation would be the impetus for changing the course of Sis' life, just as Sis' introduction of John to Marge when they were kids changed his life. After the last out was recorded, Sis left the bleachers and came down to the field to hug both John and Lloyd, and they introduced her to the team's second baseman, Richard. The rest, as they say, is history.

A few weeks later Richard took Sis to a White Sox game for their first date. Six years hence, in June of 1936 - just months before Richard was elected to the Illinois House of Representatives, kicking off one of the most iconic political careers in United States history - they were married at St. Bridget's. Among the guests were John, Marge, and 11-year-old Olivia, who in the coming years would occasionally babysit the first three of the Daley's seven children who were born before she left Chicago to attend Fordham University in New York, which led to her meeting Jack.

Before he even started studying law, Daley was already a Democratic party precinct captain by the age of 21, he worked in the City Council office as a clerk, and served as a ward committeeman. By the time he entered DePaul he was reasonably certain that he'd never practice, but he went ahead and obtained his degree, married Sis, and promptly won election to the House. In 1938 he ascended to the state senate, served six years as the Senate minority leader, and during that time was also Illinois Governor Adlai Stevenson's state director of revenue. In 1950 he was elected Cook County clerk, and in 1953 became the chairman of the Cook County Democratic Party, paving the way for his successful run for mayor of Chicago in 1955 when he ousted incumbent Mayor Martin Kennelly in a bitterly contested primary, then defeated Republican Robert Merriam in the general election.

Daley was surrounded by a phalanx of sharp-minded advisors and yes men, but when he really needed an intelligent and unbiased ear, especially when he reached City Hall and took a stranglehold of the Chicago political machine, he usually turned to his good friend, John Dupree. And rarely did the two men speak more in a single given year than 1968 when Chicago erupted in a volcano of violence as its streets became a battleground between anti-war protesters and a Chicago police force that was on high alert, by the mayor's order, to quell any threats of disruption to the Democratic National Convention by whatever force was necessary.

To have the convention in Chicago was like a lifetime achievement award for the 66-year-old Daley, a glad-handed pat on the back for all the work he had done for the party at the local, state, and national level. The last time it was held in Chicago, in 1956, he had just begun his first term as mayor. Now, he was a larger than life figure in the city, and he considered being the host mayor for the convention as one of his crowning glories. Instead, it became a blight on his decorated resume and the fallout resulted in irreparable damage to his legacy.

The seeds for trouble began germinating early in the year because of what was happening in Vietnam. Fueled by the Tet Offensive, Walter Cronkite's pronouncement that the war was no longer winnable, and the grisly nightly television images emanating from those jungles, Vietnam was tearing the nation apart, and the Democratic president - who it was quite naturally assumed would be coming to

Chicago seeking a second term in the White House - was in the eye of the storm. As early as March, peace activist groups and anti-war factions including the National Mobilization Committee to End War in Vietnam (MOBE), Students for a Democratic Society (SDS), and the Youth International Party (Yippies), were planning protest marches in Chicago during the late August convention to rail against President Johnson's handling of the war. And even after Johnson stunned the nation with his announcement that he wouldn't be accepting the party's nomination, the protesters were undeterred because Johnson's vice-president, Hubert Humphrey, was the leading candidate to head the ticket, and he was in favor of Johnson's policies regarding the war.

Daley's response to the planned infiltration was to refuse to grant permits which would allow the demonstrators to protest legally. "No thousands will come to our city and take over our streets, our city, our convention," Daley said with typical bravado and defiance.

Barely days after that statement, Daley exacerbated the situation in the wake of the assassination of Dr. Martin Luther King, Jr. Race riots broke out in the city in the hours after the tragedy, and on the West side, 11 blacks died and 20 blocks went up in flames with more than 120 fires damaging 210 buildings to the tune of approximately $10 million. Daley had to call President Johnson to request 5,000 U.S. Army soldiers be flown in from Fort Hood, Tex. to help suppress the rioting, and afterward, the mayor heavily criticized his police superintendent, James B. Conlisk, and the entire department, for what he perceived as it's too-cautious handling of the incident. During a press conference at City Hall, Daley said, "I said to (Conlisk) very emphatically and very definitely that an order be issued by him immediately to shoot to kill any arsonist or anyone with a Molotov cocktail in his hand, because they're potential murderers, and to shoot to maim or cripple anyone looting." Daley supporters deluged his office with grateful letters, but the press skewered him, and black leaders such as the Rev. Jesse Jackson called it a "fascist's response."

The day after the "shoot to kill" proclamation became public knowledge, Daley called John Dupree to gauge his reaction, and John said to him, "Richard, I understand why you said what you said, but I think you may have opened the door for some real trouble when the convention comes here." John knew the anti-war groups were coming to town, and now that Daley had derided his own police force, it was a recipe for potential disaster with the angry cops hell-bent on atoning for their alleged mishandling of the riots. Taking John's advice, Daley backed away from the statement, saying at a City Council meeting, "It is the established policy of the police department – fully supported by this administration – that only the minimum force necessary be used by policemen in carrying out their duties." Still, the die had been cast, and the police were not going to make the same mistake when the convention arrived.

By the time the delegates began flooding into his city, the mayor had transformed Chicago into a police state in the hope that the massive show of force would dissuade the dissenters from causing trouble. The area around the convention site - the International Amphitheater on the South side near the Union Stock Yards - was a veritable fortress, protected by more than 5,600 Illinois National Guardsmen, plus every member of the powder-blue shirt and helmeted Chicago police force, nearly 12,000 strong, armed not only with the standard issue firearm and billy club, but with mace, tear gas, and riot gear. In case that wasn't enough, there were 5,000 more Guardsmen on stand-by, as well as 7,500 regular army troops at Fort Hood, Fort Sill, Oklahoma, and Fort Carson, Colorado, who could be flown in within 24 hours. Further, there were more than 1,000 Secret Service agents, military intelligence officials, federal narcotics investigators, and FBI agents roaming the city with their ears to the ground snuffing out potential uprisings and conflicts.

None of which deterred Olivia in her eagerness to get to Chicago. Having never attended a convention, she had been looking forward to this all summer, especially since she and her parents would be guests of Daley, the most powerful man in Chicagoland. But as the day of her flight neared, Jack pleaded with her not to go. "Liv, I wish you'd stay home," Jack had said numerous times as reports of the impending violent dissidence usurped Vietnam in the nightly news A block. "And I don't think your parents should go into the city, either. Tell them to stay out there in Hinsdale where it'll be safe."

Naturally, the staunch Democrat would have none of it. "I'm going, and it'll be fine," Olivia said. "This is a big moment for Mr. Daley, I've known him almost my whole life, and we owe it to him to be there for support."

"Bullshit," Jack said. "Mayor Daley has enough on his mind and he won't be checking his guest list. He'll understand if you and your parents sit this one out. His town is ready to explode, and I don't want you anywhere near it."

"Jack, I know you don't care about politics, but this is the World Series to me, the Rose Bowl, or whatever other sports analogy you'd like me to use here. I've been looking forward to this all year."

"Yes, believe it or not I get it, I do. But there's this really useful invention known as the television, and we happen to have one sitting right there in the living room. Guess what? Everything that happens in Chicago will be shown right there on that tube. And here's the best part, you won't be in the middle of a fucking riot!"

Needless to say, Olivia boarded her flight at LaGuardia, after Jack sent her off with a loving, worrisome kiss. Why are the women in my life so headstrong, Jack thought to himself before saying, "Be careful."

"I will."

By the time Olivia landed at O'Hare on Sunday afternoon, it had become clear that Chicago was on the verge of boiling into a sea of civil unrest. On Thursday, Aug. 22, four days before the official start of the convention, a 17-

year-old Sioux Indian from South Dakota was shot dead by police who said he pulled a gun. The next day, the Yippies gathered en masse at the Civic Center plaza in the Loop where they nominated their own presidential candidate, Pigasus the pig. The pig and seven of the Yippies were arrested. And so it began.

The convention was formally opened by Daley on Monday night, Aug. 26, and Daley reiterated, "As long as I am mayor of this city, there's going to be law and order in Chicago." There was plenty of law, and absolutely no order over the next four bloody days that reinforced microcosmically how divided a nation the United States was.

Thousands of protesters gathered each night in Lincoln Park and Grant Park, whipped into a frenzy by leaders of the Yippies, MOBE, SDS, Black Panthers, and other satellite groups such as Allan Ginsberg, Norman Mailer, David Dellinger, William Burroughs, Tom Hayden, Rennie Davis, John Froines, Lee Weiner, Abbie Hoffman, Bobby Seale, Phil Ochs, Jerry Rubin, and Dick Gregory, preaching their New Left politics with street theater tactics. Several marches toward the Amphitheater were attempted, but all were beaten back by the mace-spraying, tear gas-throwing, club-swinging police force, and hundreds were injured and/or arrested. Night after night the protesters refueled with fury and vitriol and pressed on despite the heavy-handed opposition, and with network television cameras broadcasting the uprisings nationwide, Americans grew more despondent about the unraveling of society.

Never was this more apparent than the evening of Aug. 28 when the violence escalated nearly out of control. Approximately 10,000 gathered at the Grant Park band shell for MOBE's anti-war rally, surrounded on all sides by the police, with National Guardsmen perched on the roof of the Field Museum with rifles at the ready. As the rally came to an end, a young man began to lower the American flag near the band shell. Police rushed in to arrest him, and then several others completed the flag lowering and attached a blood-spattered shirt to be raised in its place. Police moved in again and a battle ensued, during which Rennie Davis of MOBE, whose father had been former President Harry S. Truman's chief of staff on the Council of Economic Advisers, was beaten unconscious.

David Dellinger, one of America's foremost radicals who in 1943 was arrested for failing to report for his World War II draft physical, took control at this point and instructed a march to the Amphitheater. Because they didn't have a permit, the police refused to allow them to move on the sidewalks, and the march stagnated. After an hour of heated and fruitless negotiation, the protesters tried to cross over to Michigan Avenue, but both the Balbo and Congress bridges were blocked by Guardsmen armed with machine guns. The mob moved north and was able to surge onto Michigan via the unguarded Jackson Street bridge, and then headed back south on Michigan toward the Hilton Hotel where many of the delegates, and most of the media, were headquartered. With cameras rolling, the police forcibly halted the march, and the melee became the signature event of the week, the Battle of Michigan Avenue as it was dubbed. As the police clubbed, the protesters fired back with fists and rocks and whatever else they could find to throw. Many were heard to be chanting, "The whole world is watching!" and they were right. "The conduct of the authorities here resembles the conduct of the Russians toward Czechoslovakia," said the poet, Ginsberg.

Meanwhile, inside the Amphitheater, tensions were equally stretched to the limit as the Democratic Party came unglued over its internal disagreement on Vietnam. Having defeated the Germans and Japanese in World War II, it quickly became apparent that the rising Soviet Union, and the potential spread of its Communist government, would be America's new primary enemy. Stopping the threat of Communism became paramount, and the United States decreed that it would intervene in the affairs of countries it deemed susceptible to that influence. It was this policy that drew America into the Vietnam conflict in an effort to keep South Vietnam from being overrun by Communist North Vietnam. The Democrats could not come to a unified consensus on Vietnam, with Hubert Humphrey upholding President Johnson's handling of the war, and Eugene McCarthy and George McGovern going the other way and siding with the anti-war faction in the belief that it was time to get out of Southeast Asia.

With nominations underway, Massachusetts Senator Abraham Ribicoff, in his speech promoting McGovern, said, "With George McGovern as President of the United States we wouldn't have Gestapo tactics in the streets of Chicago." Mayor Daley, standing in plain sight on the convention floor, angrily shook his fist at Ribicoff and, depending on the account, either called Ribicoff a "fucker" or a "faker." With the anti-war delegates getting increasingly agitated by what they were hearing from the stage, the police inside the arena became more and more antagonistic and scuffles broke out, again on national television. In one memorable incident, CBS reporter Dan Rather was knocked to the floor as he tried to interview a delegate who was being forcibly removed from the convention. Rather was able to recover and he told Walter Cronkite and the viewers, "Walter... we tried to talk to the man and we got violently pushed out of the way. This is the kind of thing that has been going on outside the hall, this is the first time we've had it happen inside the hall. I'm sorry to be out of breath, but somebody belted me in the stomach during that. What happened is a Georgia delegate, at least he had a Georgia delegate sign on, was being hauled out of the hall. We tried to talk to him to see why, who he was, what the situation was, and at that instant the security people, well as you can see, put me on the deck. I didn't do very well." Cronkite then said, "I think we've got a bunch of thugs here, Dan."

Like most Americans, Jack sat in the living room mesmerized by what was taking place, and he wondered where his wife was, and whether she and her parents were safe. Long after midnight, Jack got his answer, awakened by the phone on the nightstand next to his bed. When he picked up, he heard Olivia crying on the other end.

"Are you OK?" Jack said, immediately alert despite the hour. "What happened?"

"I'm OK, but we're not going back downtown tomorrow. It was awful, Jack. I've never seen anything like this. We saw on the television monitors what was going on outside the hall, all the rioting and the beating, and then the people on the floor in the building were fighting. You were right, this was a bad idea. I can't wait to get out of here."

When Olivia hung up, she sat down at the kitchen table of her parents' home in the safety of suburbia, and they talked into the early hours of the morning, lamenting the fact that the Democratic Party was irreparably broken, and that there was no way the Republican nominee, Richard Nixon, could lose the election. It was clear the Democrats should have nominated an anti-war liberal, but with only 15 states choosing their delegates by primary, Humphrey was able to secure the vast majority of delegates in the states where they were selected by county committeemen, state party officers, and elected officials. Men like Daley and his minions that kept his political machine humming.

When the convention was closed the following night, Humphrey was officially confirmed, but only the most optimistic members of the party truly believed he stood a chance after what had transpired in Chicago. The final tally was nearly 700 arrests, more than a thousand injuries to police and protesters, several hundred of those serious enough to be treated at area hospitals. And during the week of the convention, it was reported there were 308 American casualties and more than 1,100 injured during fighting in Vietnam.

22 - *Color Blind*

Arthur Ashe stood in the middle of the stadium court at the West Side Tennis Club, looked into the sun-drenched crowd of more than 7,000 mostly white faces, and told them he was "grateful that he was able to win" the first U.S. Open tennis championship. He did not mean he was grateful that his supreme talent had been enough to overcome Dutchman Tom Okker in five sets, 14-12, 5-7, 6-3, 3-6, and 6-3. Instead, he was just appreciative that, as a black man in this most turbulent of years with race relations being what they were, the death of Dr. Martin Luther King, Jr. still stirring the embers of distrust between blacks and whites, that he was allowed to play in the tournament at all.

Jack recognized what a profound statement Ashe had made, yet he was certain it was lost on most in the Caucasian-filled bleachers who nonetheless applauded the spindly, bespectacled black man anyway. Perhaps the bell would go off when they saw the *New York Times*, in its next-day edition, call Ashe's victory, "the most notable achievement made in the sport by a Negro male athlete." Even better, maybe days later they would come to understand what had really happened at Forest Hills once they read Jack's account in *SportsWorld*.

Jack had met Ashe the year before when this tournament was still called the U.S. National and was not open to professionals. He interviewed him for a story about the lack of black golfers and tennis players in the professional ranks, and during their hour-long conversation Jack had found Ashe to be a tremendously engaging and intelligent man. Wise beyond his 25 years, actually.

Born in segregated Richmond in 1943, Ashe learned early on that the color of his skin was going to create barriers in his life. Ashe's father, Arthur Sr., was put in charge of the Brookfield playground which was designated as "blacks only." There were four tennis courts not a lob shot away from Ashe's front door, and as a youth, he spent hours on those courts either playing against another neighborhood kid, or banging a ball against a wall to hone his strokes. "My arms and legs were thin as soda straws, but I soon began to get good at the game, maybe because I was born with extra quick reflexes," he said.

It was tennis that took his mind off the tragic death of his mother, who died of toxemia during her third pregnancy when he was just six years old. And it was tennis that a collegiate player named Ron Charity realized might be Ashe's ticket out of racist Richmond. Charity had also played on those Brookfield courts, and he eventually took young Ashe under his wing and taught him the finer points of the game. When Ashe began to show promise, Charity recommended that the boy spend summers at the home of

Dr. Robert Walter Johnson, a wealthy black man and accomplished tennis player and teacher who had built a court at his Lynchburg, Virginia home and conducted summer tennis camps there.

Starting at age 10, Ashe spent eight consecutive summers at Johnson's, and he became the prized pupil, winning local and national junior tournaments and ultimately earning a scholarship to UCLA, the first ever awarded to a black tennis player by the school. While at UCLA - also the alma mater of a certain baseball player who went on to break that sport's rigidly adhered to color barrier, one Jackie Robinson - Ashe took his game to the world-class level. UCLA's program was one of the best in the country, so good that Ashe began as the No. 3 player. By the time his college days were through, though, he was No. 1 and his championship victory over arch-rival Dennis Ralston of USC keyed the Bruins' 1965 NCAA team championship.

Ashe spent his college summers playing around the world. He had been competing in America's premier tournament, the U.S. National, since 1959 when Rod Laver thumped him in the first round, and in each return visit, his standing improved. His best showing had come in 1965 when, as the nation's No. 1-ranked amateur, he upset Roy Emerson - then the world's No. 1-ranked amateur - to reach the semifinals before losing to Manuel Santana. He played at Wimbledon for the first time in 1963 after being awarded a berth in the singles draw by virtue of his triumph in the Southern California district championship. Ashe figured he wouldn't be able to accept the invitation to the All-England Club because he couldn't afford to make the trip overseas, but an anonymous white woman who had been impressed by his performance, gave him $800 to cover his expenses. He gladly accepted, flew to Great Britain, and made it to the third round before bowing out to eventual winner Chuck McKinley.

After receiving his diploma from UCLA in 1966, Ashe went to West Point to fulfill a two-year military commitment. Every freshman and sophomore male at UCLA was required to take Reserve Officers' Training Corps, and after two years, he could drop out of the program. Realizing that upon graduation he would likely get drafted into the military, Ashe elected to stay in the ROTC for his entire term at UCLA. It was a shrewd move because by sticking with ROTC, he was able to serve his two years as an Army officer, and that allowed him some flexibility to play in various tournaments.

The landscape of tennis changed dramatically in March 1968 when the International Tennis Federation finally gave its blessing to open tennis, meaning pros and amateurs could play against each other in tournaments, and that excited Ashe because even though he was still an amateur, he knew he was every bit as good as most of the pros. In his first open Wimbledon in 1968, Ashe was seeded 13th and he beat pros John Newcombe and Okker before losing in the semifinals to Laver. It was Ashe's deepest advance into such a prominent tournament, and buoyed with confidence, he then defeated Bob Lutz in five sets to win the U.S. National at Brookline, Massachusetts, becoming the first American-born player to do so since 1955.

Clearly comfortable on the grass courts at Forest Hills, Ashe plowed through the early draw, and then in the second week disposed of Emerson in the round of 16, Cliff Drysdale in the quarters, and his good friend and fellow Davis Cup teammate, Clark Graebner, in a stirring semifinal. Meanwhile, Okker had taken out the legendary Pancho Gonzalez in the quarterfinals, 14-16, 6-4, 10-8, 6-3, and had beaten Ken Rosewall in the semifinals, which guaranteed him the $14,000 first prize. Okker was a registered player - in other words, an amateur who could accept prize money - while Ashe was still an amateur, eligible only for $15 per diem and a free room at the Roosevelt Hotel. Win or lose, Okker was going to cash in, but as both players were acutely aware, the title was more important than the money.

The combatants were conservative in the classic first set that extended to 26 games. Ashe's first serve was a dynamic weapon, and in the opening set he fired 15 aces past Okker. At one point in the 11th game, Ashe served two straight aces and Okker jokingly turned his back in mock surrender as Ashe prepared for his next serve. "Against him you don't get enough tennis with that big serving," Okker said. "I just couldn't return well, which is the main part of my game - to return the serve and make use of my shots. The points went too fast. How can you play tennis when you can't see the ball? Why couldn't he wait until tomorrow to start serving like that?"

However, while Ashe's serves were explosively effective, Okker's were quietly efficient. He matched Ashe service game for service game and because a set had to be won by at least two games, the players battled on in search of that elusive first service break. At 10-9, Ashe had two set points, but he pushed a forehand wide of the line and failed to return an Okker serve that brought the score to deuce, and Okker eventually won the game. But at 13-12, Ashe finally got the break that ended the 64-minute marathon. At set point, Ashe drilled a low return at Okker's feet, and when Okker could only send a meek return over the net, Ashe ripped a forehand winner.

Each managed a service break early in the second set and it appeared another long journey was ahead, but Okker also broke Ashe in the 11th game to take a 6-5 lead and then held serve to draw even at one set apiece. Ashe needed only 18 minutes to win the third set, 6-3, but Okker used a mere 20 minutes to win the fourth set, 6-3.

"Nobody can imagine, unless they've been through it, what agony you face in a close five-set match, especially in scorching weather, and more especially in a late round of a top tournament," Ashe said. "Your feet hurt, your racket hand hurts, your one-pound racket is as heavy as a shovel, your head pounds and your eyes burn from the sun. Fifth sets of tennis matches separate the great from the good."

And there you have it, the difference between Ashe and Okker. Ashe was pushed to the edge, and his greatness came bursting out. "I went back to serve the first game of the final set and everything seemed to be building," Ashe said. "My father was in the stands, so was Dr. Johnson. It was the first U.S. Open. As long as the game is played there will be only one first U.S. Open."

Ashe won the first game easily, then broke Okker in the second game. At 30-30 he deftly dropped a lob just inside the baseline to get to break point, then hit an angled crosscourt forehand winner to open a 2-0 lead. The next four games went according to serve, but Okker had an opportunity to break back in the seventh game. Here, Ashe's strategic sense bailed him out.

"I don't hammer a man's soft spot constantly because he may strengthen it," Ashe said. "I just save it as a trump up my sleeve for moments when I really need a point. So, if his backhand is shaky, I play mostly to his forehand. He thinks he's doing a lot better than he is, and when the time comes to knock him over, then I put pressure on his weakness."

That time was now, so Ashe spent the rest of this pivotal game serving to Okker's weakness - his backhand. Though he failed to put his booming first serve in play on three straight points, his second serve to the backhand side was still good enough to force three consecutive Okker mistakes. Okker returned wide on the first point to create deuce, then hit over the baseline to give Ashe the advantage, and he completed the hat trick with a netted return which gave the game to Ashe and dropped Okker into a 5-2 hole.

Ashe lost the eighth game, but then served for the match. He opened by volleying a forehand winner, then blasted his 26th and final ace of the day for 30-love. Next he forced Okker to miss a backhand, and at match point, he zipped a first serve in, ran to the net and volleyed Okker's return for a winner to end the match. The victory thrust Ashe into the world spotlight, and in a few months when his military hitch was complete, Jack had the sense that this was a man who was going to accomplish a whole lot on the tennis court, and a whole lot more off the court.

"I can't say much until I get out of the army," Ashe said, "but then I'm going to say some things and do some things. Before I'm through I imagine I'll step on a lot of toes."

And, Jack figured, open a lot of doors.

23 – Be Quick or be Dead

The men of the 3rd Battalion 26th Marines Kilo Company needed this, a night of singing, dancing, laughing, drinking, smoking, and drooling - not necessarily in that order - as the Donut Holes put on a show at base camp that did exactly what it was intended to do: Lift the spirits of the disgruntled men fighting this despicable war.

Patrick and the boys had enjoyed some down time in the past week, and the short break was capped off by an appearance by four members of the Red Cross Supplemental Recreational Activities Overseas program, the Donut Holes, or Donut Dollies as the men called them. They were single, female college graduates who signed up to do their part to assist the war effort by going to Vietnam and giving the soldiers a thrill by parading around in their short, tight mini-skirts as the men hooted and hollered. They sang and danced, played games like charades and musical chairs, or just talked to individuals who needed a soothing ear. Their shows did not compare in entertainment value to the USO productions that featured Hollywood stars and starlets, but they were more personal because the young ladies mingled with the men and learned a little about them before moving on to the next base camp.

Patrick was entranced by one of the Dollies, a redhead from Nashville named Peggy whose perfume smelled like a rose garden and whose green eyes and perfect breasts caused a stir in his fatigues. He had gawked at her almost the entire time, and was able to spend about 10 minutes alone with her after the show, just shooting the shit and trying not to get caught glancing down at her prized possessions.

Like everyone else that night, Patrick fell asleep with a smile on his face, and then was rousted in the pre-dawn hours and informed that they were about to embark on an unavoidably dangerous mission, one that had even their fearless commanding officer apprehensive. As Sergeant Major Hound Dog Harriman laid out what company command was asking them to do, Patrick bowed his head, closed his eyes, and cursed the God that his Catholic parents made him believe was really up there looking out for him.

"They're throwing us into the shit today," Hound Dog said, "and I ain't gonna lie to you boys, this is a fucked up mess. Those tits you saw last night might be the last tits some of you will ever see. You get some breakfast, and I want every one of you to write home just in case. I ain't fucking kidding. I seen a lot here, but this ain't good. But we got no choice."

There was a murmuring among the men who were all staring wide-eyed back at this Rock of Gibraltar figure because Hound Dog rarely admitted or showed concern. This guy was the ultimate survivor, a hardened warrior, already on his fourth tour and moving up in rank because the men in Hound Dog's family believed they were put on this earth to do one thing: Fight wars. If there wasn't a war to fight, they didn't know what to do with themselves, and this went back to the Civil War when his great, great, great grandfather fought for the Union and was a hero in the Battle of Gettysburg as he helped beat back the charge of the Confederates at Cemetery Ridge. About 50,000 men lost their lives in those three days at Gettysburg, but not John Robert Harriman.

Patrick saw the uneasiness in Hound Dog's eyes as he explained the mission, and he thought back to the last time his Sergeant gave off this vibe a few months back during Operation Mameluke Trust when Kilo got ambushed and lost five men in a matter of seconds. That day a phrase often recited by the troops rang true: In Vietnam, there were only two types of Marines - the quick, and the dead. It seemed like that might get put to the test again during this mission.

The 3/26 Kilo were tasked with providing security for the main supply route, National Route #1, from the Hai Van Pass at the southern boundary of Thua Thien Province, north to Phu Loc Village. None of this meant much to

Patrick because all of these villages and provinces looked the same to him. But when Hound Dog went over the particular coordinates and pointed them out on the map, everyone snapped to attention because they recognized this was a hot zone of hostile activity, a place where the VC and NVA had inflicted heavy American casualties. They knew how important that stretch of road was to get the motor convoys through, and it had to be kept clear at all cost. The enemy knew this, too, and over the past several weeks, there had been almost daily skirmishes in the region, the firefights growing in intensity as the enemy fortified its positions in the surrounding hills.

The Marines were always ready for a fight no matter how mundane the mission may have seemed, but there would be nothing mundane about this. Hound Dog made them perfectly aware that there was going to be a fight, and the best they could do was to react quickly when it started, hope they could hunker down without anyone perishing, and then rise to the challenge with all their might and secure the road. In other words, be quick or be dead. One thing was certain: This was not going to be a good day. Patrick could only hope it wasn't going to be his last day.

When Hound Dog finished his briefing, corpsman Dan Lamorello, the company medic, headed to the supply tent to load up, and he asked Patrick to give him a hand.

"Doc, I'm scared," Patrick said. "This seems like lambs being led to the slaughter."

"This whole fucking war is lambs to the slaughter, McDonald," Lamorello said as he grabbed extra rolls of gauze and vials of morphine and stuffed them into his bag, then grabbed Patrick by the scruff of his neck and told him, "You're a Marine. You do what you're trained to do and you'll be fine."

When chow was finished, Patrick walked over to the tent he shared with five others, sat on his cot, and did what Hound Dog had demanded. He wrote his death letter.

Dear mom, dad, and Kathleen:

I hope this letter finds you well and enjoying life, liberty, and the ability to go to the bathroom in a toilet, and take a hot shower in private.

Today, we are embarking on one of our most dangerous missions since I've been here, and it's my understanding that you will only receive this letter if I am killed in action. I can't even believe I just wrote that. I'm writing because my Sergeant, Hound Dog Harriman, whom I've told you so much about, ordered us to write just in case things don't go well because it will give us a chance to say goodbye if today is our day.

This is the weirdest, most morbid thing. I feel like I'm writing a suicide note, but I guess it makes sense that he wants us to do this. So many guys never had this opportunity, so I'm glad he thought of it. I respect him so much; he's as tough as they come, but he really cares about all of us.

I've never seen him this worried before a mission, so naturally I'm scared, and that doesn't make me any different than most of the guys here. Dad, I know you know how I feel. It's just that today, I'm more scared than usual. They warned us before we left that this was going to be difficult, and that some of us wouldn't survive. It just seems so insane that they would send us into such a dangerous situation, but that's what this war is.

We have been instructed to secure a main supply route that has been really active lately, and I guess it's just our turn to take a tour up there. The way it was explained to us, this road is super important and has to be kept clear, but the enemy is doing all it can to overrun us in that region.

I hope I made you proud fighting, and dying, for my country. I know it won't be much consolation if you never see me alive again, but I'm proud of myself. When I first got here and saw what it was like, I thought I'd be KIA within a couple weeks. But I have found a way to survive 11 months, and I think I've been a good soldier. I think I was a good friend to my fellow troops, and I was someone who got the job done. I still don't know what we're fighting for over here, but that should not diminish my contribution. I just hope this ends soon, and the dying stops because I've seen way too much of that.

Just know that I love you all very much, and I want to thank you for all you did for me growing up. I couldn't have asked for a better set of parents and sister. Mom, I hope the Democrats win every election for you. Dad, keep on being the greatest sports writer in the country. It was an honor being your son. Kathleen, graduate and change the world, because it needs a lot of changing. You are so special, so smart, so beautiful, and I know you will do great things.

With love, Patrick

After Patrick handed his letter to Hound Dog, the Sergeant gave it back and told him he forgot to stamp it. That meant he hadn't written the word "free" on the envelope where the stamp would normally go, one of the only perks the soldiers received while they were in country: Free mail service from Uncle Sam back home.

"I wish more things in life were free," Patrick said as he wrote the word and gave the envelope back to Hound Dog.

Patrick then began packing for the mission. When he was finished at the supply shed, he did a quick inventory: M-16 rifle in working order; three bandoleers of ammo to strap over his shoulders and across his chest; a pistol belt complete with two pouches to hold four hand grenades, with a smoke grenade and a canteen of water attached to the strap; a ruck sack to carry extra ammo and smoke grenades; a couple flares; a small fold-up shovel for digging fox holes; two days' worth of C-Rats in cans; a rain poncho; extra socks; a toothbrush; cigarettes; and a pen and note paper. About 50 pounds in all to lug around in the stifling jungle heat. Boy scout camp for killers, Patrick liked to say.

Two hours after Hound Dog stored the letters in a canvas bag and shoved them under his cot, the men of Kilo company were on their way into the shit. Literally, for Patrick, as it turned out. The C-123 transport planes had dumped probably thousands of gallons of Agent Orange into the mountainside along their route in the preceding weeks, and the powerful defoliant had started to kill the vegetation and forest, but not enough yet to deprive the enemy of the proper cover they required to execute their ambushes. About two clicks into this journey to the unknown, Patrick began to catch strong whiffs of the stuff, and his mind drifted back to some of the conversations among the guys smarter than him who swore that someday, being exposed to Agent Orange would cause serious health issues for the soldiers. But that was a worry for another day. Today, the focus when Patrick looked up at those chemically-covered hills was spotting any movement by the enemy that would tip off Kilo to a coming firefight.

It was early afternoon, about three hours on the trail under an unrelenting sun, and the men were starting to feel the effects of the heat, and the fear, and Hound Dog was scouting for a covered area to stop and take a break. But then Patrick noticed something that looked suspicious off to his left maybe 20 yards away up a slight incline, barely visible in the foliage, and he alerted Hound Dog who was about 10 yards ahead of him.

"Sergeant," Patrick said, trying his best not to speak too loudly.

Hound Dog turned around, and Patrick pointed to what looked like some kind of man-made structure. Hound Dog put up his fist to halt the march, and then motioned with his head for Patrick to go up and check it out as every man went silent and crouched down.

Patrick slipped through the brush, stepped over some rocks, ever mindful of those deadly Bouncing Betty mines, and came upon a slightly cleared out space which he immediately identified. There were four bamboo poles stuck into the ground with palm fronds positioned on top and on the sides, and in the middle there were two basketball-sized holes dug out.

"Gook shitter," Patrick said, again using a muffled voice.

Hound Dog nodded, and pointed to the ground, meaning that he wanted Patrick to get down on his knees and take a whiff to see if it was active. Patrick did, and the rancid smell made him feel like puking right there. No doubt it was active, and this was not good because that meant the gooks were somewhere close, probably ready to strike at any moment. Patrick stood up, his face contorted from the foul odor, and gave a thumbs up and a nod to Hound Dog that indeed it had been recently used. And just then, out of nowhere it seemed, came the first explosion, and the first two dead Marines on this mission. Al McAfee from Butte, Montana, and Billy Wilson from Tucson were standing side by side maybe 100 feet from the latrine, looking at Patrick as he confirmed that danger was likely imminent, and they were torn to shreds by a rocket-propelled grenade, the fucking Russians' gift to the NVA. They died instantly.

Within a split second came AK-47 artillery fire, and the men of Kilo began hitting the deck, several filled with lead and screaming in agony. Patrick took cover in the disgusting shitter and that gave him a chance to scope where the enemy was attacking from. Hound Dog was doing the same thing down below, but it was difficult to do with your head down trying to avoid getting blown to pieces. Patrick located the muzzle flashes through the thick vegetation, got up on his knees with his M-16 set to automatic and began spilling rounds into the distance, hoping to hit something. The other men who were not yet wounded gained their bearings and began firing as well, but the gooks had established their line and knew exactly how they wanted to attack and they clearly had the upper hand.

Pinned down with no escape, all Kilo Company could do was dig in, return fire, and hope they wouldn't be drawing their last breath today. Hound Dog yelled into the PRC-25 radio for Tactical Air Command support, and after giving the coordinates, he said he'd be sending up red smoke grenades in a few minutes to mark Kilo's exact position. TAC was ready to swoop in because it knew it would likely be needed, and after he was told help would arrive in about two or three minutes, Hound Dog yelled "Roger that, over," and handed the radio back to Lance Corporal Johnny Cannon from Ames, Iowa, who was always on Hound Dog's hip.

"What the hell are we gonna do, Sergeant," a terrified Cannon yelled over the din.

"We're gonna kill as many as we can before they kill us," Hound Dog said, and he wasn't kidding.

The roar of war was all around as Hound Dog tried to plot his response. He could see the NVA had them flanked to the North and West and were trying to push them into a sparsely-vegetated area to the east. Hound Dog knew that was a death wish if he moved the men that way; they had to stay put and wait for TAC to firebomb the shit out of these fuckers. Hound Dog scanned the snake line of men that stretched about 50 yards behind him and began barking his orders. He motioned to Gunnery Sergeant Eugene Mills from Los Angeles and Staff Sergeant Milo Davidson from Fargo, North Dakota to take aim with their M-60s at a position about 60 yards to the west, and he instructed Private First Class Mike Orlowski from Tampa to fire his M-79 grenade launcher toward the North flank. He looked up to where Patrick was taking cover in the latrine, and yelled, "Get some fire out there" so Hound Dog could move down the line to communicate with more of the men.

Patrick gave him a thumbs up, and on Hound Dog's signal, Patrick began providing cover as his crazy commanding officer got on his feet and, in a crouched position, scurried through the gates of hell with Cannon right behind him. Hound Dog made it to his first position just as Patrick had to stop to load the next bandoleer. Hound Dog shouted instructions to PFC Joe DeLuca of Rochester, New York, then looked up at Patrick to see if he was ready, and Patrick was. So, Hound Dog began moving to the next position when the unthinkable happened. In all the chaos, Hound Dog didn't see the trip wire in his path that was attached to a booby-trapped hand grenade. The captain's right foot stepped on the wire, and the grenade that was maybe five feet to his right detonated. The blast tore into Hound Dog's torso, chest, and neck, a devastating direct hit that would have killed most men instantly. Such as Jimmy Cannon, who took shrapnel that tore a hole into his neck and nearly severed his head.

24 - Year of the Pitcher

The last pitcher to win 30 games in a Major League Baseball season had nothing against the newest man to achieve the feat, but according to Hall of Famer Dizzy Dean, the facts were the facts.

Ol' Diz admitted to Jack during a conversation they had on the eve of Game 1 of the World Series that sure, Detroit's Denny McLain enjoyed a momentous year, posting an incomparable 31-6 record to lead the Tigers to the American League pennant. McLain became just the 19th pitcher since the turn of the century to win at least 30 games, but just the third - along with Dean (1934) and Lefty Grove (1931) - to do it since the end of the Deadball Era in 1920. He led the junior circuit in innings (336), starts (41), and complete games (28), and he struck out 280 batters while compiling an earned-run average of 1.96. Great indeed, yet in no way, at least not in Diz's estimation, was McLain a better pitcher, or had he had a finer year, than St. Louis' Bob Gibson.

"I've been saying the last five years that Gibson is the best pitcher in baseball, bar none," Dean crowed to Jack as the two sat in the box seats on the first base side at Busch Stadium watching the Cardinals take batting practice. "If I was Mayo Smith, I wouldn't pitch Denny McLain against Gibson."

264

The inference was that no one, not even McLain, was going to beat Gibson, so why would the Tigers manager sacrifice his ace, as good as he was, opposite Gibson, who had compiled a microscopic, heretofore unheard of earned-run average of 1.12 during the regular season. Pitch McLain, Dean's theory went, in games where he'd be the clear-cut favorite and would be expected to outduel any of the other St. Louis starters such as Nelson Briles, Steve Carlton, Ray Washburn, or Larry Jaster. The next day, Smith paid no heed, sent McLain out for the opener on a gorgeous, sun-splashed, muggy 80-degree afternoon in the country's heartland, and watched Gibson mow down his Tigers as if this were Williamsport, Pennsylvania, and they were representing Detroit in the Little League World Series.

Gibson struck out a World Series record 17 men and the Cardinals coasted to a 4-0 victory, a spectacular beginning to the defense of their 1967 world championship. In a year that had already become known as the year of the pitcher, this was one of the most remarkable pitching performances not only of 1968, but in history. Gibson crafted 144 pitches, permitted four singles, a double, and a walk, and punctuated the afternoon with an exclamation point by striking out the side in the ninth inning - Al Kaline, Norm Cash, and Willie Horton. They had combined during the regular season for 71 home runs and 201 RBI - to shatter ex-Dodger great Sandy Koufax's record of 15 strikeouts in Game 1 of the 1963 Fall Classic against the Yankees.

Gibson's 17 whiffs tied a Cardinal team record set by none other than Dean himself in 1933, and left baseball observers with their mouths agape. "Great pitchers like me and Gibson don't fool around with the hitters," Dean told Jack and a knot of other scribes outside the Cardinals clubhouse after the dominating Game 1 performance. "We both like to throw the ball with something on it, and we don't throw to spots. When you pitch to spots and go for the corners, you take something away from your power pitch."

Gibson's emergence from the ghettos of Omaha, Nebraska to World Series record-breaker was a fascinating tale, particularly when you consider the fork in the road he faced when his college days at Creighton University came to an end. Who knows what would have become of Gibson if, in 1958, Cardinals general manager Bing Devine hadn't waived a $4,000 bonus contract offer at him with the caveat that he quit playing basketball and concentrate solely on baseball? Meadowlark Lemon, the ringleader of the world-famous Harlem Globetrotters, had a pretty good inkling. "I thought Bob was a better basketball player than a baseball player," Lemon once said of Gibson, his teammate for four months bridging the end of 1957 with the beginning of 1958. "I think Bob could have played with any NBA team. He was that good." Perhaps, but a decade later, it was certainly looking like Gibson made the proper career choice.

The youngest of Pack and Victoria Gibson's seven children was born in 1935, three months after Pack died of tuberculosis. As if that wasn't enough of a hardship as the

266

Great Depression was still choking the life out of families, particularly Negro families, Gibson spent much of his dirt-poor childhood dealing with a heart murmur, hay fever, asthma, and rickets - a disease caused by Vitamin D deficiency characterized by imperfect calcification, softening, and distortion of bones. Still, Gibson overcame his health issues and blossomed into an outstanding athlete, starring for the local recreation center basketball and baseball teams established by his older brother, Josh. When Gibson reached high school, he gravitated toward basketball, due in part to his skill for the game, but also because the baseball coach at Omaha Technical High would not allow him to try out for his team because he was black. When a new coach took over in his senior year, Gibson was welcomed to the team and became the first black student at the school to play baseball, six years after Jackie Robinson broke the color barrier in Major League Baseball.

Gibson could switch hit, play all three outfield positions, catch, and did a little pitching, yet while he excelled in his one year on the varsity, he felt basketball was going to be his ticket to college. The two-time all-state forward dreamed of playing at Indiana University, only to be rebuffed in a letter sent by the school informing him that it already had its quota of Negro players. Cardinals scout Runt Marr had seen him play baseball, and offered a modest minor league contract, but Josh demanded Bob go to college, and he wound up at Josh's alma mater, Creighton, right there in his hometown of Omaha, the first black to attend on a basketball scholarship. By the time he graduated he was the Blue Jays' all-time career leader in scoring average (20.2 points per game). Each spring he would suit up for the baseball team just for the fun of it, thinking all along that he would eventually make a career in professional basketball.

However, his prowess on the hardwood drew very little interest from the NBA, and with so many minor-league baseball teams to fill, baseball scouts took keen notice of Gibson's senior year performance, a 6-2 pitching record and a .333 batting average that was tops in the Nebraska College Conference. He was no bonus baby phenom, but bird dogs from the Yankees, White Sox, Athletics, Dodgers, Phillies, and Cardinals all inquired about whether he'd be interested in signing after graduation. Baseball seemed the prudent choice, but basketball had a grip on him, especially after Gibson played a game against the Globetrotters when the traveling troupe passed through Omaha, and he was told afterward by owner Abe Saperstein that he'd like to sign Gibson to a players' contract.

Gibson saw this as a way to attract the attention of the NBA, and he agreed to join the Globetrotters on one condition: Saperstein would let him play minor league baseball in the Cardinals' system that summer of 1957, and then join the Globetrotters after the baseball season. Saperstein agreed, but after four months on the road, the ultra-competitive Gibson grew tired of the carnival aspect of the Globetrotters where winning the games was secondary to entertaining the masses. Devine sealed Gibson's basketball fate with the bonus offer, and Gibson left the Globetrotters to pursue a career in baseball that now was clearly headed for one destination: The Hall of Fame.

Gibson made his major-league debut with the Cardinals in 1959, earned his first All-Star Game invitation in 1962 when he won 15 games, then over the next five years won 18, 19, 20, 21, and 13 games, and led St. Louis to World Series championships in 1964 and 1967, winning the MVP in both.

Now came this dazzling display in Game 1 against the Tigers, followed by another superb outing in St. Louis' rain-plagued 10-1 triumph in Game 4 at Tiger Stadium when he allowed just five hits while striking out 10 to give the Cardinals a commanding three games to one lead. Thus, when the resilient Tigers won the next two to force a deciding Game 7, Gibson took the mound having won seven of his eight career World Series starts, completing all eight and allowing a mere 13 earned runs while striking out 84 and walking 16 for an ERA of 1.62. No man in baseball history had ever won seven straight World Series starts, and with a record five games recording at least 10 strikeouts, he was now two ahead of the second-place man on that list, Koufax.

Had it not been for one bad inning in Game 7 - the top of the seventh at Busch Stadium when the Tigers touched him for three runs after he'd retired the first two men easily, snapping a scoreless tie and keying their 4-1 Series-clinching victory - Gibson very possibly would have pitched the Cardinals to their third championship in five years, and taken home his third World Series MVP award.

Instead, that honor went to Detroit's portly portsider, Mickey Lolich, who pitched the Tigers to victories in Games 2 and 5, and then, on just two days' rest, outdueled Gibson in the deciding seventh game, giving up five hits and a meaningless run with two outs in the ninth inning.

"You all thought I was an improbable hero, but I came sneaking through," Lolich said to the gathered media inside the sweaty, raucous visitors' clubhouse. "There's always been somebody ahead of me. A hitter like Al Kaline, a pitcher like Denny. It was always somebody else; never Mickey Lolich. But now my day has finally come. It's wonderful, isn't it, to take a shower in champagne?"

Of course, this was the only way the 1968 baseball season could end; in the year of the pitcher, someone would hurl a brilliant game, though Gibson, not Lolich, was the likely source. During this scoring-challenged season there had been 339 shutouts, 82 games had ended 1-0, and only six batters had topped .300 (Boston's Carl Yastrzemski being the only man in the AL). It was enough to create panic in the commissioner's office, and baseball's hierarchy was already discussing rule changes for 1969 to help the hitters by lowering the mound, and shrinking the strike zone. Yet of all the pitching feats accomplished, leave it to Don Drysdale - who earlier in the season had set major league records for consecutive shutouts (6) and scoreless innings pitched (58 2/3) - to sum up just how good Gibson had been. "Bob Gibson with a 1.12 ERA; that's almost obscene," Drysdale said before the Series began.

Gibson finished with a record of 22-9, completing 28 of his 34 starts with 13 shutouts and a league-low average of 5.8 hits allowed per nine innings. In the six games he did not finish, he was lifted for a pinch-hitter, meaning he was never relieved all season. In the nine games he lost, the Cardinals scored one or zero runs five times, and provided a total of just 17 runs overall. There was one stretch in the summer when he gave up two runs in 95 innings (one of which scored on his own wild pitch) as he put together five straight shutouts, nearly matching Drysdale before the newsprint had dried on the recounting of Big D's record.

Game 1 of the Series was his show as he outclassed McLain, who was lifted for a pinch hitter after five innings having allowed three runs (two earned) on three hits and wondering what the hell Mayo Smith was thinking. "I just had bad control," McLain said. "I was making good pitches, but they weren't going where I wanted them to go." Jack listened to McLain's explanation, then asked him what he thought of being pulled. "Yes, I was very surprised. When you pitch 336 innings like I pitched this year and get yanked, yes, you have to be surprised. He didn't tell me anything; he just sent somebody up there." But giving Gibson his due, McLain added, "That's the greatest pitching performance I've ever seen by anybody."

Lolich sent up a warning flare in Game 2 with a complete game 8-1 victory as he gave up six hits and struck out nine while his teammates battered four Redbird hurlers for 13 hits. Lolich even hit his first big league home run.

The Series shifted to Detroit and St. Louis' Ray Washburn and Joe Hoerner shut down the Tigers on four hits for a 7-3 victory while Tim McCarver ripped a go-ahead three-run homer in the fifth inning. Tigers star Al Kaline recognized the problems this loss created because looming in Game 4 was Gibson. "I'm not saying I don't think we can beat Gibson, I'm saying it's going to be tough," Kaline said. "You have to respect the guy, he's the toughest in pressure situations."

Gibson was tough no matter what the situation, and Kaline was proven correct when Gibson locked up the Tigers again, and assisted his own cause with a home run, the second of his World Series career, giving him another line all his own in the record book. McLain was again the foil, and he gave up four runs on six hits before a 74-minute rain delay - which had come after the game had originally been delayed 35 minutes - ended his day. Leadoff man Lou Brock had a double, triple, and home run, drove in four runs, scored twice, and stole a base.

However, with three cracks to win the Series, the Cardinals failed each time. Brock opened Game 5 with a double, scored on Curt Flood's one-out single, and Orlando Cepeda crashed a two-run homer. Four batters into the game Lolich was down 3-0, but over the next 8 1/3 innings, the Cardinals never scored again. Detroit pulled within 3-2 in the fourth, then won it in the seventh when Kaline's bases-loaded single plated the tying and go-ahead runs and Cash tacked on an insurance run with a RBI single, both off Hoerner who had relieved Nelson Briles.

Game 6 was a romp, 13-1 for the Tigers, as Jim Northrup's grand slam highlighted a 10-run third inning that gave McLain - coming back after his short Game 4 stint – his 32nd and final win of the season.

So on to Game 7, Gibson vs. Lolich, and for six innings the combatants matched 1968-style zeros, the year of the pitcher, as it were. In the bottom of the sixth, the Cardinals scratched out two singles, but Lolich picked off Brock, the best base stealer in the world, and then he picked off Flood to squelch any potential uprising. "I can't remember picking off two men in one game, let alone one inning," Lolich said.

Right there, the game tilted in Detroit's favor and the Tigers pounced on the opening in the top of the seventh. Gibson struck out Mickey Stanley and induced Kaline to ground to third and all seemed fine for St. Louis as Gibson had now retired 20 of the first 21 men he'd faced. But then Cash singled to right, Horton singled to left, and Northrup hit a laser to center field. At first, it looked as if it would be the third out. Instead, Flood, one of the finest center fielders in the game, misread the flight and took three steps in, realized his mistake, and couldn't catch up to the ball as it soared just over his outstretched glove and rolled to the wall. Northrup pulled into third with a two-run triple, then trotted home when Bill Freehan doubled to left-center. "I don't want to make alibis; I should have made the play, but I didn't and that's all there is to it," said Flood. Gibson refused to blame his road roommate, saying only, "There's no way you can win if you don't score runs."

And the Cardinals couldn't do it. In their final three at-bats they had one batter reach via an error in the seventh, one by a single in the eighth, and then Mike Shannon hit a solo home run with two out in the ninth before McCarver fouled out to Freehan behind the plate to end it.

"I think I pitched well enough to win in most circumstances," said Gibson, "but the other guy pitched a better game."

It wasn't too often that Gibson could ever say that, especially in 1968 when he was the best pitcher in the year of the pitcher.

25 - DEROS

Patrick McDonald had been counting the days to DEROS almost from the moment 11 months earlier when the DC-6 transport plane dumped him into the cesspool that was Vietnam. Date Eligible for Return from OverSeas. December 20, 1968. That date was burned in Patrick's memory, and his sole purpose in life was to make sure he still had a life when the calendar flipped to December 20. That's when the Marine Corps would thank him for his service and let him go home to begin the transition into becoming a human being again. They gave you the option to sign up for another tour after some R&R, and some guys like Hound Dog Harriman did it because they felt Vietnam was where they belonged. Patrick knew Vietnam was not where he belonged. Sayonara, shit hole. He just prayed he'd make it to the day when he could say that.

By now Patrick was a short-timer, meaning a Marine who was in the final stage of his 13-month tour in country. The Marines had an accompanying saying that went along with DEROS. It was comprised of the number of days he had remaining on his stint, followed by the word "wakeup." In Patrick's case, when he had risen from his bunk on this hot and steamy Vietnam morning, swatting the incessant gnats away from his face, he mumbled to himself "58 and wakeup." Fifty-eight days until he'd wake up, pack his gear, and get on the first DC-6 leaving from the air base in Da Nang, destination civilization.

Patrick had learned many things during his time as a grunt, and one was that war was a highly individualized experience for each soldier. In many ways, his father Jack told him, it was a little like baseball in this respect: You are part of a battalion of men and you must work together for the greater good of the mission, just as in baseball you are part of a team focused on the singular goal of winning the game. But in baseball, when you're in that batters' box, it's just you against the pitcher. Your teammates can't help you hit the curveball, or get good wood on the heater. And in war, you are encapsulated within your own personal war where your primary objective is to get in, get out, and never look back. From the day you arrive until the day you are lucky enough to depart, a Marine is embroiled in his own struggle to reach his end game alive, with limbs and vital organs intact, and his mind still functioning. And if everyone else in the battalion, the division, the regiment, the company, does the same, you share the bond of survival of the fittest. Or maybe better put, the luckiest. Hooo raahhh!

As the days ticked ever so slowly off Patrick's calendar and his DEROS came into focus, Patrick also came to understand that it was only human nature to feel a bit more trepidation than normal about going out on a mission. He had seen this throughout his time at war, dozens of men who became skittish on patrols because they knew they were so close, yet so far away. Never was it more apparent than in the last couple months of active duty, where every step in those shitty jungles could be your last, and what a shame it would be to almost make it out alive because almost doesn't count. You lived with that fear every day, but it multiplied the shorter your time became, and in many cases men fought to toe the fine line between their mortality and the mission almost as hard as they fought Charlie.

As the men of Kilo Company tip-toed down National Route #1, their necks in perpetual pivot, their eyes wide open, and their hearts beating out of their chests, Patrick and his comrades knew that line had never been finer. They had been in some deep shit the past few months, starting with that mess at Khe Sahn, and then Operation Mameluke Thrust, but this just felt so different. The enemy was lurking, almost salivating, in the hills that bracketed this road, and while they couldn't see those crafty gook bastards, they knew they were there, ready to pounce. The quick and the dead. The Marines who weren't quick on this day were going to be the Marines who would be dead. But no one could have imagined one of the dead was going to be Hound Dog.

He didn't die right away. The pain screamed from every pore in his body as the blood gurgled out of the holes created by the grenade blast. Patrick couldn't believe what had happened, and before he could process it, his first instinct took over and he leaped out from his cover in the latrine and began running down the hill to his fallen commanding officer. Fuck DEROS. Fuck it all. As soon as he emerged, the enemy took notice, then took aim, but somehow Patrick made it to Hound Dog's shredded body without taking a hit. When he got there and saw Hound Dog's innards exposed, he knew there was nothing that could be done. This tough bastard, from the toughest family Patrick had ever heard of, was toast. But he wasn't dead. Not yet. He looked up at Patrick, somehow managed to lift his left arm so he could grab Patrick's collar to pull him down close, and in a gravelly voice barely above a whisper, he told Patrick to "Mail those fucking letters." Patrick nodded, and seconds later, Hound Dog's eyes fell shut forever.

There was no time to mourn. Kilo Company was now rudderless, its leader gone, under fierce attack, and Patrick's only thought was to get himself and as many of the men as he could out of this death trap alive. Kill them before they kill us, as Hound Dog would say. It wasn't his responsibility; there were others who out-ranked him, but he was the man who was right next to the dead bodies of Hound Dog and Jimmy Cannon, in possession of the radio and the region map, and he needed to act. He crawled over to Jimmy and winced at the mortal wound that had nearly torn his head off, grabbed the PRC-25 radio and barked into the handset, hoping someone would answer at the other end.

"Command, command! This is Private First Class McDonald, Kilo Company, over! We're taking heavy fire, Sergeant Major Harriman is dead, we need TAC support immediately, over!"

The radio crackled to life within seconds, and some Major told Patrick to calm down, help was on the way, and he double-checked the last coordinates Hound Dog had provided, then asked Patrick if he could confirm where they were. Patrick found the map in Hound Dog's ruck sack, nervously stared at it trying to decipher the area, and was able to confirm Kilo's position.

"Ninety seconds out, send up your red smoke grenades so we can pinpoint your location, over."

"Roger that, over," Patrick said, and then set the handset down.

The gooks did not let up. The attack continued mercilessly, and knowing they had inflicted damage, they were smelling blood. It seemed hopeless, like there was no way out of this mess as tracers were zipping past Patrick as he tried to locate company medic Dan Lamorello. When he found him about 20 yards behind his position, it looked like he was working on someone, though Patrick couldn't tell who it was. Just then, a rocket-propelled grenade detonated equidistance between Patrick and Lamorello, and PFC Willie Shaw from Athens, Georgia was in its deadly path.

The explosion was followed by Shaw's primal screams of agony because his right leg was completely severed. Again, Patrick's instinct surged and he grabbed the radio and the map, and crawled the 10 yards to where Shaw was lying there, blood squirting from the upper part of his leg that was still attached to his body. He was nearly overcome by the ghastly sight, but kept his shit together and tried to comfort Shaw as he removed the trouser leg of the fatigues from the torn off limb, and tried to stanch the bleeding.

Shaw was clawing at Patrick, pleading for help, and Patrick knew he needed to get some morphine from Lamorello's bag.

"Hang on, hang on, Willie, lemme go get some medicine from the doc, he's right over there," Patrick said.

"No, no, no, don't leave me man, don't leave me!"

"Willie, you gotta lemme get the morphine man, I'll be right back."

Patrick pried himself loose and despite the danger, rose to his feet and sprinted the short distance to Lamorello, diving on his belly when he got there.

"Doc, Shaw's leg is cut right off; I need morphine!"

Lamorello was working feverishly on a wound in PFC Ziggy Donato's chest and couldn't leave the funny kid with the three packs a day smoking habit from New York City.

"In there," he said, pointing to his bag. "Take what you need. You remember what to do?"

"Yeah, yeah, I got it."

"Did you call for air support?"

"Yeah, I gotta send up smoke grenades," Patrick said.

Patrick grabbed the morphine and some gauze, nodded to Lamorello, then retreated to whence he came. He was a few feet from Shaw and ready to hit the ground when he felt the searing pain of an AK-47 round tear into his right shoulder, just above his chest. And before the blood had even started to squirt, a second round caught him in the left thigh.

Patrick's eyes rolled to the back of his head, the intense pain washing through him, and everything went hazy as he lay there not sure if he was alive or dead. He could still hear Shaw screaming, could still hear explosions all around, so that was his indication that while he wasn't the quickest Marine, he wasn't yet a dead Marine. Somehow, he had managed to keep his grip on the morphine syrettes and the gauze intended for Shaw. After a few seconds of gaining his wits, Patrick surmised that despite the pain he was in, Shaw was worse off, and he could still try to help his comrade. He rolled onto his stomach and crawled back, his movements greatly hindered by his wounds. He made it to Shaw, but before he could attend to him, he reached into his ruck sack, fished out his smoke grenade, pulled the pin and let it fly. Then he found another on Shaw, and did the same, hoping that was enough to identify their location so the B-52s wouldn't douse them with the coming napalm. Patrick turned back to Shaw who had quieted down because he was slipping into unconsciousness. He plunged a syrette into Shaw's upper thigh, then removed the blood-soaked pant leg and wrapped all the gauze he had on Shaw's exposed stump, hoping that it would be enough to prevent Shaw from bleeding out.

All that work had taken Patrick's mind off his own pain, but as he sat there holding the gauze in place, he knew he had to do something to manage his own wounds or he might black out and be no use to Shaw. He had grabbed an extra syrette from Lamorello in case one wasn't enough for Shaw, but now he needed it for himself, so he plunged it into his leg. Just then, PFC Billy Watkins of Chapel Hill, North Carolina arrived to see if he could help.

"Cut my shirt off, then cut it in half," Patrick said. "Take one part and wrap it around my leg, and take the other and wrap it around my shoulder."

Watkins did what he was told while Patrick reached down to grab the radio headset.

"Command, command, this is PFC McDonald, Kilo Company, over. Red smoke is up, we need that air strike now, over."

"Kilo Company, we're on the way, thirty seconds out. What's the situation, over?"

"Still hot sir, still taking fire. We've got some wounded, some dead, we're gonna need the Hueys fast, sir, over."

"Hang tight Kilo, we'll get you outta there. B-52s should be in range. Get ready, over."

Watkins worked to get Patrick's bleeding under control, while Patrick tried to keep pressure on Shaw's horrific wound, and then came that beautiful moan of the B-52s arriving, and then the hot orange fire bombs exploding on the enemy, burning those bastards to a crisp. Three strikes in all, a devastating blow to the enemy, and as the planes flew away, all you could hear from those hills across the way were the gooks who survived, screaming as their flesh melted.

Within minutes, a Dustoff Huey crew - Dedicated Unhesitating Service To Our Fighting Forces - found an open area to land, and they were able to get Patrick and the rest of the wounded out of there. Before he was loaded onto the helicopter, Patrick waved Lamorello over to where he was laying on a canvas stretcher.

"You did good, soldier," Lamorello said as he inspected the two dressings that covered the holes in Patrick's body. "You saved Shaw's life. He's going home without a leg, but he woulda been going home in a box if not for you. You know what they say, 'the face of the coward is the back of his head as he runs from the battle.' Shaw saw your face."

Patrick managed a smile, but then remembered the seven men who were going home in boxes because of what had happened in this miserable region. "Doc, Hound Dog gave me a job, but I ain't gonna be able to do it, so can you?"

"Sure thing."

"He stashed the bag of letters under his cot. He told me to mail the ones for the guys who might die. Can you take care of that?"

Lamorello looked at Patrick, his young face covered with jungle grime, his body ravaged by two bullet holes, and he couldn't help but respect this kid for his courage and bravery and his compassion for his departed fellow soldiers.

"Done. And I'll rip yours up because guess what? It's DEROS day for you, Patrick McDonald from Garden City, New York."

26 – Gloved Fists

On the very day that Jack nearly lost his life - June 6, 1944, the historic D-Day landings at Normandy when Jack took a Nazi bullet to the shoulder which ended his service in World War II - the seventh of James and Dora Smith's 12 children was born in Clarksville, Texas. That coincidence, that tiny morsel of a connection, combined with the fact that Tommie Smith was also going to be a gold medal favorite, automatically qualified the sprinter as the athlete Jack wanted most to meet and perhaps profile for *SportsWorld*'s special edition preview of the 1968 Summer Olympics. So, between Arthur Ashe's historic triumph at the U.S. Open, and Detroit's World Series victory over St.

Louis, Jack had flown out to Lake Tahoe for the United States men's and women's track and field Olympic Trials.

It was there, nearly a mile and a half above sea level amidst the majestic pine trees of the Sierra Nevada mountains, where Jack broke through Smith's initial wariness of the far too inquisitive white man with the notebook and all the questions. And Jack's hours of interaction with Smith in the days leading up to the competition revealed a compelling story marked by impoverished beginnings, a young life of hard work and hardship, his overcoming every obstacle to achieve athletic excellence, and the accrual throughout his journey of sociological awareness and a corresponding steely courage to stand up and rail against the indignities heaped on all blacks, but in particular what he and his fellow black athletes had encountered in their climb to the pinnacle of sport, the Olympics.

Yet Jack could not have imagined just how captivating a figure Smith would become a few weeks later, in the moments after his glorious dash to the 200-meter gold medal. Only then, on that October 16 evening, did Jack truly recognize the depth and the spirit and the bravery of Tommie Smith, when he and fellow American and bronze medalist John Carlos stood on the medals podium in front of 50,000 people in the Olympic Stadium and millions more across the world watching on television and made a statement that would never be forgotten.

There they were, carrying their shoes to reveal black socks that represented black poverty. Smith wore a black scarf and Carlos black beads to signify the lynchings their people had suffered. And most noticeably, each man raised a black-gloved fist into the air as the *Star-Spangled Banner* played, striking a blow not so much for the rise of Black Power, but to protest American society's continued and repulsive failure to allow all men to be equal, regardless of their color.

In the near week Jack spent in Lake Tahoe with Smith and some of the other athletes including Carlos, Lee Evans, Leon Coleman, Bob Beamon, Larry James, Jim Hines, Charlie Greene, Ralph Boston, Willie Davenport, Erv Hall, Ronnie Ray Smith, Mel Pender, Ron Freeman and Vince Matthews, no one ever talked about doing something demonstrative should they be so fortunate to be in the position of having a medal draped around their neck. Yet as soon as Smith and Carlos walked back onto the track for the ceremony, and Jack noticed their stocking feet, he could sense something was coming. When it came, it was as poignant a moment as Jack could ever remember witnessing at an athletic venue. "It was not a gesture of hate; it was a gesture of frustration," Smith told Jack afterward.

It may not have had the significance of Rosa Parks refusing to sit in the back of the bus in Birmingham; of James Meredith - with the help of President Kennedy and the National Guard - integrating the University of Mississippi campus; or of Vivian Malone and James A. Hood doing the same at the University of Alabama, walking right past indignant Governor George Wallace who had famously stated, "segregation now, segregation tomorrow, segregation forever." But in the world of sports, America's playground in comparison to the mayhem that was gripping the country and other parts of the world in 1968, theirs was a colossal gesture, a throwing down of the gauntlet to declare that the United States would not be whole until it changed its ways regarding race relations. What these two young men were trying to prove is that even though a few months earlier a white man murdered Dr. Martin Luther King, Jr., his dream of equality for all men would never die, not if they had any say in the matter.

When Jack initially approached Smith about writing the profile, Smith rebuked his effort, and it was not hard to understand why. Given the climate, why should Smith trust Jack? For all he knew, Jack was just another in the Caucasian-dominated media who had an agenda aimed at denouncing the cause, and he certainly had quite a platform to advance it, the pages of the nationally-renowned *Sports World*. Talking to Jack could potentially be a tremendous mistake, but when Jack told Smith where he was on the day 24 years ago when Smith was born, Smith smiled and said, "You had that one in your back pocket, didn't you?" Jack smiled back, and Smith - who had been a member of the Army ROTC in college - said, "Sir, I respect any man who fought for his country, so I'll answer your questions."

Once Smith was comfortable, he opened his soul like a faucet, details pouring out about a life Jack could not have fathomed. Smith was born to a cotton sharecropper father and an Indian mother. James Smith taught himself how to read by studying the Bible when he wasn't out in the fields picking cotton, or tending to the hogs and cows. The family moved from shack to shack in Texas, wherever there was cotton for James and his sons to pick, until one day he sold the animals and told Dora and the children to pack their meager belongings; they were getting on a bus headed for Northern California, in search of a better life.

James wanted his children to be educated, so while he continued to pick cotton in the sprawling fields of the San Joaquin Valley, Tommie went to school. Learning was a struggle, but he persevered, and by the time he reached the seventh grade, his magnificent body began to fill out and his natural athleticism had coaches clamoring. He out-ran every kid who ever sidled up next to him, and when he advanced to Lemoore High School, he became the star of the football, basketball, and track teams. As a junior, he ran the 100-yard dash in 9.6 seconds and long-jumped 23 feet. He also began running the 200 and the 440, and as his times decreased, colleges began to take notice and he ultimately accepted a track-basketball scholarship to attend nearby San Jose State.

It wasn't long before Smith realized his future was in track, so he opted out of playing basketball, and became one of legendary track coach Bud Winter's superstars at a time when the program was an incubator for aspiring Olympians. At various points during Smith's enrollment, Carlos, Evans and Ronnie Ray Smith were Spartans, and Smith told Jack that during those days, world records were being set about every two weeks. Counting his participation in relays, Smith alone broke or tied 13 records before he graduated with a bachelor's degree in Social Science.

When he wasn't setting cinder and tartan tracks ablaze, Smith was growing intellectually, his learning difficulties behind him, and he was becoming acutely aware of the angry world he was living in and how stacked the odds were for men and women of his color. It was at this time Smith met Harry Edwards, a former discus thrower at San Jose State who went on to earn his Masters' degree from Cornell and had returned to San Jose State as a visiting sociology professor. With the campus becoming a magnet for black activism even though its black population was minuscule, Edwards possessed the strongest, most piercing voice regarding the abhorrent treatment of black people in the U.S.

Though his pulpit was microscopic compared to that of Dr. King's, he had begun to make a name for himself, particularly when he challenged the segregation policies of renting apartments in the campus area. He founded the United Black Students for Action, and that group's vociferousness and the potential for a race riot led to the cancellation of San Jose State's 1967 football season opener against Texas-El Paso, the first collegiate athletic event ever cancelled under the threat of racial protest. Through that opprobrium, the UBSA transformed into the Olympic Project for Human Rights, and under the banner of the OPHR, Edwards called for the meeting of top black athletes in Los Angeles to discuss the merits of boycotting the '68 Olympics.

At that gathering, which Dr. King learned of and gave his blessing to, a set of demands to the U.S. Olympic Committee were drafted. The first was the barring of South Africa from the Mexico Games due to its apartheid practices. They asked that International Olympic Committee president Avery Brundage resign because of his allegedly racist views, both against blacks and Jews. They requested a black man be added to the U.S. Olympic Committee. And in a matter unrelated to the USOC, they sought the rescinding of Muhammad Ali's recent ban from boxing for refusing to go to Vietnam, and that he be reinstated as heavyweight champion. If the demands were not met, the black athletes would not represent the U.S. in Mexico.

Brundage took umbrage to the power play and responded, "If these boys are serious, they're making a very bad mistake. If they're not serious and are using the Olympic Games for publicity purposes, we don't like it." This from a man who, in 1936 at Adolf Hitler's Berlin Games, convinced the U.S. Olympic Committee to bench Jewish sprinters Marty Glickman and Sam Stoller for the 400-meter relay race because the Americans were clearly going to win, and he feared a Jew receiving a gold medal would be a tremendous embarrassment to the fuhrer. The same man who, two years later, was paid back by Hitler when the madman awarded Brundage's construction firm the contract to build the German embassy in the United States. The same man who, in 1940, had been kicked out of the America First Committee, a Nazi solidarity group that was trying to keep the U.S. out of the war in Europe, for being too pro-Hitler. This man, Brundage, was calling into question the ethics of a potential black athlete boycott?

In a bizarre period of time early in 1968, the IOC did indeed kick South Africa out of the Olympics, inexplicably reversed course and re-admitted the country, then ultimately bowed to overwhelming dissidence from several nations including the Soviet Union and told the South Africans that in the best interest of the Games, they should stay away. Not surprisingly, Brundage did not resign, Ali remained banned from boxing, and not until after the '68 Olympics was African-American Jesse Owens - the four-time gold medal winner from the Berlin Games - given a position on the USOC.

Though the intentions of OPHR were notable, as the summer of '68 approached, the black athletes were not unified, split almost down the middle on whether to go through with the boycott. Some were militantly in favor, such as UCLA basketball star Lew Alcindor who decided he wasn't going to play on the U.S. team, boycott or no boycott, and didn't. Others were opposed because as 100-meter gold medal favorite Jim Hines opined, they had worked so hard to have the chance to participate in the Olympics and the best way to make a statement would be to win a medal, preferably gold, and prove their superiority. Smith was clearly on the fence, but when the threat of the boycott dissolved, he never had to take a side.

With the boycott off the table, Smith's attention turned to making the team, and the Trials at Echo Summit were a thing to behold. This site, with its running track oddly wrapped around tall stands of pine trees and huge granite boulders which blocked the view of the races at certain points, was picked for the Trials because it was slightly higher in elevation than Mexico City's breathtaking 7,350 feet and thus would be an ideal place to prepare for the lung-taxing thin air the athletes would be competing in at the Games. Four world records were broken - Carlos (19.7 seconds in the 200 meters), Evans (44.0 in the 400 meters), Geoff Vanderstock (48.8 in the 400-meter hurdles), and Bob Seagren (17 feet, 9 inches in the pole vault) - and when the tallying was complete it was clear this would be one of the strongest track and field teams the U.S. had ever assembled. It was so good that Smith finished second to Carlos in the 200 final, securing his place on the team, though he was confident that once he got to Mexico he would win the gold and do something to focus the world's attention on America's racial divide.

He partly intimated that when interviewed by ABC sportscaster Jim McKay at the Trials. Smith was asked about the status of the boycott and he said it was his belief it was off, but went on to add, "Jim, I can't give you no concrete evidence or no concrete answers on what might happen at Mexico City; all I can say is you can expect almost anything."

The American men went on to dominate the track and field competition, winning 12 gold medals, seven by black athletes. Smith in the 200, Hines in the 100, Evans in the 400, Willie Davenport in the 110 hurdles, and Bob Beamon with an astonishing world record leap in the long jump. Also, blacks comprised all of the positions on both the 400- and 1,600-meter relay teams. Six other medals were won by black American men, including Carlos' bronze in the 200 when he somehow was edged out for the silver by Australia's Peter Norman.

Overall, it was a superb two weeks for the American Olympic team. They ruled the pool as the men and women's swimming and diving teams combined to win 23 golds. In boxing, George Foreman won the heavyweight gold, Ronnie Harris the lightweight gold. In basketball, the U.S. remained undefeated all-time in the Olympic tournament (63-0) and captured the gold for the seventh consecutive Olympiad as Jo Jo White, Spencer Haywood, and Charlie Scott played the starring roles, the tournament culminating with a 65-50 victory over Yugoslavia.

Perhaps it was a shame that so much of the American success, and the fact that it took home more gold (45) and total medals (107) than any other nation, was overshadowed by what took place on that victory rostrum in the grand stadium. Or, as Jack conveyed in his column, perhaps those riveting moments when those two gloved hands were thrust into the air would bring about change in a country that so desperately needed to change.

Smith, wearing bib number 307, set an Olympic record of 20.37 seconds in winning his first 200 heat, won the quarterfinal in 20.28, and shaved another smidgen of time off with a 20.14 in winning his semifinal. Carlos ran the fastest heat, a 20.12 in his semifinal, setting the stage for a captivating final, provided Smith could run. There was high drama at the stadium when Smith felt a twinge in his left thigh just as he crossed the finish line in his last heat and he immediately reached for the muscle, admitting afterward that with all the hate mail he had received the past year, he actually at first thought he might have been shot. As he slowed to a jog and then to a stop on the track, he was limping noticeably and there were murmurs throughout the crowd as the announcer on television intoned that this could be disastrous for Smith, possibly the difference between a gold medal and nothing at all. Smith bent over in pain, his hands on his knees, as a fellow competitor, Edwin Roberts from Trinidad and Tobago, offered a caring pat on the back and unlaced and removed Smith's shoes for him.

With the final just two hours later there was grave concern Smith wouldn't be ready. Instead, the American trainers iced him down, his old San Jose coach Bud Winter worked him out in a practice area, and as the start of the race neared Smith gave the nod that he felt he was good to go. Smith was in lane three, Carlos in lane four, and at the gun both men started cleanly, Carlos exploding to the early lead, Smith comfortably paced. At the turn Carlos was a meter and a half ahead, and while Smith was running smooth and feeling no effects from the thigh injury, he knew he'd have to find a kick or he wasn't going to catch his teammate. He did, reaching an otherworldly gear with just under 100 meters to go, his powerful stride in perfect form, and once he caught Carlos there was no stopping him. He ran an immaculate race and 15 meters from the tape he knew it was over. Not only did he win, he did it in a world record time of 19.83 seconds which may have been fractionally better had he not extended his arms in premature glee to resemble a jet - Tommie Jet they often called him - before crossing the line with a proud and beaming smile on his dark face. Carlos fell victim to the surprising Norman's late charge, and the Australian nipped him for the silver.

The race was historic, the first sub 20-second time ever. What happened thereafter was more historic. Smith huddled with Carlos to share his plan when they made it to the medals stand. "I'm with you," was Carlos' reply. As Smith and Carlos were preparing themselves, Norman said, "I believe in what you believe in, and I want to help." Smith had no response because truthfully, what could Norman do? Besides, he only had two gloves. Well, what Norman did was notice an OPHR pin, the same one being worn by Smith and Carlos, affixed to the jacket of a member of the U.S. rowing team named Paul Hoffman. Norman asked if he could borrow it, Hoffman gladly obliged, and off Norman went to make his own personal protest and cement his place in history as the white man in the iconic photo that shows two black men behind him in black stocking feet with black gloved fists raised high.

You see, Norman knew racism, and appalled it. Growing up in Australia in a devout Salvation Army family that believed strongly in equality for all men, Norman had seen his country long deny basic human rights to its own Aboriginal people, going so far as to take their children and give them to white families to be raised, in some cases the white men raping the black girls "to breed the blackness out of them" as stated in the White Australia Policy. Only a year before had Australia awarded citizenship to its Aborigines, though acceptance was tepid at best. This was Norman's opportunity to support the Americans' cause, but to speak out against his own nation.

If Smith was nervous before the race, he was more nervous after, and when Jack asked what was going through his mind in the moments before the ceremony, he said, "I was praying underneath the bleachers, I was praying on the walk up to the victory stand, and I was praying the entire time I was up there."

Naturally, there was a firestorm, led of course by Brundage. Officially, the U.S. Olympic Committee announced the next day it was suspending Smith and Carlos and ordering them to vacate the Olympic Village within 48 hours. However, it was clear that Brundage was the impetus behind this action and that he likely told the USOC if it didn't reprimand Smith and Carlos, the entire U.S. contingent would be asked to leave. "I had said that if there were any demonstrations at the Olympic Games by anyone, the participants would be sent home," Brundage said. "That demonstration, I think, aroused resentment among all who saw it. There's no place for such things, and the boys involved were sent home."

The punishment only hardened the black athletes' resolve. When Beamon stunned the world with his leap of 29 feet, 2 1/2 inches, and Boston joined him on the rostrum as the bronze medalist, Beamon's track pants were rolled up to reveal black socks, and Boston was shoeless, as Smith and Carlos had been.

When the Games were closed and Jack returned to the States, he was stunned by the reaction from some of the American media. *The Los Angeles Times* referred to the Smith-Carlos gesture as a "Nazi-like salute" and the *Chicago Tribune* opined they were "an embarrassment visited upon the country, an insult to their countrymen" who had performed "an act contemptuous of the United States."

Really? All around the country there had been violent protests of Vietnam - hell, Jack's own daughter, Kathleen, had been involved in one at Columbia. The Democratic Convention had devolved into a week of police-induced chaos on the streets of Chicago. Dr. King and Robert F. Kennedy had been murdered in cold blood. Cities had been burned and looted by race rioters. Around the world there had been mammoth uprisings in France, in Prague, and in Mexico just before the Olympics began. And this is what respected newspapers like the *Times* and the *Tribune* were upset about? Two black athletes, quietly, non-violently, even respectfully, raising their fists in a simple plea for a chance to live their lives the way America's majority lived.

At the post-ceremony press conference, Smith said, "If I win I am an American, not a black American. But if I did something bad, then they would say 'a Negro'. We are black and we are proud of being black. Black America will understand what we did tonight."

As Jack wrote, all of America, and the world, should understand what those two men did that night in Mexico City.

27 – Is This America?

All of it could wait. Pro football. College football. The start of the NBA and NHL seasons. After the month he'd just had, traveling to the Olympic Trials in California, covering a seven-game World Series, then heading straight to Mexico City for the Olympics, nothing was going to prevent Jack from taking some well-earned vacation time to spend with his son, Patrick. *SportsWorld*'s editor, Mark Brantley, was wise not to challenge Jack on this.

Was it unplanned? Would Brantley have to reconsider some coverage plans for a few weeks? Yes, and yes. But family trumps everything, especially when a family member was coming home from the Vietnam War with two bullet holes in his body and a desperate need to be loved and cared for.

"We'll figure it out," Brantley had said to Jack. "I hope Patrick's doing well. And great job on this Tommie Smith/John Carlos thing."

The day before Jack was to leave Mexico City at the conclusion of the Summer Olympics, as he was trying to put the finishing touches on his story, the phone rang in his hotel room. On the other end was Olivia, already talking before the second syllable of his "hello" had echoed through the receiver.

"Patrick's coming home, he's coming home," Olivia said in a tone mixed with excitement and concern. "He's wounded, Jack. He was shot in the shoulder and the thigh, but they said he was going to be OK and he's being sent home. He's coming home! Our baby's coming home!"

At first Jack couldn't get any words out, the thoughts were running through his head too fast to single out just one. What happened? How badly was he injured? By OK, did that mean he was alive but might not walk again or be able to live a normal life? When is he coming home?

Jack stuck with, "What happened?"

Olivia launched into a re-creation of the conversation she had with the Marine official who initially scared the shit out of her when he identified himself on the phone because she naturally leapt to the conclusion that Patrick had been killed in action. The official explained, in finite detail, what occurred on the mission, making sure to emphasize that a primary reason for his being wounded was that he had acted heroically to help save a fellow Marine. He said Patrick had been transported to the Naval Support Activity Station Hospital at Da Nang where he underwent successful surgery overnight to remove the two rounds he had absorbed, and that he was resting comfortably and would be allowed to call home later in the day. He then shared the details of Patrick's travel itinerary back to the U.S. Once he was suitably recovered and fit to fly, he would leave the air base in Da Nang bound for Okinawa for processing which would take at least a day, then on to Travis Air Force base in Northern California, halfway between Sacramento and San Francisco. From there Patrick would be bussed down Interstate 80 to Treasure Island Naval Base in the middle of San Francisco Bay where he would go through the official military discharge. When all that was finished, he would be taken to San Francisco International Airport for a direct flight to La Guardia in New York and the start of his transition back to his old life.

"So you haven't talked to him yet?" Jack asked.

"No, I think they're going to set something up today."

A wave of pride surged through Jack. His son was a military hero. He'd helped save at least one life, and who knows how many more. But best of all, his son was not dead. He would be coming home, his service in Vietnam complete. They say in peace sons bury their fathers, and in war fathers bury their sons. This was two wars, and two McDonalds wounded in action but not killed, and that was all a military parent could hope for.

"I'm writing all day in my room, so call me when you hear anything. Have you gotten ahold of Kathleen or your parents?"

"No Jack, you're the first one I called. Kathleen is probably in class so I'll try to get a message to her through her RA, and then I'll call mom and dad. They're going to be so relieved. When I answered the phone and he said he was calling from the Marines, my heart just stopped."

"Yes, I imagine I would have reacted the same way. Well, if he's going to be fine and recover fully, I guess trading two bullet scars for two months off his tour is worth it. I'll bet he feels the same way."

Olivia managed a light laugh, then said she wanted to make her calls so the line would be clear in case Patrick was trying to get through.

"OK, I love you," Jack said. "I'm leaving tomorrow morning and if all goes well, I should be home late tomorrow night. Remember, call me as soon as you hang up with him."

Two weeks later, the TWA jet carrying Patrick and 12 other returning soldiers - some injured, some not - touched down at Travis, and a palpable surge of excitement coursed through the stuffy cabin. They were on American soil. Finally. The stars and stripes flapping in the breeze, the true symbol of the very freedoms they had been sent to Vietnam to protect. They were not back home with their families yet, but they were back in their own country, the one they had been so bravely and courageously risking their lives for, and they were anxious to see what kind of welcome home they would receive. Within minutes, they were wondering where the hell they were because this couldn't have been the United States.

So many days for Patrick in 1968 had been difficult as he tried to stay alive amid the danger all around him in those faraway jungles. Many days were worse than others, the fear compounded by sadness and depression from watching fellow Kilo Company Marines die on the battlefield. For Patrick, some men had perished right in his arms, and in moments like those when you are helpless to prevent the life of another human being from extinguishing before your eyes, you truly understand the horror of war. But what he was subjected to on this afternoon at Travis felt even worse; gut-wrenching, vile, confusing, an utter betrayal of human decency. The very people the Marines told him he was fighting for in the stand against Communism and the preservation of the American way were gathered outside the air base dressed in their blue jeans, sandals, tie-dye t-shirts, and bandanas for the express purpose of denouncing the returning soldiers as if they were motherfucking Charlie his own self.

As Patrick and the other men, whom he did not know before their flight, collected their duffle bags on the tarmac, they could hear the chants from beyond the chain-link fences, and could read the placards. "Baby Killers!"; "Thou Shalt Not Kill"; "Remove U.S. Troops From Vietnam"; "I Hope I Live to be a Draft Dodger." Patrick looked at them and he wondered aloud, "What the fuck is wrong with these people?" as some of the other soldiers nodded to him in agreement, equally appalled and perplexed.

Like all the soldiers in Vietnam, Patrick knew some of what was going on back home. His parents' letters detailed much of the war-related strife - the uprisings on the college campuses, the mess in Chicago, the riots that had ensued in the aftermath of the assassination of Dr. Martin Luther King, Jr. and how all of it was tearing the country apart in what had become one of the worst years in American annals. The men talked to some of the journalists and TV reporters and cameramen covering the conflict in the field and they provided snippets of information, and Patrick and the rest of Kilo Company often discussed what they'd heard in their down time around the barracks, field camp, or mess hall. They understood this was the most unpopular war in the history of the nation, but while the protesters could scream all they wanted, the bottom line was that every American who was sent to Vietnam was merely a pawn in a miserable situation. Only a small percentage of the men and women in country - military lifers like the dearly-departed Hound Dog Harriman - truly believed in what the United States was doing over there. Guys like Patrick felt they were performing their patriotic duty, doing a job they had been told to do, but the reality was that most of the men in Vietnam were just trying to make it through each day without getting their legs shredded by a claymore mine or their skulls blown up by an AK-47 round or three.

They were American citizens, just like the assholes beyond that fence. They'd done their time, and whether the protesters disagreed with their participation was irrelevant. They were home now, and they didn't deserve this.

"Men, this shit happens almost every day here," said the officer who greeted the flight. "It's despicable, but it's the way it is. Most of those fuckers out there would shit their pants if they came face-to-face with a gook in the jungle. You men are heroes, they're a bunch of piss ants. You remember that, but you also remember that you have to rise above it. You can't let them get to you, you can't be weak and stoop to their level. Keep your head down, and don't confront anyone because it just creates a shit storm. Be strong. Be Marines."

It only got worse when the men boarded a bus for the transport to Treasure Island. The gates opened at the exit, the bus began rolling through, and here came eggs and tomatoes being hurled at the windows which were closed because they'd been warned not to slide them open for this very reason. The protesters taunted them as if they were serial killers because in their minds, that's what the soldiers were. Every muscle in Patrick's tired and damaged body twitched as he surveyed the insanity, and it took every ounce of energy he had to restrain himself from opening his window and yelling at his fellow citizens to go fuck themselves.

As the bus motored its way toward Treasure Island, a million thoughts raged in Patrick's mind. What had he or any of these soldiers done wrong? Why were they being made to be the scapegoats? Do these people really think it gave him a rise to go half a world away to kill other human beings, and even worse, nearly be killed countless times?

The official discharge process took several hours, and Patrick lost track of how many times he had to sign his name on the never-ending stream of forms being pushed across the table by the processing officer. But he would have sat there and signed all day if that's what it took to get his honorable discharge. There wasn't a thing he would miss about his time as a Marine. Certainly not boot camp, and certainly not his time in country. He would always look back with pride on how he served in Vietnam, how he had helped his fellow Kilo Company men in their time of need, how he fought bravely in so many bloody battles and racked up more than his share of kills. Better them than me, was the saying. He didn't appreciate the two scars that would forever grace his body, but if the alternative was a wooden box, he'd rub those scars ever so fondly and savor every breath he took.

During the long trip from Okinawa to the Bay Area, Patrick wasn't able to get much sleep as he ran through so many scenarios regarding his immediate future. He'd heard the disheartening tales of men coming from home the war and being unable to find their way. Some struggled with the after-effects of the war, psychologically damaged, and there was no shame in that. Having seen what they had seen, you were damn fortunate if you avoided the often debilitating malady known as post-traumatic stress disorder. Others had left broken homes, or otherwise unsatisfactory lives, to join the Marines, and now they were confronted with the harsh reality of returning to those situations to find that nothing had changed, and things may have gotten worse.

Patrick vowed that his story would be different. He had advantages, for sure. He came from a solid, loving home, and thanks to his father's well-heeled position as a national sports columnist, the McDonald's lived a very comfortable life in their suburban Long Island neighborhood. Patrick would have his old bedroom to come back to, home-cooked meals prepared by his doting mother, and the luxury of time to plot a course for what was to come next. And best of all, he knew he'd have the love and support of his parents and sister, no matter how long it took to figure things out.

The first thing Patrick saw when he emerged from the jet way that connected the plane with the Pan-Am terminal at LaGuardia was the sign, held by his sister Kathleen, that read, "Welcome Home Patrick!!!" Then he saw his mother jumping up and down with glee, waving as if her hand was on fire. And then he saw his father, smiling, stoic as ever, knowing what it felt like to be coming home from a war wounded, but unbroken. He locked his eyes with Jack, answered his father's wink with a nod, and then prepared to be engulfed by his mother and sister after barely a few steps.

Goodbye Vietnam, Patrick thought as he kissed his mother and sister, and shared a manly hug and handshake with his father. Every moment of it sucked, but it did not beat him. Patrick McDonald did not win the war, but he won his personal battle, and a life that seemed rudderless before he enlisted now seemed filled with possibilities.

28 - Harvard Beats Yale 29-29

When Jack told *SportsWorld* editor Mark Brantley of what he thought his next assignment should be, he received the exact response he expected from his immediate superior.

"Are you serious?" Brantley said over the phone when Jack informed him that he wanted to cover the 85th renewal of the Harvard-Yale football game the weekend before Thanksgiving, the same weekend on which some of the biggest games of the 1968 college season were also being played, games that would surely impact the race for the mythical national championship.

"Why the hell would you want to cover a game between two teams no one gives a shit about?" Brantley said as he took a long, smoky drag off his cigarette, fully prepared to debate Jack on the issue, and perhaps wield executive power to veto the idea, something he didn't often do with his national columnist.

Jack knew Brantley had a viable case. Unbeaten and No. 1-ranked USC, with its soon-to-be Heisman Trophy-winning tailback, O.J. Simpson, was hosting arch-rival UCLA at the Los Angeles Memorial Coliseum looking to clinch the Pac-8 title and thus secure the conference's bid to the Rose Bowl. At the big horseshoe in Columbus, Ohio, second-ranked and unbeaten Ohio State was playing host to once-beaten, fourth-ranked Michigan, "that team from up north" as Buckeyes coach Woody Hayes always referred to the hated Wolverines. The winner would earn the Big Ten's berth in the Rose Bowl, and if Ohio State and USC both won, they would be playing in a no-doubt-about-it national championship game in Pasadena on New Year's Day. Two classic, long-time rivalry games, and both with big stakes, so yes, either would have made for compelling reading in the pages of *SportsWorld*.

Jack wanted to do something a little different, and his argument was this: The Ohio State-Michigan and USC-UCLA games were both being shown on national television, part of a natural time zone doubleheader, so college football fans would have the luxury of watching both if they choose. And for those who missed the telecasts, they would have every opportunity to read accounts in their Sunday morning newspapers because both games had drawn huge media interest and would be covered by dozens of outlets including the two main wire services, Associated Press and United Press International. By the time *SportsWorld* hit the newsstands five days after these games had been played, subscribers likely would have had their fill; it would be old news, something *SportsWorld* always fought when it came to event stories, so why not give them something off the beaten path? Harvard-Yale was delicious for this purpose, and Jack sold it hard to Brantley.

"Look at it this way: Beyond the game, think about all those white-collar Harvard and Yale alums who might skip the *Wall Street Journal* for a day and buy the magazine instead," Jack said. "Think about how that would look for our advertisers. You don't think we'd score some points with the bean counters upstairs? I can just see Martin calling Franklin on the phone and reeling off the profit margins for the issue. By the way, you know Franklin is a Harvard man, right?"

"Oh, you know just what strings to pull, don't you?" Brantley said in a sarcastic tone, acknowledging that yes indeed, he knew *SportsWorld* CEO Franklin Xavier Stevenson earned his undergrad business degree at Harvard, and that managing editor Martin Abrams would barely be able to contain his boner if an article about Harvard-Yale increased newsstand sales and opened up potential new advertising clients. "The master puppeteer, Jack McDonald. How long have you been working on this pitch? You probably already booked your hotel, didn't you?"

"Well," Jack said, "as soon as we hang up I was gonna get right on that. Pretty sure there's a Hilton in Back Bay with a vacancy waiting for me to fill."

"Why Harvard-Yale? Why should we be paying attention to this game? It means nothing on the national scale. It doesn't impact the bowls because Ivy League teams don't play in bowl games. I just don't see what I'm getting here."

"Mark, you can't seriously deny that you don't know how intense the Harvard-Yale rivalry is," Jack said incredulously. "This is Army-Navy without the fatigues and the marching. These schools have been battling each other for supremacy since the mid-1800s. You know they had a regatta in 1852 and it was the first intercollegiate sporting event in this country's history. They've been going at it ever since, whether it's rowing, fencing, football, or physics. This is what college sports should be about. Not all the money, all the glory, all the championships; it's about the competition. This is a good story, and aren't we supposed to be all about the best stories?"

"Since when did you become such a sanctimonious prick?"

"I'm not being sanctimonious; I'm just spelling it out for you. I'm telling you, I can really make this sing. Do you realize that the only football rivalry older than this is Lehigh-Lafayette? Plus, this is the first time since 1909 both teams are unbeaten coming into The Game, so it actually will be for a championship. It might end up being a great game as well as a great story."

"Jesus Christ, you better be right Jack or this is gonna go over about as well as a fart in the confessional booth. OK, pack your fucking tweed jacket and book it."

Jack arrived in Cambridge Friday afternoon, in time to take in the Crimson's last practice before what would be the final football game for all of the Harvard seniors. O.J. Simpson was going to be the first pick in the next pro football draft, but there would be no pro football futures for anyone on this squad. This was it, perhaps the last afternoon of true organized athletic competition before all, or at least the vast majority of them, would take their Harvard sheepskins to Wall Street, or a courthouse, or a banking institution, or any number of other respected occupations. No one went to Harvard to play football; you went to soak up a world-class education, and if football was something you were also proficient at, well, that was a nice diversion in the autumn from the grind of a notoriously challenging institutional-wide curriculum. The same held true at Yale, though the Bulldogs did have one player whose future would likely be in pro football. Running back Calvin Hill was the rare Ivy Leaguer with enough raw talent to be on the radar of every pro team, and Jack was looking forward to sitting down with the young man later in the evening at the team hotel, but for the other Yale seniors, this, too, would be their sporting swan song.

Although both teams were 8-0, Yale was the clear-cut favorite and those who paid any attention to Ivy League football gave the Crimson little chance to win. The Elis had won 16 games in a row dating back to 1967, including a season-capping victory over Harvard at the Yale Bowl when they blew a 17-0 lead by allowing 20 straight points before pulling it out in the final two minutes when resourceful quarterback Brian Dowling threw a 66-yard touchdown pass. Yale had rolled through its first eight games in 1968, its slimmest margin of victory a 25-13 conquest of Cornell in late October. Its excellent offense, led by Hill and Dowling, had piled up 288 points operating from a well-conceived Wing-T variation that included motion, shifting, and zone-busting passes. Harvard wasn't nearly as proficient on offense, but its eight consecutive victories were the result of a stifling defense which ranked No. 1 in the nation with a yield of just 7.6 points per game. Only two opponents had reached double figures against the Crimson, and in their previous five games, all Ivy League victories, they had allowed a mere 27 points.

Not bad for a team that had almost come unglued prior to the season when a player revolt in the late summer during preseason practice nearly came to fruition. The seniors on the roster felt coach John Yovicsin didn't care about them because this was their last year, and the younger crop of players was more intriguing and meant more to the future of the program. The seniors considered themselves the "forgotten guys" and were ready to walk, but only because senior halfback Vic Gatto was named captain did they elect to stick it out and, in essence play for him rather than Yovicsin. Eight straight wins, and now here they were, face-to-face with their fiercest rival with a chance to finish off Harvard's first undefeated season since 1920.

"We've got everything to gain," Yovicsin told the gathered press after practice. "My lads aren't going to put their undefeated record on the block without putting up a fight. To beat us they must score a lot of points because we're going to get across that goal line."

Yale's football history dwarfed that of Harvard's. The Bulldogs were America's original sporting powerhouse, and no iteration of the New York Yankees - be it the era of Babe Ruth, Joe DiMaggio, or Mickey Mantle - could match the sheer dominance of Yale football. From its first year of competition in 1872, through 1912, the Bulldogs were awarded the college football championship 26 times and won 348 games while losing 24 and tying 25. Otherworldly would be an apt description of the hold Yale had on the college game. As the sport grew in popularity thanks to the emergence of schools such as Notre Dame, Army, and Navy, the competitive balance began to shift, but the Bulldogs remained one of the elite programs through the World War II years. After a spate of relative mediocrity, they were back on the prowl under fourth-year head coach Carm Cozza. When they took the field at Harvard Stadium on a sunny 41-degree late fall New England afternoon, the Bulldogs had not won a national championship since 1927, but they had three Ivy League crowns to their credit - including 1967 - and owned an unassailable all-time record of 627-176-50.

Jack spent time gathering some color for his piece, and he found the ticket distribution for the game rather interesting. Harvard gave 9,000 tickets to its undergrads, the highest ever doled out. To fill the requests of the alums, officials prioritized by oldest graduating class, and by the time they got to the class of 1949, they were out of tickets. Approximately 15,000 tickets were shipped to New Haven, with each student allowed a maximum of four, each alum two. Yale ticket manager Jack Blake told Jack his phone never stopped ringing for three days until they sold out.

Speaking of phones, Jack learned of a man, Harvard class of 1935, who lived outside Chicago and could not travel to the game. His solution to stay up on the action? He enlisted his Boston-based nephew to tune into the local broadcast on his transistor radio, and leave it next to the mouthpiece of the phone. He figured it was going to cost about $25 in long-distance charges, but it would be money well spent.

He probably wasn't feeling that way late in the first half when the Yalies, behind another superb performance by Dowling, were cruising to a 22-0 lead and were on the verge of turning the game into a laugher, not to mention create an uncomfortable situation for Jack with the powers that be at *SportsWorld*. Jack could just hear Brantley crowing at the score when it popped up on the Prudential Scoreboard during the Ohio State-Michigan clash. Not that Brantley had a leg to stand on, being that the Buckeyes were on their way to thrashing the Wolverines 50-14.

Jack had learned all about Dowling in the week before · kickoff, which is why he wasn't at all surprised by what he was seeing from the kid in the first half. If Yale wasn't an all-male institution, Dowling would have been the guy with the harem of pretty co-eds trailing behind, giggling and hanging on his every breath as he sauntered through Hewitt Quad. He was smart, handsome, the boy next door, everybody's All-America. And most of all, he was a winner. He hadn't lost a football game in which he started and finished since the end of sixth grade, a streak of 65 consecutive victories. Yale's last defeat, the 1967 season opener? Yep, Dowling was out with a broken wrist. He had more than a hundred scholarship offers when he left St. Ignatius High School in Cleveland, all of which would have provided a free ride through college. His father told him he'd pay the $2,000-a-year tuition to Yale – no athletic scholarships in the Ivy League - because a degree from Yale would mean something.

Dowling led the Yale freshman team to a 6-0 record, and after dabbling with basketball, tennis, and baseball that first year on campus, he focused his energy on football as a sophomore. That year he suffered a knee injury that forced him to miss virtually the entire season, and he missed three games as a junior. With Dowling on the field, his Yale teams were 21-0; without him, they were 5-6. It was enough to inspire a student named Garry Trudeau to create a comic strip for the campus newspaper, the *Yale Daily News*, called "bull tales" in which the main character was named B.D. (after you guessed it) who paraded around with a football helmet forever perched on his head. And now, as his final act for old blue, Dowling was orchestrating a surgical rout of Harvard. When Dowling hit Del Marting with a touchdown pass and then a two-point conversion pass, it was 22-0 and Harvard Stadium was mute, save for the Yalies waving their white hankies and chanting "We're Number One, You're Number Two!!!"

Harvard's starting quarterback, George Lalich, had enjoyed a solid season, but he had been unable to get anything generated on this day, so after the Crimson recovered a Bulldog fumble at the 36, Yovicsin sent little-used junior Frank Champi - a former javelin thrower who was fourth-string at the start of the season - into the fray. "He looked scared to death," offensive lineman Tommy Lee Jones said. "It all looked overwhelming to him."

Yet within a couple hours, Champi's name would resonate forever more in Harvard football lore.

"When I woke up this morning, I felt strange, you know?" Champi said afterward. "I had this feeling that I'd play in the game and that I would do well. That's why when I got into the game, I never felt shook. It was like I was dreaming. I still had a little trouble getting the feel for a while, but I had no doubt I could do it."

Here's what he did.

Taking possession following a fumble by Hill, Champi directed a 12-play, 64-yard drive that ended with his 15-yard touchdown pass to Bruce Freeman on a third-and-six play, and though a bad snap foiled the extra point, leaving the score 22-6 at intermission, there was hope in the Crimson locker room.

Despite the spark Champi provided, Lalich, the senior, was back under center for Harvard's first possession of the third quarter, but he was stopped cold again on three downs and the Crimson punted. However, when Yale's Mike Bouscaren fumbled that punt and Freeman recovered at the Bulldogs 25, Champi came trotting onto the field to a thunderous ovation, and moments later he fired a 23-yard pass to Pete Varney that moved the ball to the 1 to set up Gus Crim's touchdown plunge that made it 22-13.

Two more Yale fumbles thwarted offensive possessions which resulted in a scoreless quarter for the Bulldogs, their first in the last 25, but Harvard was unable to capitalize on either. Early in the fourth quarter, Yale managed to stop bobbling the ball long enough to piece together a 45-yard drive that ended with Dowling, of course, running in from the 5 for a touchdown that gave the Bulldogs a seemingly safe 29-13 cushion with 10:44 left to play.

More than seven minutes later, with Yale driving to what would have been a nail in the coffin score, Bob Levin coughed up the Bulldogs sixth fumble of the day, but with Harvard 86 yards away from the Yale end zone, and only 3:31 remaining, needing 16 points just to tie, bleak would still be the best way to describe the Crimson predicament. The Yale faithful certainly felt that way. Unfazed by Levin's fumble, they kept waving their hankies and taunting the Harvard fans with their "We're Number One, You're Number Two!!!" chant. And then slowly but surely, their confidence began to dwindle until it ultimately faded to mute as Champi made like Dowling during a spellbinding stretch of football that produced one of the greatest, not to mention unlikely, college football finishes in history.

Staring at third-and-18 from the Yale 38, Champi dropped back to pass and was hit and lost control of the ball. With both fan bases screaming, a fortuitous bounce sent the ball into the hands of unsuspecting Harvard tackle Fritz Reed and the big guy lumbered 23 yards to the 15 for an incredible first down. On the next play, Freeman caught a Champi pass at the 5 and fought his way into the end zone with 42 seconds to go. The Crimson had to go for two, and it appeared all was well on the Yale side when Champi's pass to Varney fell incomplete. Alas, a rather innocuous interference penalty gave Harvard a mulligan, and from the 1, Crim ran in the two-pointer to cut Harvard's deficit to 29-21.

The stadium was electric – all 40,280 on their feet - and the old concrete bowl probably buckled ever so slightly when the Bulldogs muffed the onside kick and Harvard's Billy Kelly fell on it at midfield. Dowling stood there on the sidelines in disbelief, and it was revealed later that he asked Cozza if he could go into the game to play defensive back. He may have been tempted, but Cozza said no because he didn't want to break the spirit of the man he would have to take out in that situation. So, Dowling, who'd made 32 interceptions during his high school career as a two-way player, watched as his unlikely counterpart, Champi, made history.

On first down, Champi scrambled for a 14-yard gain, and a 15-yard facemask penalty assessed to Bouscaren on the tackle was tacked on, moving the ball to the 20 with 32 seconds remaining. Two straight incomplete passes drained the clock to 20 ticks, but on third-and-10, a gutsy draw call to Crim gained 14 yards and gave the Crimson a first-and-goal at the 6 with 14 seconds left. Champi was sacked for a two-yard loss, and he called his final timeout with three seconds to go. Yovicsin sent Gatto - who had been hobbled by a hamstring injury suffered earlier in the day - back onto the field, and instructed Champi to throw him the ball, and damned if he didn't do just that. Champi was pressured immediately, managed to scramble away, and somehow, after what seemed like minutes rather than seconds, saw Gatto open in the far left corner of the end zone. Champi reared back and let fly and the ball landed safely in Gatto's arms to make it 29-27 with no time remaining.

"I got hit, I thought someone was breathing down my neck, I scrambled, I threw off my wrong foot," Champi said, recounting the play. "Gatto was open for a moment. I just threw it in his general direction. After that, I remember feeling a sense of inevitability. I thought, 'We've come this far.' I was very confident. It was inevitable."

The inevitability didn't happen for nearly 10 minutes as the delirious Harvard crowd poured onto the field in glee, apparently forgetting that Harvard still needed to convert a two-point play or else the magnificent rally would be incomplete. Once order was restored, Champi settled under center for the final play. He took the snap, rolled slightly to his right, stopped, and looked back to his left where Varney was running a quick slant to the middle. The big end had inside position on his defender, Ed Franklin, and Champi drilled it right into his belly for the game-tying conversion. "On the conversion," Champi said, "it was a simple roll throwback to Varney. It's impossible to stop if thrown right, and Pete is so big, there was no hope to stop it."

He was right, and bedlam ensued. The Crimson ran onto the field and mobbed Champi and Varney, while the Bulldogs stood frozen, unable to process what had just happened, even as the field was being over-run once again by Harvard fans.

Honestly, Jack couldn't believe it. When he pitched the idea of covering this game, he could only have dreamed it would have gone this way. "You never know, it might end up being a great game as well as a great story," he remembered telling Brantley on the phone.

And so it was 29-29, a tie on the ledger of both teams, but no one was arguing the fact that it felt like a tremendous Harvard victory and an equally appalling Yale loss. Two days later, in the *Harvard Crimson*, the headline was absolutely perfect: Harvard Beats Yale 29-29.

"When you've done what we just did, you've lost," Yale's Weinstein said, refusing to accept that the tie still meant the Bulldogs shared the Ivy championship with the Crimson. "It's the same as a defeat. We don't feel much like champions."

Cozza, gracious in defeat, couldn't help but take a poke at the officials who certainly seemed to call it a bit in Harvard's favor down the stretch. "Harvard had momentum, but they also had help," Cozza said. "I don't question the integrity of the game officials, but they sure as hell got caught up in the emotion of the game and it cost us. But how can I say that without detracting from those Harvard kids who were great. If we hadn't fumbled six times, we could have named our score. It was almost like a nightmare, really. I don't know how else to explain it. We feel like we lost it, even though we didn't. Something like that won't happen again in 1,000 years."

When Jack filed his story Monday morning, he called Brantley to alert him of its arrival.

"It was a pretty good game," Jack cracked.

"You're one lucky bastard McDonald, one lucky bastard. By the way, who do you like in the fifth at Aqueduct today?"

29 - Saving 1968

The eight-foot-tall white spruce was an exquisitely well-shaped Christmas tree, no low hanging branches, full throughout the middle, and then tapered up to a perfectly symmetrical triangle. Naturally, it was trimmed just the way Olivia liked it with white lights wrapped all the way around, decades-old homemade ornaments dangling from the branches, and silver and gold tinsel strands to fill in the gaps. At its base, set up on a white bed sheet, was the Nativity scene complete with miniature statues of the baby Jesus flanked by Mary and Joseph, with various angels, shepherds, and sheep on the periphery. And there was a gold star - made by Kathleen when she was in third grade - perched at the very top.

The mistletoe was hung from one of the cross beams in the foyer where you entered the house. Garland was draped all the way up the rail of the staircase that led to the second floor of the four-bedroom Colonial, as well as across the mantel above the fireplace which was crackling with three logs in full flame on this cold, wintry Garden City Christmas Eve. And throughout the main floor there were seasonal decorations that Santa Claus himself would have suggested to Mrs. Claus for their North Pole living space.

In the kitchen, there was a beehive of activity. The filet mignon - a family tradition on the night before Christ's

324

birthday - was broiling in the oven; the potatoes were boiling on the stove; Kathleen was preparing the salad by cutting carrots, peppers, and cucumbers to mix with the lettuce; Olivia was placing the muffins and dinner rolls in a wicker basket lined with a white linen napkin; and Olivia's mother, Marge, was at the sink, keeping pace with the dishes.

And where were the men? As usual, in front of the television, though there was no viewing pleasure, which was an impending problem. Just minutes before guests from around the neighborhood would begin arriving for the annual McDonald Christmas Eve dinner party, Jack was fidgeting with the rabbit ear antenna atop the 23-inch Admiral color console situated in the corner of the family room opposite the tree.

"No, move it to the left," Patrick told his father, who had moved the thin metal prongs into just about every conceivable angle without much success in achieving picture clarity.

"No, go back, move it a little to the right," Patrick said as he sat on the brown leather couch, crutches propped up against the arm, still in convalescence nearly two months since his return from Vietnam. Suddenly, the screen snapped to attention, and Patrick held up his hand in a stop motion and said, "OK, right there."

Jack slowly pulled his hand away as if for some reason doing this carefully would matter, but as soon as he did the screen went fuzzy again and the picture began flipping vertically. "What am I supposed to do, stand here and hold the damn things all night?" Jack said with a burn of frustration flaring from his nostrils.

"Give little Kevin next door a couple bucks to come over and hold it for us all night," Patrick said with a wry smile that instantly irritated Jack.

"Or you could go get some tin foil," said John Dupree, who was sitting in the recliner smoking his pipe, reading *Newsday*, and smirking at his son-in-law's impatience.

Jack stomped into the kitchen, grabbed the Reynolds Wrap, ripped off two sections, went back into the family room, wrapped the silver foil around the rabbit ears, and voila, the picture improved immediately, except for a feint ghosting that was tolerable. "Works every time," John said, returning his focus back to the newspaper while Jack rolled his eyes upward into his sockets.

Ordinarily the TV wouldn't be on. Olivia wouldn't allow it, not on her favorite night of the year, one she spent weeks planning, a ritual that dated back more than 20 years. Normally, Perry Como, Johnny Mathis, and Engelbert Humperdink Christmas albums would be spinning on the hi-fi, providing the ambience behind the din of lively conversation produced by the six to eight couples that filled the house. But this was a special occasion because on this Christmas Eve of 1968, American astronauts Frank Borman, Jim Lovell, and Bill Anders were making worldwide history by becoming the first men to orbit the moon as part of the Apollo 8 mission. This was the first human journey to another world, an event that could not be missed, and Olivia's party wouldn't be the only one put on hold with predictions that this would be the most-watched television program in the history of the medium.

Recognizing its significance, Olivia, meticulous planner that she was, altered the schedule of the evening to allow her family and guests the opportunity to watch the telecast which was slated to begin in the eastern United States at 9:30 p.m., or thereabouts. So, dinner would commence at eight bells, with the coffee, dessert, and post-meal liquors to be served just before the astronauts said hello through the magic of television to share their incredible pictures from a quarter million miles away, truly one of man's greatest feats.

Jack's memory was legendary, and he could vividly recall the day when President John F. Kennedy announced his desire for the United States to explore the moon. In the early morning hours of Thursday, May 25, 1961, a water pipe burst at Garden City High School forcing the cancellation of school. With clear skies and the temperature in the mid-70s, a glorious spring day in the city, Jack pounced on the opportunity to take Patrick to Yankee Stadium for that afternoon's ballgame against the Red Sox. Even though Mickey Mantle wasn't in the lineup - thus stalling his race with teammate Roger Maris to break Babe Ruth's single-season home run record - the Yankees jumped on Boston starter Billy Muffett for five runs before an out was recorded in the second inning. Johnny Blanchard and Tony Kubek each hit two-run homers, and that was all Whitey Ford needed as the Yankees went on to a 6-4 victory.

When they returned home to Garden City, Olivia had dinner ready, and when the meal was finished and the kitchen was tidied up, Jack and his wife settled in front of the television - this one a black and white 19-inch Philco model - to watch the news. Walter Cronkite led his broadcast with the story that earlier in the day President Kennedy - in office barely four months - threw down the gantlet as he stood before Congress and proclaimed:

"I believe this nation should commit itself to achieving the goal, before this decade is out, of landing a man on the moon and returning him safely to Earth. No single space project in this period will be more impressive to mankind, or more important for the long-range exploration of space; and none will be so difficult or expensive to accomplish."

Jack looked at Olivia and said, "That's a little ambitious, don't you think? We can't even get the potholes on the LIE fixed."

Ever since the race to space was consummated on October 4, 1957 when the world awoke to headlines announcing that the Soviet Union had launched man's first satellite, Sputnik 1, the United States had been playing catch up. A month later, Sputnik 2 went up with a dog named Laika aboard, and with the Americans and Soviets already locked in a Cold War struggle, the United States had to get its shit together, and fast. Congress, at the urging of President Dwight D. Eisenhower, immediately accelerated its space program by establishing the National Aeronautics and Space Agency, and passed legislation to revamp America's public school curriculum to emphasize science and math, subjects vital to the training of future space scientists.

NASA started the Mercury program in 1958, and its objectives were to place a manned spacecraft in orbital flight around the Earth, investigate man's performance capabilities and his ability to function in the environment of space, and recover the man and the spacecraft safely. Within three years, on May 5, 1961, just three weeks before Kennedy's ultimate challenge, astronaut Alan B. Shepard Jr. became the first American to enter space. Shepard's Freedom 7 flight launched from Cape Canaveral, Florida and lasted 15 minutes, during which he climbed 115 miles above the Earth's surface before splashing down in the Atlantic Ocean some 300 miles from the Cape. The launch, seen by millions on live television, branded Shepard a hero and he was feted with parades in Washington, New York, and Los Angeles, and received the NASA Distinguished Service Medal from Kennedy.

However, the Soviets were still in the lead because one month earlier, Soviet Union cosmonaut Yuri Gagarin had become the first human to fly into space during a 108-minute orbital flight. So, NASA's response was the concurrent creation later in 1961 of the Gemini and Apollo programs, Gemini to serve as a more demanding informational and testing platform which would bridge the way for Apollo to eventually go to the moon.

Pleased by NASA's progress, Kennedy said in a speech at Houston's Rice University in September 1962:

"We set sail on this new sea because there is new knowledge to be gained, and new rights to be won, and they must be won and used for the progress of all people. For space science, like nuclear science and all technology, has no conscience of its own. Whether it will become a force for good or ill depends on man, and only if the United States occupies a position of preeminence can we help decide whether this new ocean will be a sea of peace or a new, terrifying theater of war." He later added, "But why, some say, the moon? Why choose this as our goal? And they may well ask why climb the highest mountain? Why, 35 years ago, fly the Atlantic? Why does Rice play Texas? We choose to go to the moon in this decade and do the other things, not because they are easy, but because they are hard, because that goal will serve to organize and measure the best of our energies and skills, because that challenge is one that we are willing to accept, one we are unwilling to postpone, and one which we intend to win, and the others, too."

Gemini steamed forward through the mid-1960s, 10 manned missions in all, unfazed by America's myriad problems, not the least of which was the assassination of Kennedy in November 1963. But Kennedy's death did not slow the pursuit of the moon because President Lyndon B. Johnson had long been a staunch supporter of NASA and had advised Kennedy in 1961 on the importance of space exploration. He maintained the backing of NASA, and by the end of 1966, it was time to begin the final stage: Apollo.

It did not begin well. In January 1967, the three-man crew of Apollo 1 - Gus Grissom, Roger Chaffee, and Edward White - were killed during a launch rehearsal at Cape Kennedy when the cabin caught fire and the trapped astronauts could not escape the defective Command Service Module. With both houses of Congress opening investigations into NASA, and NASA conducting its own internal inquiry, the Apollo program's planned manned missions were put on hold for 20 months, though NASA made good use of the time by fixing the flaws of the CSM and perfecting its procedures and training methods. When Apollo was given the go-ahead to resume, the clock was ticking rapidly, but there was still a tremendous belief that an American flag would be thrust into the lunar surface before the end of 1969.

Confidence began to wane, though, in the summer of 1968. Attached to the Saturn V rocket launcher were two vehicles: The CSM transported the three astronauts into space and then eventually back to Earth, while the Lunar Excursion Module was operational only in space. Once in the moon's orbit, two astronauts moved to the LEM, undocked it from the CSM, then piloted it to the moon's surface for landing. When exploration maneuvers were complete, they re-docked to the CSM, and once they were safely aboard, the LEM was forever discarded and the CSM would bring the astronauts home.

The CSM was working to perfection and hitting all its benchmarks, but the LEM was found to have engineering flaws. The conclusion was that it would not be ready to perform its upcoming Apollo 7 and Apollo 8 lower Earth orbit test missions, so Apollo program manager George Low proposed an intriguing and potentially dangerous change to the mission schedule.

Because neither Apollo 7 nor 8 would be landing on the moon, only orbiting it, Low came up with the idea to leave the LEM behind, and attach only the CSM to the Saturn V launcher. Apollo 7 astronauts Walter M. Schirra, Donn F. Eisele, and Walter Cunningham were tasked with conducting the CSM-only Earth-orbital test in October, making them the first United States crew to enter space. And if all went well, the Apollo 8 crew of Borman, Lovell, and Anders would take the next step in late December and make world history by becoming the first humans to leave Earth orbit, reach the moon, orbit it, and return safely to Earth.

Ordinarily, this would have been a difficult sell to the NASA hierarchy and President Johnson because the accelerated timetable would place incredibly taxing training demands on the Apollo 8 crew now being asked to fly about three months ahead of their initial schedule while also performing an entirely new mission. Also, the Saturn V launcher had experienced some instrumental failures on two test flights, and though the technicians believed those had been ironed out, it was a concern. The Apollo 1 tragedy was still an open and painful wound, and NASA likely would not have survived if something had gone wrong in space and the Apollo 8 astronauts could not be returned to Earth.

There were so many reasons not to attempt this, but one overriding reason why they felt they had to. According to the CIA, the U.S. was on the brink of losing yet another round in the race for the moon. Their intelligence - which later turned out to be incorrect - indicated that the Soviets were shooting for a one-man orbital mission to the moon before the end of the year, and were well along in their testing. Originally, NASA wasn't planning to attempt this until early in 1969 with Apollo 9. With the pressure to beat the Soviets so great, the decision was made to go for the moon in December, hopefully ahead of the enemy.

"Any idea that the Apollo program was a great voyage of exploration or scientific endeavor is nuts," Borman said years later. "That wasn't the primary mission; the primary mission was to go to the moon ahead of the Russians and meet the President's mandate. The real reason that I was in the program, and the real reason that the program existed, was because it was a battle in the Cold War, and we started from behind and we won; it's as simple as that."

Apollo 7 performed flawlessly, and it was all systems go for a December 21 launch of Apollo 8 from Kennedy Space Center at Cape Canaveral. It took three days for the spacecraft to travel to the moon, reaching on Christmas Eve morning, and so began 10 full revelations over the course of 20 hours. During the first three, the astronauts took pictures and video of the moon's surface, recon for where subsequent Apollo missions would be able to land. It wasn't until the fourth revelation, when Borman rolled the spacecraft away from the moon and pointed its windows to the vast horizon, that the Earth came into view a quarter million miles away in all its circular blue and white beauty. "Oh my God! Look at the picture over there. Here's the Earth coming up," Borman excitedly blurted out. Lovell and Anders were as much in wonderment as Borman, and Anders grabbed one of the cameras and snapped, among many, the now famous photograph which was later titled Earthrise.

As Olivia, Kathleen, and Joan were clearing the dinner table and getting ready to serve coffee and dessert, Jack led the exodus to the family room and made sure everyone had someplace to sit or stand for the broadcast from space. It was a tight fit, but the room could accommodate the crowd, and Jack said a silent prayer when he pushed the power button on the television, hoping the picture would cooperate, which it did.

Right on schedule at 9:30, "Good evening, Apollo 8 is in its ninth and next to last full orbit of the moon," said Walter Cronkite as the CBS News coverage began, silencing the McDonald family room. Cronkite provided a brief recap of what the astronauts had accomplished, and then a simulation of the spacecraft alongside the moon's surface appeared on screens all across the world, accompanied by a live audio feed from the NASA ground control command center in Houston. Eventually, the voices of the astronauts came online, and, after some technical difficulties, the simulation was replaced by the live television feed from the on-board camera pointing out the window of the CSM showing their view of the moon.

It was a tedious broadcast in that virtually no one watching really knew what they were looking at despite the detailed explanations by Borman, Lovell, and Anders, but it was fascinating nonetheless. They closed the 30-minute program by reciting verses 1 through 10 of the Book of Genesis. "We are now approaching lunar sunrise and, for all the people back on Earth, the crew of Apollo 8 has a message that we would like to send to you," Anders began, and all three took turns reading until Borman signed off by saying, "And from the crew of Apollo 8, we close with good night, good luck, a Merry Christmas, and God bless all of you, all of you on the good Earth."

With that, Jack stood before his guests, raised his vodka gimlet, and toasted the brave men who had founded a new frontier, but perhaps the finest summation of this achievement, and what it meant to America, came in a telegram Borman received shortly after he, Lovell, and Anders returned safely to Earth three days hence Christmas Eve.

"Thank you Apollo 8; you saved 1968."

Epilogue – Welcome Back to Miami

When the Apollo 8 broadcast was finished, Walter
Cronkite told viewers to stay tuned to CBS for a special
airing of *60 Minutes*, a newsmagazine-style program that
had debuted in September and was already getting rabid
ratings because of the breadth and topicality of its
investigative journalism.

This heart-wrenching edition, not exactly joyous Christmas
Eve viewing yet nonetheless compelling, featured reporters
Mike Wallace and Harry Reasoner interviewing Coretta
King and Ethel Kennedy, the grieving widows of Dr.
Martin Luther King, Jr. and Robert F. Kennedy.

And thus, within a couple hours on network television came the perfect encapsulation of 1968: Americans spilling tears of joy witnessing the awe-inspiring and somewhat miraculous achievement of America's journey into space, followed by a reminder of all the tears that had been spilled over the tragic and senseless deaths of two of the country's brightest and most influential men.

It had been a year like no other in American history, a year marked by unthinkable tragedy, by violent protest and revolt, and by a wholly unpopular war that seemed confusing, never-ending, and seemingly unwinnable at the horrific cost of far too many young lives. But at the opposite end of the spectrum, it had been a year of mankind-changing advancement, of coming-of-age political and cultural awareness, and of tremendous athletic achievement that at least in some small way helped to assuage everyone into feeling that there was still hope, there was still good, and that perhaps brighter days were ahead as the calendar turned to 1969.

For Jack and his family, 1969 began as a working vacation of sorts with Jack on assignment covering Super Bowl III between the upstart New York Jets and the powerful Baltimore Colts in Miami, and Olivia, Patrick, and Kathleen along for the week, enjoying a much-needed break from reality, not to mention winter. After all, it had been quite a year for the McDonalds, too.

Patrick's life perpetually in harms' way in Vietnam, with every day skirting death and marked off the calendar a victory unto itself, and then his tour of duty coming to a harrowing but fortunate end for him: That day along National Route 1 when the firefight broke out and Hound Dog Harriman and so many of Patrick's fellow grunts were shredded to death, yet he somehow escaped with non-life threatening wounds that served as his ticket out of the shit. Not a day had passed where Patrick hadn't replayed in his mind the horror of those few minutes and wondered why he was one of the lucky ones who lived, the worst of it at night when he'd wake up from the nightmares in a cold sweat.

For Kathleen, it had been a year of emotional uproar, but also a year of spiritual growth and maturity. The war had torn her in half because on the one hand, she fully supported her brother and his efforts over there, and she was so very proud of him. But on the other hand, she came to loathe America's involvement and became a sympathizer to the protesting masses, even going so far as to participate in the SDS-led uprising at Columbia and ending up arrested and booked into a Harlem jail cell.

That day when her father had come to bail her out was a turning point in her life, the moment when she crossed into womanhood and became a person who could think for herself and make choices that suited her best interest, no matter whether her mother or father or anyone else agreed. She felt empowered by the experience and realized that if she stayed true to herself and her beliefs, nothing could stop her from achieving whatever goals she would ultimately set. With this new strength, she went against her parents' wishes and flew out to California to spend the summer with her cousin Daisy in search of new adventures, rather than sit in a newspaper office back in New York City serving an internship that may or may not have meant anything to her future.

When she came home she was strong, confident, worldly almost, and though she would always be their little girl, Jack and Olivia realized she was no longer a little girl. Kathleen had begun mending fences with Jack when he had visited her in San Francisco, and before she began the fall semester of her junior year at Columbia, she promised to be studious and responsible, and in return she asked Jack to loosen his grip and treat her like an adult, and have faith in her decision-making. Reluctantly, and with a kiss and a hug, he agreed to try.

Of all the McDonalds, no one was more pleased to bid farewell to 1968 than Olivia. As a mother, worrying about your children begins at conception and it never really dissipates 'til death do you part. So, to have watched the nightly reports from Vietnam which brought the horror of the war right into her living room, and then not knowing for weeks at a time whether Patrick was dead or alive, was almost too much for Olivia to take.

And as if she wasn't already sleep-deprived, her precious daughter added extra layers of angst, first by getting caught up in the dangerous insurrection at Columbia, and then making the choice to gallivant around California with her famously carefree cousin. All summer Olivia could not get the picture out of her head that Kathleen would return to New York with a flower in her hair, a bag of weed in her jeans pocket, and a life plan of becoming a Rolling Stones groupie.

Amidst this bubbling cauldron of consternation, there was also the unraveling of her beloved Democratic Party which she witnessed first-hand at the ill-fated convention in Chicago. As a result, Republican Richard Nixon won the election, an event that Olivia predicted would send the country into cataclysmic decline. Yes, apolitical Jack had rolled his eyes at that one.

Quite a year indeed, so as a Christmas morning surprise, Jack announced that he was taking everyone to Miami with him for the Super Bowl. He'd have to do some work, naturally, but there would be plenty of time for the beach, for shopping, for dining, and maybe even to catch a nightclub act or two.

On a warm and sunny morning a few days before the game, work and recreation came crashing together. The McDonalds were gathered at the crowded pool deck of the Galt Ocean Mile Hotel; Olivia and Kathleen hoping to alter the ghostly color of their New York skin, and Jack and Patrick seated at an umbrella-covered table, Patrick reading Tom Wolfe's book, *The Electric Kool-Aid Acid Test*, and Jack engrossed in the sports section of *Miami Herald* where the front page blared the headline, "Namath Guarantees Jet Victory."

Almost on cue as Jack read about Joe Namath's boast of certain victory the night before, there was a murmur followed by oohs and aahs as the wildly popular quarterback of the Jets came strutting out bare-chested, wearing only a plaid bathing suit and sandals, and plopped himself down on a sky blue and white lounge chair to grab some rays before that afternoon's practice.

It took all of about a minute before Namath was surrounded by reporters in a semi-circle in front of him, with fawning women and excited children behind him and on his flanks. "This wasn't the way I planned it," Namath said with that Hollywood smile of his, intimating that he had naively hoped to come down and relax, open some of his fan mail, and sign a few autographs if any were requested.

Having given Jack three days of complete access a little more than a year ago for a cover story in *SportsWorld*, Namath was well acquainted with the nationally-known columnist and gave him a pleasant hello. He acknowledged the presence of a couple of the New York writers that he knew by name, including one of Jack's good friends, Larry Merchant of the *Post*, and he also nodded to a young CBS radio reporter named Brent Musberger, whom Jack had met only a couple days earlier.

"Did you really guarantee a victory last night?" Jack asked Namath.

Namath had attended a dinner in the Playhouse Room at the Miami Villas where the Miami Touchdown Club was honoring him as pro football's most outstanding player for 1968. During Namath's speech, a Colts fan shouted from the back of the room, "The Colts are going to kick your ass." Namath didn't skip a beat, and he said what he and his Jets teammates had actually been thinking for the better part of a week. "Hey, I got news for you; we're going to win Sunday, I'll guarantee you."

"So, you don't think that might piss off the Colts a little?" Jack asked.

"I don't care, and if they need that to put on their bulletin board to get them ready to play, then they're in big trouble," Namath replied.

Gold. Namath was gold for a sports writer. Jack had come to learn this when he did his big piece on the quarterback after he'd become the first man in pro football history to surpass 4,000 yards passing in a season. But this was gold-plated gold, and it was going to make for a deliciously juicy story come Sunday if the Jets were to go on and beat the mighty Colts at Miami's Orange Bowl.

Jack stayed with Namath for about 15 minutes before returning to the table where Patrick had been watching with pride his relatively famous father doing his sports writer thing.

"Good talk?" Patrick asked.

"He's a character," Jack replied. "But for his sake, he'd better win that game Sunday."

Patrick wasn't much of a football fan, baseball was his favorite sport, so he wasn't really sure whether the Colts or the Jets were the better team. "Can they win?"

"You know what, I think they can," Jack said.

Just another interesting day at the Galt Ocean Mile Hotel. It was not lost on Jack that one year ago, almost to the day, he had sat at this very pool deck across from then Green Bay Packers coach Vince Lombardi, listening to the great man's declaration of retirement, which came with the warning that Jack wasn't to breathe a word of it to anybody until after the Super Bowl. And it struck Jack how his world – both personally and professionally – had so drastically changed in the year between his conversation with Lombardi and this one with Namath.

Patrick was still in Vietnam; Kathleen was still a veritable child; Lyndon B. Johnson was the president; Dr. Martin Luther King, Jr. and Robert Kennedy were very much alive and trying to figure out ways to get America headed in the right direction; Jack hadn't kissed the hands of Catherine Deneuve and Brigitte Bardot at a fancy hotel in France; Mickey Mantle was still a Yankee; pro golfer Bob Goalby wasn't being painted as a math dunce; no man of Mexican descent had ever won golf's U.S. Open; no black man had ever won one of tennis' grand slam events; no Major League pitcher had ever thrown six consecutive shutouts; no one had ever long-jumped 29 feet in the Olympics or anywhere else; and the only gloved fists people were interested in belonged to the greatest boxing champions.

And one year ago, who could have ever imagined that a brash, long-haired quarterback would openly guarantee that his under-appreciated team from the ragamuffin AFL would whip the champions of the established NFL in the game that decided the champion of pro football, and then actually go out and do it?

It's what made sports so great, and it was why Jack was convinced he had the greatest job in all the world. Even in a year wrought with so much tension and grief, Americans had their sports to take their minds off everything, if only briefly, and it was Jack's job to chronicle as much of it as he could. Not a bad gig, and Jack often thought of something Chief Justice of the United States Supreme Court Earl Warren once said: "I always turn to the sports section first. The sports page records people's accomplishments; the front page has nothing but man's failures."

About the Author

Sal Maiorana is a native of Buffalo, New York and a journalism graduate of Buffalo State College, class of 1984. He is currently in his 32nd year as a sports writer for the Rochester (N.Y.) *Democrat and Chronicle*, and his primary beat for the past 29 years is coverage of the National Football League's Buffalo Bills, making him the longest-tenured day-to-day beat writer in franchise history.

He is a 2009 inductee into the Frontier Field Walk of Fame which honors Rochester's most decorated athletes, coaches, administrators, teams, and media personalities. He is also a two-time Rochester Press-Radio Club Sports Writer of the Year award winner, has been recognized once by the American Legion as Rochester's Sports Writer of the Year, once as the Rochester Media Association Established Professional honoree, and has won numerous New York State Publishers' Association and Gannett News Service citations for his work with the *Democrat and Chronicle*.

His freelance work has appeared in numerous publications and online web sites including *The Sporting News, Golf World, Golf Week, USGA Journal, USA Today, PGA Magazine, Lacrosse Magazine*, NFL.com, CBS Sportsline, and Pro Sports Exchange.

He is also the author of 20 books. For information, please go to his Amazon author page to see all the titles.

He is married to the former Christine Charlton, and has three children; daughters Taylor and Caroline, and son Holden. And lest we forget, their dog, Buddy.